NEWS
A Consumer's Guide

NEWS
A Consumer's Guide

IVAN AND CAROL DOIG

Prentice-Hall, Inc., *Englewood Cliffs, New Jersey*

Library of Congress Catalog Card Number: 72–2496
Printed in the United States of America

ISBN: P 0-13-615617-7
        C 0-13-615625-8

10 9 8 7 6 5 4 3 2 1

Prentice-Hall International, Inc., *London*
Prentice-Hall of Australia, Pty. Ltd., *Sydney*
Prentice-Hall of Canada, Ltd., *Toronto*
Prentice-Hall of India Private Limited, *New Delhi*
Prentice-Hall of Japan, Inc., *Tokyo*

Acknowledgments

Hanna Arendt, *Eichmann in Jerusalem*, The Viking Press, Inc. Reprinted by permission.

Robert Alan Aurthur, "The Wit and Sass of Harry S Truman," *Esquire*, August 1971. Reprinted by permission of Esquire, Inc.

Victor Bernstein and Jesse Gordon, "The Press and the Bay of Pigs," reprinted from the *Columbia Forum*, Fall 1967, Vol. X, No. 3. Copyright 1967 by The Trustees of Columbia University in the City of New York.

Daniel J. Boorstin, *The Image*, Atheneum Publishers, 1962, p. 61. Copyright 1961 by Daniel J. Boorstin. Reprinted by permission of Atheneum Publishers.

Wallace Carroll, "Ralph Waldo Emerson, Thou Shouldst Be Living at This Hour," *Nieman Reports*, June 1970. Reprinted by permission of the Nieman Foundation and the author.

Lewis Chester, Godfrey Hodgson, and Bruce Page, *An American Melodrama*, The Viking Press, Inc. Reprinted by permission of The Viking Press, Inc. and Andre Deutsch Ltd.

David Deitch, "Case for Advocacy Journalism," *The Nation*, November 17, 1969, pp 789–91. Reprinted by permission of *The Nation*.

Robert J. Donovan, "The Rules Have Changed," *Nieman Reports*, March 1970. Reprinted by permission of the author.

Richard Harwood, "The News Business: Can Newsmen Do Better on the Facts?" *The Washington Post*, August 22, 1971. Reprinted by permission of the author.

Elliot Horne, *The Hiptionary: A Hipster's View of the World Scene.* Copyright © 1963 by Elliot Horne and Jack Davis. Reprinted by permission of Simon and Schuster, Inc.

Jeanie Kasindorf, "He Just Prays It Will Be an Easy Day." Reprinted by permission from TV GUIDE ® Magazine. Copyright © 1971 by Triangle Publications, Inc., Radnor, Pennsylvania.

John Keasler, "A non-violent paper? Try it—it's murder!" *Editor and Publisher*, May 31, 1969. Reprinted by permission of the publisher.

A. J. Liebling, *The Press.* Reprinted by permission of The Author's Estate and its agent, James Brown Associates, Inc. Copyright © 1961 by A. J. Liebling.

"Manila," United Press International, September 27, 1967. Reprinted by permission of United Press International.

William McGaffin and Irwin Knoll, *Anything But the Truth* (New York: G. P. Putnam's Sons). Reprinted by permission of the publisher.

"Most of California Hit in Nader Report Wrap-up," August 27, 1971. Copyright 1971, *Los Angeles Times*. Reprinted by permission.

Tim Reiterman, "Two Faces of Berkeley—and the News," *Chicago Journalism Review*, 11 E. Hubbard St., Chicago, Ill. 60611, subscription $5 for one year.

Diane K. Shah, "A Fashionable Bacchanal," *National Observer*, February 15, 1971. Reprinted by permission of the publisher.

Rebecca West, *The Meaning of Treason*, copyright 1947 by Rebecca West, The Viking Press, Inc. Reprinted by permission of the publisher.

Thomas Whiteside, "Selling Death," *The New Republic*, March 27, 1971. Reprinted by permission of The New Republic, © 1971, Harrison-Blaine of New Jersey, Inc.

"The Word from Olympus," from *The Unsatisfied Man*, Colorado Media Project, Inc., April, 1971. Reprinted by permission.

Contents

Acknowledgments

A number of people lent us time and effort during our work on this book.

Our first thanks must be to Jean Roden; what marvelous fortune it is to have a reference librarian, a diligent editor, and an enthusiastic friend all in one.

Linda and Clint Miller gave us careful reading, as they have done more times than even long friendship should have to put up with.

Ann and Marshall Nelson provided prompt help; rarely do authors have the good luck to have their work read by an editor and a lawyer within a single household.

Jan Bateman contributed much toward honing our original ideas into book form.

Our gratitude, too, to other good friends who read chapters for us: Bill Chamberlin; Tom and Ro Holden; Bill and Carelyn Reeburgh; and Denzil Walters. Joyce Greenfield did her usual excellent job in typing the manuscript rapidly and accurately. Melvylei Stone's quick and cheerful help made our library research a lighter task. The staffs of the Shoreline Community College library and the University of Washington library were unfailingly attentive to our research problems, and good people to spend time with besides.

William Caldwell of *The Record* of Bergen County, N.J., Professor Neale Copple of the University of Nebraska, and Professor Ben H. Baldwin of Northwestern University have our thanks for reviewing the manuscript and offering excellent suggestions for strengthening it.

As we have thanked them in the past for other hard work and attention to detail, now we thank Ainsley Roseen for his proofreading and Bessie A. Ringer for her help on the index.

And finally, we're indebted to two nettled news consumers who did much to inspire our work, Frank Muller and Betty M. Thomas; and to Sandra Messik and Bill Oliver at Prentice-Hall.

About the Authors

Carol Doig is associate professor of communications at Shoreline Community College in Seattle, teaching courses in basic journalism, English, and media criticism. She formerly was a reporter and education editor of the *Asbury Park* (N.J.) *Press*, assistant wire editor of the *Everett* (Wash.) *Herald*, and associate editor of *Together* magazine. She's held two jobs in the field of public relations. For several summers, she worked as an instructor and counselor in the National High School Institute at Northwestern University, and has taught reporting at Northwestern and magazine article writing at the U. of Washington. She has bachelor's and master's degrees in journalism from Northwestern.

Ivan Doig is a free lance writer and, in the research for magazine articles, a professional news consumer. Among the magazines in which his articles have appeared are *American West, Parents', McCall's, Bell Telephone, Writer's Digest, Yankee, Kiwanis, Editor & Publisher, Journalism Quarterly,* and *Forest History.* During duty in the Air Force Reserve, he served as a public information specialist. Formerly an editorial writer for Lindsay-Schaub Newspapers in Illinois and assistant editor of *The Rotarian* magazine, he has taught magazine article writing at Northwestern. He has bachelor's and master's degrees in journalism from Northwestern, and a Ph.D. in U.S. history from the U. of Washington.

NEWS

A Consumer's Guide

Chapter 1

Anchor Man, Digger, Prime Timer, Arouet, and You

Among the most fragile of all our products is information. Particularly the brand labeled "the news." News comes apart quickly in your head. And there's considerable likelihood that the news will have flaws even before it reaches you. In short, the news generally is odd goods, very possibly gone awry somewhere along the line.

Yet, anyone who needs information provided by the media, from weather reports to battle reports, has no choice but to be a news consumer. Because our daily packaged information is a vital commodity, this book is a do-it-yourself kit for the consumer—you.

Critics and defenders of news operations swirl all around us, offering judgments about newscasters, editors, programs, publications. Who to believe? Newsmen may be suspected of justifying their own products. The critics who assail them may have an interest in manipulating news for their own profit.

So, be your own critic, with the help of this consumer's guide.

That means knowing something about how the news media work and what can be expected from them.

Then it means learning about some tools with which to evaluate the news. Learning how to judge whether a news story is accurate. How you can discern when the news has gaps in it. How you can tell when a report is biased. How to uncover your own biases as you hurry through the day's news, extracting some parts and forgetting others.

By the end of this book, you'll have gone through a set of techniques which should make you a smarter news consumer. You'll learn how to tell a flawed news product on the one hand, and a self-serving complainant on the other. You'll learn, too, to sort your daily way through personalities and problems which forever accompany the news. As a starter, meet four symbolic companions who share the chapter title with you . . .

The television scene this evening is like looking down into a dollhouse where the figurines are in revolt.

The crowd, jam-packed on the convention floor, surges even more thickly around the TV reporters. Outside in the streets of Chicago, young demonstrators are mocking the Democratic national convention, this diorama of American politics 1968, and here in the arena, Mayor Daley's security force is taking the resentment out on the news media.

Boxed in a studio above, a network anchor man looks on, the most familiar voice in America calmly describing the hubbub. Suddenly, CBS reporter Dan Rather is slugged, bent double from a stomach punch by a security man.[1]

The anchor man's voice is different than anyone has ever heard it over the television set.

"I think we've got a bunch of thugs here," Walter Cronkite says angrily.[2]

The newspaper this morning is not running the columnist's words as usual at the top of its editorial page, snugly close to the most prestigious masthead in America. He's held the spot a long time; more than a dozen years before, President Eisenhower said the New York Times writer was using his column to tell the White House how to run the country.[3] But his current words are front page news.

The first star journalist to hurry into the People's Republic of China when relations between the United States and the mainland Chinese thawed in 1971, the columnist waits impatiently to dig into interviews with the Peking leadership. For some reason, his Chinese hosts kept him stalled in Canton for two days.

Now they tell him, at the same time that they tell the rest of the world: White House adviser Henry Kissinger was in Peking during those days of delay, secretly arranging plans for a visit to China by President Nixon.

As the columnist remembers it afterwards from a bed in Peking's Anti-Imperialist Hospital, word of that missed story and his acute appendicitis attack coincided.

"At that precise moment, or so it now seems, the first stab of pain went through my groin," James Reston writes.[4]

The President of the United States is going on TV and radio tonight. His speech was worked out in longhand on a yellow legal pad, and here in the last hour before his prime time appearance he goes over the typed copy.[5]

His predecessor, Lyndon B. Johnson, used for most of his television appearances an automated speaker's stand, an elaborate invention with built-in Teleprompters and arms of sound equipment extending alongside the President so supportively the contraption was nicknamed "Mother."[6]

The President before that, John F. Kennedy, made intricately rhythmic language and inspirational quotations about power and responsibility his television trademark.

This President has his speeches typed out the way an e e cummings poem appears on paper, words grouped into natural phrases on fields of white for ease of scanning and delivery.[7]

A few minutes from air time, he walks into the Oval Office and sits down at his desk. Soon a light glows on the camera in front of him, and he looks up from the words patterned across the pages.

"Good evening, my fellow Americans," Richard M. Nixon begins.

The thinker lived near the border in those years, ready to hurry across the magic line to safety whenever he enraged the government.[8]

Slight and sarcastic, he was one of history's dangerous men. By the time he was 30, a trail of banned and burned publications lay behind the thrusts of his intellect. To the discomfiture of Europe's established order, the thinker survived 53 more years. His weaponry: wit and ideas.

God is always on the side of the big battalions, he said.

When the crown regent sold half the horses in the royal stable, the thinker said he should rather have disposed of half the asses in the royal court.

Posterity gave Francois Marie Arouet a rare reward for the snap of his phrases. It credits him with memorable lines whether or not he said them. So, the sentence which shields the basic freedom is attributed to this thinker:

"I disapprove of what you say, but I will defend to the death your right to say it."[9]

Tonight and this morning and across the years, these four live with you. By invitation of history.

Time replaces the names with new ones—except that of Arouet, who characteristically stole a march on the procession and made the change himself, to the pen name of Voltaire. And time changes the way messages come and go in the household, and how they're seen and heard. But the why stays the same. Through all the headlines and the dial-clicking and the lofting of wise thoughts, you are together with these familiar strangers for an inescapable reason. The symbolic figures Cronkite, Reston, Nixon, and Arouet—and you —all deal in a commodity called *news*.

Somewhere back in the gathered urges that make us what we are, the impulse for community took hold. Ever since, human beings have projected across the spaces between them information of one sort or another.

Now, after our trek out of the forest and the village, we are continually aware of the great world coursing into our own spheres. What eventually is sorted into a news consumer's head from these bewildering encounters depends on how a Reston gathers news stories or misses them, on a Cronkite's frame of mind as he views an event, on the way a Nixon communicates through the media with a national constituency, on the power of a Voltairean idea.

The best you can do about the predicament of having to depend on these others, as well as yourself, is to watch carefully. You are a consumer of a peculiar commodity. News is tricky, and hard to judge. But it is a commodity we need for that part of us which makes decisions, that part of us where the impulse for community is rooted deep. This book suggests some ways to overhaul your news consuming habits, and to work on the confusion of reports you get each day from the media.

Chapter 2

"Oh, come on, Harry! It can't be as bad as all that!"

If It's Good, Is It News?

Today an array of U.S. citizens estimated at more than 200 million persons did not participate in a public protest of any sort.

Is that news?

During a protest at Kent State University on May 4, 1970, troops of the Ohio National Guard shot into the crowd, killing four students.

What actually happened?

Every time a news story appears in print or on the air, the newsman is answering questions such as these. We call his responses his news judgment. The newsman has some definition of "news," and working from it he singles out occurrences which seem to him to be news stories. These stories he believes to have news "values"—elements of timeliness, proximity, or some other attribute which, in his eyes, make them important for the reader to know.

But the news consumer also answers questions such as these, and often very differently. We see and hear what we want to see and hear, and we read into the news what we want to find there. In short, the consumer does his own editing and rewriting. Some of the lights he works under are his own—prejudices, enthusiasms, suspicions, all the wattage of his emotions. Some are society's, the subtle lusters which color the way entire generations see the world.

A person has, then, two fallible sources for the news which ultimately enters his head: the newsman's judgment and his own.

The Nose for Which Newsmen Are Famous

A young reporter was sent to check a telephone tip that a piscatory aroma was smelling up a posh neighborhood along the New Jersey coast. She returned to report that her investigation had been fruitless; that is, odorless.

"Couldn't find a fishy odor, huh?" chided the night editor, tongue snugly in cheek. "Just goes to prove you have no nose for news."

The talented newsman long has been credited with such a nose, as if he had been born with an acute proboscis which leads him to stories much as a Geiger counter leads a prospector to uranium.

The process, though, is not like that. Uranium already is there, waiting to be discovered. News does not even exist until someone defines it into existence. And how it is defined depends on an uneasy balance of established practice and what counts in a particular society at a given time.

A newsman first inhales ideas about news in the same way as people around him—by hearing and reading the product called news as he grows, and by listening to his parents and others comment about what they hear.

When he decides on news as a profession he is likely to take college courses in which professors and textbooks explain news to him. Then he goes to work for experienced editors who are explicit, and sometimes profane, when a young reporter fumbles a story which the editors consider news.

In this way established views of news pass, sometimes with modifications to meet changes in the world's ebb and flow, from one generation of newsmen to the next.

Take as examples of news views the remarks of two network newsmen with long seniority on television's evening reports.

"Placidity is not news," declares David Brinkley of NBC. "If an airplane departs on time and arrives on time, it isn't news. If it crashes, regrettably, it is."[1]

Walter Cronkite of CBS, whose evening news arrives in the living room distinctly different in style from NBC's, states his viewpoint in strikingly similar terms. Responding to a college coed who wanted news coverage of the majority of students who quietly went to class while others marched and demonstrated he said, "It's a little bit like having to report all the cats that aren't lost that day."[2]

If that's what news is not—and few newsmen have been heard to disagree—what is the product which newsmen strive for?

Trying to fully explain news gets so sticky that many an explainer nervously seeks a glib way out. One of the more enduring pseudo-definitions, for instance, pontificates that "news is what editors say it is."

But listen to David Brinkley again. "News is the unusual, the unexpected."[3]

Complementing that view, the man with whom he shared the NBC news spotlight for fourteen years, Chet Huntley, describes news as "the warts on society's skin. The aberrations."[4]

It's helpful to remember, while struggling to contain the term news, that newsmen do have individual quirks and preferences, as well as intuitive responses to events, that defy tidy classification.

Walter Cronkite, for instance, has reported manned space exploration from its infancy and maintains a genuine enthusiasm and expertise which means that news of astronauts and space flights commonly get more attention on his CBS evening report than on the competing television news shows.

Less profoundly, publisher James Gordon Bennett considered dogs eminently newsworthy for his New York Herald and Paris Herald. Standing fast in Paris when most of the populace fled before the oncoming German army in World War I, Bennett wrote for the Paris Herald a lengthy story under the headline, **Routine of Canine Life in Paris Upset by War.**[5]

What's News?

Journalism professors, books, editors and reporters often explain news in terms of characteristics or values. Legitimate news stories, they say, possess one or more of these values.

Their rosters of news values commonly include a story's timeliness, its proximity to the reader, the prominence of the people involved, the significance of the event, and a human interest category which welds an array of humorous, bizarre, tragic and unusual news about ordinary people. Some newsmen and analysts would add conflict to the list.

News values weren't developed in the light of a smoky fire as neolithic newsmen pondered what to chisel into stone for their first issue. News developed to serve informational needs, and thoughtful people later looked at the product and, to try to understand it better, searched for its elements so that they could talk about it with greater precision.

The harried small town editor who rasps to his newest reporter, "Go see what that strike down at the shoe factory is all about; it's gonna affect a lot of people," demonstrates his news values, though they've become reflexive and he probably won't stop to explain them elaborately.

The strike down at the shoe factory has timeliness because it was called today; proximity because it's in the town served by the paper; prominent citizens are involved in the negotiations; it's significant to the area's economy; and one among many human interest angles includes the personality conflicts that fused the deadlock.

On the other hand, a story in which a single news value predominates may make a newspaper's first page. Here's one that did:

> MANILA (UPI)—A Philippine Air Force helicopter Tuesday rescued a fear-struck farmer from a coconut tree where he sought refuge for 59 days.
>
> Quirino Berja, 48, was plucked from his 60-foot-high perch in Binalonan Town, about 180 miles north of here, and was flown to Manila for a medical examination.
>
> The rescue team reported that Berja was pale and could hardly talk. Berja also whacked one of the rescuers on the forehead before consenting to leave his treetop sanctuary.
>
> Berja climbed the tree July 30 after he had been chased by an angry mob following a heated argument with Binalonan residents during his daughter's wedding reception.

He lived on food and soft drinks supplied by friends. He hauled up the rations with a rope tied from the treetop, and protected himself from intruders by hurling empty pop bottles and coconuts.[6]

Human interest, that. Undiluted. This story happened far from U.S. readers, to a man they don't know, and the bizarre incident transmits no great significance in terms of the world's fate. A certain timeliness is there, since he was rescued yesterday, but that isn't paramount.

To further weaken it journalistically, the report is pocked with holes—that is, it poses more questions than it answers, and does not answer some obvious ones. A few of them:

What kind of argument could have driven a man into a tree for two months?

What kind of man could be driven?

Had he behaved astonishingly before?

Who tried to get him down before the Philippine Air Force was summoned?

What did they say?

What did he say?

What happened to the daughter?

Did this wreck her wedding? Her honeymoon? Her marriage?

Despite these omissions—some readers might say because of them—the story of the treed father-in-law is intriguing.

Whatever else we say about news values they are, at best, simply a useful way of talking about news. They won't unerringly lead newsmen to stories. Indeed, some reports containing multiple news values can best be described as non-news.

May 2, 1971: Tricia Nixon's White House wedding is forty-one days away. *The Chicago Tribune* runs on page one a five-column story with pictures of Tricia and Lynda Johnson Robb. The Trib copydesk gives the story an honest, non-news headline: **No Advice on Wedding, Says Lynda.** The first paragraph uninforms the readers:

> Lynda Johnson Robb, the nation's last White House bride, doesn't plan to offer any advice to Tricia Nixon who in June becomes the next.[7]

The story oozed downhill from that nadir. Timeliness, prominence, and human interest could not rescue it from crashing insignificance.

Another shifting point about news values is that their relative importance can fluctuate. Our current concept of timeliness didn't mean much in Colonial America, when news from Europe routinely took months to sail its way across the Atlantic. But once the ship arrived, people wanted to hear the old news as soon as possible. One enterprising Boston coffeehouse owner—coffeehouses served as centers of information in those days—took to rowing out to ships before they docked, then scrambling back with the reports so his customers would get the news first.

This can be termed the element of discovery within the concept of time-liness. Although the events were long past, their reports were new to the colonies. That discovery factor holds with stories as diverse as the Dead Sea Scrolls,[8] found more than nineteen centuries after the biblical days they describe, and the love letters from President Warren G. Harding to a lady not his wife, which came to light forty-one years after Harding's death in 1923.[9]

The discovery factor operated in the My Lai massacre of March 16, 1968, which finally exploded into the media in November, 1969,[10] and won investigative reporter Seymour Hersh a Pulitzer Prize.[11] It's clear in the Pentagon Papers, commissioned by Secretary of Defense Robert McNamara in June, 1967, and crusted with bureaucratic dust by the time they were wedged out into the press, in defiance of a "Top Secret—Sensitive" stamp in June, 1971.[12]

Today, many editors rate timeliness below a story's significance, and below the journalistic principles of fairness and accuracy. The swing in such opinions since the turn of the century shows how remarkably a news value can change.

By the late nineteenth century, the telegraph, transoceanic cables, tele-phones, transportation improvements and fast presses had moved the country light-years from the plodding pace of colonial days. Some publishers were enthralled with the speed they could get news to the readers, perhaps even within the same day. Timeliness ruled during the era of yellow journalism, and William Randolph Hearst, who loved the spirit of the chase, was its ultimate disciple.

Hearst was first with the news if he possibly could be.[13] As a young San Francisco publisher he hired a tug to rescue a fisherman in seas so rough the Coast Guard wouldn't budge. He sent special trains across the state to speed-ily deliver his Sunday papers, forcing dismayed competitors to match his extravagance. Also, he went aloft in a balloon, wrote stories about how it all looked from up there, and sent them to his newsroom via carrier pigeon.

Moving to New York to challenge Joseph Pulitzer for newspaper riches there, Hearst careened into the Spanish-American War. Hiring the steamship *Sylvia*, he installed himself, a staff of newspapermen, a photographic dark-room, and typesetters equipped with a lightweight press. Hearst personally covered some of the fighting in Cuba and interviewed one of his own reporters after the enthusiastic employee got carried away, joined a charge and went down with a bullet in his shoulder.

"I'm sorry you're hurt," the reporter remembered Hearst saying, "but wasn't it a splendid fight? We must beat every paper in the world."

Since Hearst's most rambunctious years, the idea of speed unfettered by accuracy or significance has been replaced by a more sober view of the news. It isn't unusual now for editors to hold a story until important details can be added or until a charge can be answered by the person accused. Part of the print media's toning down of timeliness obviously has come about because they can't hope to beat radio and television to spot news. Instead, editors are trying to map out more territory in background and interpretive reporting.

"Scoop is a dying art," says David Halberstam, who won a Pulitzer Prize for his Vietnam reporting. "What is important is judgment and balance."[14]

And so, with most of the forty-seven volumes about U.S. involvement in Vietnam at their disposal, the New York Times did not rush into print with the "Pentagon Papers." Instead, in a rented hotel suite a special detail of Timesmen, carefully sifted the material for six weeks.[15]

Take note, though, that along with this forbearance was the hope that no one else would publish similar material before the Times was ready.

Is Good News No News?

Does bad news drive out good? Many consumers and critics, and some newsmen, believe it does, and a constant drumfire of complaint has rocked newsrooms and executive suites.

"The widely prevalent concept of what constitutes news is a narrow destructive concept—a sick concept destructive to society as a whole," in the view of Dr. Herbert A. Otto, a New York psychologist. He has urged that the media give more time and space to reporting discoveries in science, to coverage of arts and literature, and to "the positive things that people do."[16]

KIRO-TV, the CBS affiliate in Seattle, in the spring of 1970 began publicizing itself as the city's "good news" station and running at least one story labeled that way each evening. Such tidings of comfort made the station an early entrant into a field that soon became popular as pinpoints of "good news" lighted up across the country.[17] For many, the listenership ratings seemed to turn on. But in Seattle, television critics wondered whether good news amounted to no news.

"KIRO has gone as far as to place a Good News sign behind the announcer—perhaps for those who can't immediately tell the difference," grumbled Frank Chesley of the *Seattle Post-Intelligencer*. "It smacks of huckstering. It cheapens the dissemination of information by reducing it to the level of TV melodrama—the 'good news' as a sort of comic relief. Would a 'bad news' sign be used behind a story on the Mideast crisis?"[18]

Despite such raps, the *Wall Street Journal* reported, KIRO allotted $100,000 during the first "good news" year to publicize its product, including major ads in newspapers and billboards around the city.[19]

According to rating services, the TV executive's holy writ, KIRO's local news audience was lowest of the three network stations when the campaign began.[20] The station predicted it would rise to number one. But after a year and a half of "good news," it was where it started out in the ratings, dead last.[21]

Across the country, other stations which adopted variations of the good news policy reported increases in listenership at first. Then ratings of some of the stations began to tail off, and some followed the lead of WLS-TV in Chicago in cutting back toward a regular format.[22]

Newspapers also reported mixed results. After a few months of a good news feature called "The Brighter Side," the Arizona Republic in Phoenix pulled back from three times a week to once.

"It's like all things; it just loses its wallop," said managing editor J. Edward Murray. "We skimmed the cream (of good news stories) off the community and the novelty wore off. Even readers who feel most strongly that editors select only negative news realize after looking at a good-news column for a while that it's not news. They pick up a newspaper to find out what is new, different and off the norm."[23]

KIRO's anchorman and news director, Clif Kirk, disagrees. He thinks the Seattle station's "good news" is news, and that it isn't used in place of more significant stories. All it does is remind listeners that not every piece of news is negative.[24]

"In the normal pacing of the show we would probably have that story in there anyway," he said of the at-least-one-heartening-story-per-newscast formula. "It's more a matter of calling the viewer's attention to the fact that we do have it than a matter of us really doing much that's different from what we did before we had what we call good news."

Historically, the news media have handled much besides bad news, from the routine of weddings, sports, beauty contests and sweepstakes winners through polio vaccine and environmental cleanup.

The honorable tradition of good news includes human interest stories by the late Ernie Pyle. Pyle earned fame reporting on GIs during World War II, but even before that he wrote of ordinary but interesting people as he traveled around the U.S. as a newspaper reporter.

Since 1967, CBS has had Charles Kuralt reporting On the Road in much the same spirit. There he is, riding white water in Alaska, interviewing a crossroads poet in Illinois, listening to a nonagenarian brickmaker from North Carolina who has volunteered as a one-man aid mission to Guyana.[25]

On the same network, Heywood Hale Broun has brightened the weekend with funny, slickly written sports reports.

Objections have been raised, however, against even trying to classify news as good or bad. Often it is a matter of perspective. Good to whom?

"The 'good news' concept implies that a qualitative judgment can be made about news," television columnist Frank Chesley wrote. But he doubts it. "When Mike Wallace (of CBS's *60 Minutes*) blew the whistle on the Navy's $3.9 billion investment in the M-48 torpedo—which never did work—THAT was good NEWS. That was excellent 'new information,' although the Navy, which admitted trying to squelch the story, didn't think so."[26]

KIRO's news director Kirk seems to agree. "Good news is to some extent in the eye of the beholder, and what's good news to one man may not be good to his neighbor." But he adds, "Nevertheless, there are stories that accent the more positive aspects of our day-to-day living . . . stories of success . . . stories of people doing something for their neighbor, and so forth."[27]

If newsmen are not primarily responsible for the world's bad news, and if a number of newsmen in fact have been eager to shake the image of malevolent messenger, perhaps something else is at work here. Pleasant news seems to have an inverse relationship to significance; the good stories seem to be less important than the bad ones. Perhaps they just seem to be, because good news doesn't interrupt our stability. We don't brood about happiness.

To try to gain a perspective, the *Miami News* decided on a variation of the good news theme to find out what would happen if a metropolitan daily eliminated all stories of violence for just one day.

The decision exorcised all violence, including that in features and sports. Not even the comics were spared. "B.C." was axed for clubbing a snake. And then, as John Keasler tells it:[28]

> One thing happened, quite naturally, and happened early—the biggest running story in weeks blew wide open before first edition deadline. A Miami fugitive sought for murdering a policeman was captured in a shoot-out.
>
> The *News* editors were climbing the wall, but they held firm to their commitment. They led early editions with a garbage-worker strike story and the pink edition, five star final for street sales, rolled out with a lead story on an ex-$4-a-day waiter being awarded $3,000,000.
>
> It was a harried managing editor, Howard Kleinberg, who at the end of what seemed like an endless day, said, "Well, we did it—I think we proved a lot, for the whole newspaper business. But I sure as hell won't ever do it again . . ."
>
> The non-violent day was Kleinberg's idea. Like all newsmen, he had grown up with the incessant plaint from subscribers: "Do you have to print all that violence? Why don't you people put good things in the paper?"
>
> Editor Sylvan Meyer, under "An Edition Without Violence," wrote an explanation at the top of Page One which, in part, said:
>
> "What we have omitted today are the details, and the emphasis, on what often amounts to a numbing portion of gore, inhumanity and strife . . .
>
> "What does this prove . . . ? What it may prove is that there is no answer to the oft-heard complaint that 'newspapers emphasize violence'. . .
>
> "This de-emphasis of violence for this one day may demonstrate that we, as readers, would not receive from our paper an accurate and complete picture

of the world around us if the paper practiced such deliberate selectivity every day and tried to shield us from reality . . ."

In the inner sanctum of news decisions, it suddenly appeared that May 16 was the most violent day in human history.

"The first stories I saw were two armed robberies and a bloody campus riot," said Kleinberg. "Then, at 7:15, what do we get but the nightmare—the shoot-out capture of the fugitive."

There was last-minute pressure, from wildly frustrated editors, to drop the whole idea.

"We were tempted," said Kleinberg. "Then we decided—good or bad—we would stick to the commitment. What could we do? Announce we would wait for a non-violence day until some nice day when there wasn't any violence?"

What was the reaction of readers on that day?

"We were primed to face anger from all sides," Kleinberg said. "We got one furious call, that first day. A subscriber raised tee-total hell about 'Orphan Annie' being left out. We had to read it over the phone."

One other reaction was a bit disturbing. In what Editor Meyer termed a "concession to reality," a short index headed "Violence in Brief" had given bare outlines of deleted major stories.

Larry Jinks, managing editor of the *Herald*, called Kleinberg to ask if the *Herald* could buy an ad beneath the index which said: "For details, see your *Miami Herald*."

For days after the non-violent issue, letters of praise mounted in volume to the *News*. (Along with some less happy ones which spoke of "censorship.") The issue was called a "gallant gesture," "humanitarianism" and other nice things. But, one which might be pertinent for other editors said, in full:

"To the Editor, *Miami News*:

"All right. You win. A newspaper with no violence is hardly a newspaper and I'll try to remember. I'm mad at the world as it is, and not the news or reporters. J. David Houser."

An even more pertinent in-trade comment might be Kleinberg's summing up of staff opinion.

"Trying to put out a newspaper without violence could kill a man."

The Consumer as Editor and Rewrite Man

The newsgatherer's decisions on the nature of news shape the stories which come to the consumer. Now for the snipping and shaping that go on in the workroom behind our own foreheads—that is, the effects of the mental wraiths which govern any consumer's perception of the news.

First, and probably most obvious, is his comparatively small sum of invested time. The reader or viewer in his easy chair will consume in minutes a story the reporter slogged away at all day, or maybe several days. Not surprisingly, that story will have a different impetus in the reporter's head than in the consumer's.

Newsmen live with some stories. *The Atlantic* has hired topnotch reporters to spend many months to put together a single article for the magazine. On assignments of the sort, Dan Wakefield spent four and a half months traveling throughout the nation for a report on the public mood about Vietnam,[29] and Ward Just invested eight months in researching a study of the U.S. military.[30]

Or, the reporter's perspective may have deepened from having spent every working day for years on the topic he is writing about. This is beat coverage, the practice of assigning a reporter to one specific topic: city hall, the Supreme Court, public schools, labor unions. A newsman such as the late Meyer Berger of the *New York Times* may grow so savvy about his entire city he becomes a sort of municipal wizard.[31] More likely, he will work towards expertise in a single beat. Legislative reporter Tom Littlewood of the *Chicago Sun-Times* covered the Illinois state legislature for several years, then moved on to his paper's Washington bureau to report on Congress.

Such is the expert reporter's depth, and even the inexpert one has to spend much more time and enterprise on his particular item of news than is ever visible in print or on the air.

On most stories, the news consumer cannot extend his own perspective as far. But he can go beyond shallows of living room laziness.

Simply reminding himself that his own perspective is at work foreshortening the news is the basic effort. Lamentably few of us have perfect memories. Our minds mostly remember highlights. No matter how carefully a reporter tells a complex story, the consumer a few minutes later may recall only big bold outlines of the news item.

Occasionally that's enough. *Japanese Bomb Pearl Harbor* hit the entire American populace as powerfully as a telegram with the single word WAR. Most often, such a billboard perspective won't be adequate:

Congress May End Draft, but . . . Opposition senators threatened . . . The Administration is studying . . . It is unclear . . . A Pentagon manpower study . . . Troop commitments in the Far East and Europe . . .

Candidate X Appears to Be Leading in His Race for Office, but . . . Young voters casting their first ballots may . . . Campaign funds are short . . . His voting record on . . . Lukewarm crowds at his speeches . . . He would be the first candidate here ever to . . .

The qualifiers may swirl on and on, far beyond the unwary reader's memory span.

The consumer, then, must take care to pay attention to nuances of the news he takes in so rapidly. No one without a photocopying machine for a brain can remember all the nuances, but we can remember there *are* nuances. If you don't remind yourself that a story scanned into your head has limber qualities which give way very quickly, you're not getting the news. Your abrupt perspective is letting through only headlines, and most likely inaccurate screamers at that.

So, the time a consumer is able to spend on the news is one rudiment which shapes his reception of a story. More subtle factors are not entirely of your own doing. Layered in with your own feelings are society's opinions.

Many a reader and viewer, for instance, will expect that some of the commotion all around is actually progress. They may not admit this, or in fact, may deny it or be unaware of such a slant in their thinking. But rebel or establishmentarian, most of us are powered through life by some expectation that tomorrow somehow is likely to be more worthwhile than today.

Here in Western civilization, such hopes have had bright trappings at least since the seventeenth century, when Isaac Newton began to tease a theory of gravity out of the mysteries of the universe. Once man learned to use formulas in even the invisible realms of nature, science was on its way to the atom smasher. The Industrial Revolution tooled science's new ideas into factories, and the Technological Revolution installed assembly lines for consumer goods. As the heirs of those vast trends, we have Progress ever with us: new medicines, new automobile styles, the transistor radio, the 747 to Paris.

One place a person likely will not get a lifting sense of progress, however, is in the news.

For a nation historically in a hurry, there is little progress to be found in a decade of war in Vietnam, or in racial crises 350 years after black and white began living together on this continent, or in the jangling clamor of an election campaign nearly 200 years after our two-party system began evolving.

News which does flash forth as progress—heart transplants, moon shots —may turn out to be spectacular for its uniqueness rather than its value for the individual citizen.

In short, much of the day-by-day news will be a disappointment for a mind attuned to progress. Progress, in the dictionary definition of "movement toward a goal," is best calculable where objects are concerned—a laser adapted for a new surgical technique, for example. Much of the news has to do with the products of our heads, not our hands, and its display in print or broadcast seldom enough is tidy or comforting. Legislation, war, opinion, debate, prejudice; countless staples of the news derive from the invisible world of thought, and anyone with an eye for progress will not find it nearly so readily as in the visible world of made objects.

Progress shades the news in the reader's mind from a second direction— the point our mechanical dexterity occupies at the moment. Innovation still is going on in the news business in a big way. But we're talking here about how developments already on the scene affect our expectations about a story. A span of technical tricks which took us from the quill pen to the television set also instilled ideas about what size and shape we want our news to come in.

First, man learned to telegraph words across large spans of distance. The next step was to skip the wires, and send words by radio. Then came pictures with the words—television. The package the news came in became more and more handy, more and more unitary.

By now, the consumer is accustomed to receiving the news in small chunks, within a regular time segment—the time he spends reading the morning paper, or listening to the radio while driving to work, or watching the evening news on television. He wants his news in a hurry, and he wants it in a familiar form he won't have to struggle with.

This puts demands on the reporter that affect news stories. The news consumer should be aware that material is being left out because of space limits, or that a complex story is being simplified.

Take the daily chaos of a political campaign. It is almost impossible to report. The consumer probably would be horrified and retire to a cave if it were reported to him in its full confusion. New York Times columnist Russell Baker once described the campaign reporter's daily travail:

> The writing is done by the reflexes, usually on airplanes, on buses, or at open-air press tables with a 60-piece brass band blowing patriotic airs into your ear and a few hundred hot blooded lady politicos fighting for standing room on your typewriter.[32]

Nor is politics the only topic difficult to interpret. Practically everything but the baseball scores must be simplified one way or another. And the consumer should look at everything but the baseball scores with that in mind.

A news story passes through many fingers and craniums on its way to the consumer. Then the consumer sees in the story what he wants to see anyway. Historian Carl Becker once called this recreating the world in our own image.[33]

Admittedly, a person needs mental bedrock of one sort or another. Going through life remaking our beliefs every day would quickly drive us neurotic. But a belief held in the face of honest evidence to the contrary is not mental bedrock, it's just rocks in the head. You should be aware of how much you are distorting the evidence—re-editing the news—to fit your own beliefs.

Think back to the news of May 4, 1970, as capsuled at the beginning of this chapter. One news consumer will know, as clearly as if he had been there shouting curses at the Guardsmen, that the Kent State killings were slaughter by trigger-happy National Guard gunsels at the orders of the Establishment. Another will know, as definitely as if he had been there looking through the sights of an M–1 rifle, that the killings were a proper measure of law and order against the radical thugs infiltrating the campuses to instigate revolution.

The careful critic will try to discern what the situation was, according to eyewitnesses and evidence, and make tentative judgments from there. It is the more painful way to read the news, because judgments are much more likely to go against your wishes if you allow them freedom. But it is the only way to be at all accurate about what is happening in the world.

Just as the reporter has a typewriter or microphone as a tool for producing a story, the consumer has tools for examining his own reaction to that story. We've known for more than half a century about stereotypes, and we still have them and let them get the better of us. The explanation Walter Lippmann wrote in 1922 sums up our craving:

> They may not be a complete picture of the world, but they are a picture of a possible world to which we are adapted. In that world people and things have their well-known places, and do certain expected things. We feel at home there. We fit in. We are members. We know the way around. There we find the charm of the familiar, the normal, the dependable; its grooves and shapes are where we are accustomed to find them.[34]

Stereotypes, simply put, are security blankets for the brain. The consumer is most apt to take in the news with his stereotypes comfortably snug around him. In news coverage of race relations in America, he will see the center stage figures as demons or heroes. If the news media presents information to the contrary, he writes it off as bias—the media's, not his own. He knows what those people are like, regardless of what the news says. The consumer faithful to his stereotypes mentally rewrites the reporter's version of the facts.

Not only do we adjust the news to fit our stereotypes; if the news doesn't square with the major preconceptions which govern our lives, we may banish it entirely, refuse to believe it.

In 1770, Captain James Cook sailed into Botany Bay on the southeastern coast of Australia. The natives there had never seen a ship before, and Cook's *Endeavour* was 106 feet long and titanic with masts and sail. Yet, a naturalist aboard the *Endeavour* noted in his journal, the aborigines ignored this fantastic new sight, going about their village life "to all appearance totally unmoved by us."[35] The visitation was too strange to be comprehended, and so the primitives ignored it.

We are not so far from those aborigines. When the wholesale deaths caused by U.S. infantrymen in the Vietnamese village of My Lai came to light and numerous eyewitness accounts and even photographs attested to the holocaust, many Americans still professed disbelief. Their reaction seemed to be that My Lai never happened, it wasn't as bad as the media made it out to be, and the villagers deserved it anyway. Such news stories shatter too many beliefs to rest easily with the consumer. The easier way is to obscure distressing news with old dogmas.

Such are some of the major disagreements between the newsman's viewpoint and the consumer's. But are they in fact serious? From protest marches to
sensitivity sessions to election campaigns, our society resounds with the faith
that betterment is a matter of adjustment. That two sets of good intentions
disagree is not to be admitted. Write it off as a "problem in semantics."
Bickering is merely "breakdown in communication."

But as far as the affair between the newsman and the consumer is concerned, this notion that differing viewpoints actually are so much alike that
only a little good will is needed to bring the two together is baloney.

News earnestly reported and fairly presented probably will be uncomfortable for you as a consumer a good percentage of the time, and you aren't
going to like such unease.

As was evident when we examined the reasons news is selected by
newsmen, the news sometimes will be choked with tragedy, venality, horror,
homicide, and every other objectionableness known to man. The publications
and the broadcasts may upset the equilibrium you have achieved through
stereotyping. Sooner or later, you will think the world is going to hell at a
supersonic rate.

When the news upsets the consumer from time to time, he almost certainly will resent becoming upset. But that consumer—and you, and all the
rest of us struggling through the twentieth century—ought to realize what it
is he resents: the message, not the messenger.

The newsman brings to the consumer what writer Rebecca West once
called "the facts that put together are the face of the age; the rise in the
price of coal, the new ballet, the woman found dead in a kimono on the
golf links, the latest sermon of the Archbishop of York, the marriage of a
Prime Minister's daughter."[36]

Like it or not, we must have the news.

"For if people do not have the face of the age set clear before them,"
Miss West continued, "they being to imagine it. . . ."

"Great news! Mass media are pushing ecology. Pass it on."

Drawing by Henry Martin; © 1971 The New Yorker
Magazine, Inc.

The News Apparatus

News stories are made, not born. Made by workers and machines that refine random happenings into bundles of information.

So, one bogey word flung at the media is true. News is "manufactured." The messages which come to your eye or ear are borne by electrode and gear and circuitry and pulley, a whole sophisticated tangle of industrial apparatus.

News travels, too, on the same underpinning you find beneath products as diverse as pig iron ingots and cough drops—the American corporate structure, designed for sales and profit.

And whichever corporation the news comes to you from, it's probably much the same as the competitors' versions. Television, magazines, newspapers, radio all feature a topic and, before the glut passes, leave you feeling that you've been told more than you want to know. Time and again you will see the news media bunching around a topic—civil rights, ecology, militant women—and playing it big until the next phenomenon appears.

Suspicious, no?

Suspicious, yes; conspiratorial, no. At least since the textile workers of northern England smashed equipment in the Luddite disturbances of the early nineteenth century, citizens have been somewhat leery of machines themselves, of the power and profits the machinery feeds to ownership, and, most of all, of the effects giant industry has on their lives.[1] Here at our own millisecond of history, the manufacturing process does have its effects on the news, and so on us, but in ways more subtle and less wicked than the news consumer probably suspects.

Imagine, for a few paragraphs, a newspaper reporter named Dana Schmierkase.

As with most newsgatherers on any working day, reporter Schmierkase is covering not the White House nor the latest brushfire war overseas, but a plain story right here in town: a school board meeting.

The voters a few days ago turned down a bond issue, and tonight the board members are trying to hack through the impending financial problems. As Dana enters the auditorium of the Millard Fillmore High School a few minutes before 8 p.m., parents and students are still streaming in.

The meeting opens, discussion begins: cut sports, defer building projects, close some schools, fire some teachers and administrators. Amid it all, Dana takes notes, asks followup questions later.

Back at the newsroom, the reporter settles at a typewriter to put together a story for the morning paper. First, a telephone call to get comments from the townsman who led opposition to the bond issue. Next, information from the newspaper's library—recent clippings on the vote in this bond election, background on other bond issue failures around the area.

When the story is written, Dana hands it to the man handling the flow of news copy on that shift, usually the city editor or the managing editor. He skims the story and passes it to a copy editor, telling him what size headline he wants on it.

The copy editor begins penciling. He tightens sentences, checks for accuracy. The reporter has spelled Fillmore with a lone "l"; that Schmierkase better learn to get names right, the copy editor mutters. He reads two paragraphs which seem flimsy. Trimming them from the story, he tells the reporter he wants instead some comment from a school board member who missed tonight's meeting but who may be the swing vote on whatever budget cutting the board does at its next session. Dana makes the phone call while the copy editor writes the headline.

The story next goes to composition—through the mechanical maze of typesetting, casting, plating, and printing which inks the story into the newspaper read over the breakfast coffee.

In scant outline, that is the newsgathering process of all the media: reporting, editing, production.

If Dana Schmierkase were writing for a magazine, the topic would be bigger—perhaps a report on school bonds being voted down in several different cities—and the story longer. For radio, a shorter story, perhaps with recorded comments from the board meeting. For television, both sound and film would be added.

But if the basics of the news business are similar all across the industry, the refinements are not. Each news medium works out of its own history and its own collection of special quirks.

Publications: The Eternal Footprint

Levering the pressure down on his modified wine press, Johann Gutenberg in about the year 1448 brought Western civilization the invention of movable type.[2]

Those words stamped on paper by the German printer carried the reproduction of language from hand to machine. It meant that the ideas of mankind could be passed through time less laboriously, and in plentiful facsimiles which would reach the common man as well as the learned noble. With movable type, the alphabet truly became the footprints of civilization.

In the English-speaking world, the newspaper has been the quickest version of mass printing for a little more than three centuries. "Journals," and thus journalism, began appearing in England early in the seventeenth century, and nosing into the scene around them. Editor Ned Ward of the *London Spy* may have been the original investigative reporter, with his visit in 1699 to a workhouse for small-time convicts: " 'Prithee, friend,' said I to a surly bull-necked fellow . . . 'what are you confined to this labor for?' "[3]

The most lackadaisical of modern newspapers fall below Ned Ward's quota of curiosity, but both technique and manpower have swelled at all offices of today's News-Times-Herald-Journal-Press-Tribune-Star-Sun.[4] By the time of the Civil War, refinements in the cylinder press made it possible to print on high speed streams of paper, the mass production needed for big metropolitan dailies.[5] Technicians have been trying to further refine the complex printing operation ever since—Mark Twain lost a fortune on a typesetting machine which had 18,000 separate parts, at least one of which was sure to be out of kilter—to the point where the computer now is entering the printing process.[6]

Count heads out beyond the machinery, and you find that newspaper staffs have grown prolifically since the days of the journeyman editor-printer about a century ago. Even a small daily may have a staff of several dozen, and on the metropolitan papers the manpower runs into the hundreds. On any daily paper today, with a gamut of coverage from politics to PTA, many of those newsmen will be specialists in a single topic.

Aside from similar staff structure and production methods, today's dailies have another feature in common; they rely on national syndicates for most of their news stories. The Associated Press and United Press International, with several thousand employees each, send hundreds of stories by teletype every day to papers that buy their services.[7] Wired into the national news enterprises which so amply rap out stories to fill white space, the "local" newspaper may have fuller coverage of the U.S. Department of State than of the city hall a few blocks away.

Magazines come into print at the pace newspapers used to—monthly or weekly. Publishing less rapidly allows a chance to prepare longer, more carefully crafted articles. Against this is the disadvantage that slower production schedules make it harder to cover recent events. *Newsweek* and *Time* perhaps straddle most successfully. Each will run background articles up to several thousand words long, but also can get a story as late as Sunday morning and have it on newsstands nationwide on Monday.[8]

Magazines have taken a financial shellacking in recent history. The giants have lost advertising revenue to television and specialized publications. In the 1960s such venerables as *Collier's* and the *Saturday Evening Post* went out of business, *Look* followed in 1971, and others have been hurting badly. Even so, some of the most vigorous reporting still comes by magazine, in a lineage of useful snooping which goes back at least to 1858, when *Leslie's Weekly* exposed the marketing of unhealthy milk.[9]

Radio: The Voice Box

Radio came like a genie in the night, the first medium to travel on air. From the evening when a few crystal sets picked up the 1920 presidential election returns being broadcast by KDKA in Pittsburgh, radio news promised a fascinating immediacy, so fascinating that newspaper publishers tried to shackle the swift new competition.[10] When wire service stories grudgingly were granted to broadcasters in 1933, radio was not allowed to use news less than twelve hours old.[11]

That didn't last long, and by the time Europe was nearing war in the late 1930s, radio was doing a compelling job both with spot news and with analysis of events. From the Munich crisis in 1939 until World War II ended in 1945, radio was probably more effective with quick news than television would have been. Instead of the repetitiveness of looking at a living room war, listeners were lured by the nightly suspense of hearing newsmen broadcast across the oceans. Precisely because the audience couldn't see what was happening, attention was sharpened.

Master reporters such as Edward R. Murrow talked the news eloquently. Here is Murrow, giving his countrymen one of the first reports from the Nazi concentration camp at Buchenwald:

> There were two rows of bodies stacked up like cordwood. They were thin and very white. Some of the bodies were terribly bruised, though there seemed to be little flesh to bruise . . . I tried to count them as best I could and arrived at the conclusion that all that was mortal of more than five hundred men and boys lay there in two neat piles. . . . [12]

With the country shifting to habits of television viewing in the early 1950s, radio news became a mobile service, the quick report available by car radio or transistor packet. The news operations of many stations now are rip-and-read—stories torn directly from a wire service teletype and recited into the mike—or a telephone stint, with a reporter or two scrambling around town and calling in terse reports.

Some stations do better. KAIM in Honolulu broadcasts an afternoon roundup of analyses and editorials from newspapers around the world.[13] At WCCO in Minneapolis, the director of community affairs travels out into communities from Montana to western New York, reporting back to his station staff about the needs and interests he hears from townspeople.[14] But by and large, radio now provides the smaller news details a consumer wants: headlines, traffic reports, weather forecasts.

Television: The Gossamer Screen

His eyebrows penciled dark to show up better on the receiver, John Cameron Swayze reads the news in front of a camera.[15]

The year is 1933, and Swayze's noon telecasts for W9XBY, the experimental station owned by the *Kansas City Journal Post*, trickle out only to idlers watching the few receivers on display in store windows. But those darkened eyebrows are the mark of the future. The visual image would be added to news in the living room.

Two decades passed, and Swayze showed up nationwide as anchor man for NBC's evening newscast, with Douglas Edwards his rival across the channels on CBS.[16] With the experience of two more decades since television truly became national, network news operations have grown to staffs of hundreds.[17]

Television news at its best is superb service for the news consumer. The combination of pictures and spoken word can put a story into the living room with a wallop—our fellow humans killing or being killed, marching for their causes, looking us in the eye as they talk into the camera, the whole cantankerous and fascinating chronicle of our era. So potent is television, in fact, that we don't yet know how our society has changed because it has seen first-hand the civil rights movement, the Vietnam war protests, and the war itself.

Two types of reportage can be done more forcefully by television than by any other medium yet invented: coverage of events as they happen, and the documentary style of investigation.

The news consumer can sort through his own memory for unforgettable flashes of live news: Tom Pettit of NBC shouting "He's been shot! Lee Oswald has been shot!" in November, 1963;[18] the 1968 Democratic convention, when Chicago police clashed with protestors chanting "The whole world is watching"; man stepping onto the moon in July, 1969.

In documentary work, the networks over the years have hit so hard on military matters, poverty in America, the racial climate, and many other topics that outraged reactions were turned against television itself.

But at its normal level—the local level, the 700 commercial stations—television news is usually far from superb. There are honorable exceptions, quite a few. KYW-TV in Philadelphia, which as an affiliate of the Westinghouse Broadcasting Company has that chain's tradition of vigorous news coverage, one night devoted five and a half hours of evening time to detailed discussion of plans for a national bicentennial celebration in 1976.[19] KCRA-TV in Sacramento has been broadcasting an hour and a half of local news each evening. Enterprising coverage from the Sacramento station's news staff of seventy persons has included extended interviews, stories from a roving correspondent in northern California, and a KCRA camera crew's reports, shown in thirty nightly segments of five minutes each, about the nations of eastern Africa after ten years of independence.[20]

Many stations, however, fail to put across the news with any real impact. Television is impermanent, a picture quickly come and quickly gone. This gossamer thinness of reality is even more troublesome when a TV news show is a succession of spiritless film clips and too-brief recitals of events. Local television news shares, too, the distraction common in the network news programs. As the *Survey of Broadcast Journalism* put it in 1969:

> With as many as twenty products or services being advertised in each half-hour segment, commercials must inevitably diminish the impact of given events by sharing with them and imparting the familiar gloss of trivia to the half-listening mind.[21]

Machinery Marches On

On the screen, planes whine down in quick attacking dives, their bomb bursts blossoming in deadly pattern there in the Asian delta country. The men and machines of combat are virtually right here in this room. The war comes home to the American viewing public.

The news consumer sits in a movie theater this night in January, 1938, and the on-screen warfare rumbles in China, where the U.S. gunboat *Panay* has been bombed by Japanese planes.[22] Newsreels, which have since passed entirely from the national scene, were a technological phenomenon thirty-five years ago.

If this book had been written then, or even twenty-five years ago, it would have been about newspapers, magazines, movie newsreel, and radio. Now it is mostly about newspapers, magazines, and television. What it would be ten or fifteen years from now, there's no solid way of knowing. The news machinery changes along with the rest of our technological culture.

Some of tomorrow's apparatus is already in sight: television cassettes, more versatile communications satellites, computerization and electronic editing in the wire services and publishing plants. At this writing, cable TV is becoming bright on the horizon. Some seers talk of vast variety and quantity of information once cable begins delivering several dozen more channels of programming to your living room set. But predicting just what the effects of any technology will be is only guesswork.

Sometimes innovation doesn't faze us much. The credit card, for instance, means the gas station attendant no longer has to make change, but there he stands, still dribbling the last drops into the tank to bring the sum to an even number. And no one would have thought Americans would submit to constant surveillance, yet we meekly shop at stores under the eye of closed circuit television. And more of us will be strolling televised streets such as those of Mount Vernon, New York, where television cameras were installed in the spring of 1971 to watch the downtown area twenty-four hours a day.[23]

Other times, the new can be a cultural earthquake. The innocent discovery that a gas called neon would glow when electrified has flicked on a glitter all across the face of the American landscape.

The best we can do about the future is to read ahead a bit from changes already happening. Some subtle but powerful ones are affecting the news a consumer gets.

Through a system which has been coming into use for several years, a newspaper can receive wire service news stories coded onto paper tape, much like stock market ticker tape. The tape can then be fed into automatic typesetting machines. A dandy saver of effort, manpower, and wages, but impossible to edit as easily or as well as the old way in which an editor simply penciled in changes and corrections.

So, the tendency is to save time and trouble by not making such changes —to feed stories into the production machinery just the way they arrive from the wire services. As anyone who has seen the errors and dismal writing which crop up in wire service reporting will know, such non-editing is a giant step for mediocrity. Some newspaper managements, such as those at the *Providence Journal and Bulletin*[24] and the *St. Louis Post-Dispatch*,[25] have resisted tape for the sake of preserving their own craftsmanlike editing. Other managements see only the dollar signs and hurry to install the automatic news.

The same trend is heading to the day when the paper's wire editor won't even get a teletype copy of the story along with the tape. UPI and AP both are perfecting computer operations which can provide a newspaper so much wordage that no one can read it all. Instead, the local editor will read brief descriptions of each story, then call up on a video screen anything he wants to look at more fully. This use of descriptors instead of full stories doesn't bode well for feature stories, which rely on deftness of topic and writing rather than magnitude of importance and which catch an editor's eye as he skims the wire copy.

News machinery is as relentless as any other gadgetry. The more mechanized you get, the more the machines dictate your time. Television's cameras, lights, sound and film editing equipment, and videotape provide the medium its special impact in presenting the news, but such paraphernalia also gobble up time.

Robert G. Abernethy of KNBC-TV in Los Angeles once decided to see how much enterprising news coverage he, as one reporter, could put together daily in the face of television's time and technical demands.

"So I tried various ways to spend my days," Abernethy recalls. "I went out covering stories, came back in and put the film together. I stayed in the office and put together a package of national and international news, re-writing the wires and using the NBC News Program Service tape. I tried combinations of the two. Covering a story, the most I could get on the air was four or five minutes. Doing a national and international package, the most I could get on was about seven. And this was a full day's work."[26]

Say a television station has an hour program of local news each night, as many now do. That's a total of forty-five to fifty minutes of news space. It would take the day's work of seven topflight newsmen such as Robert Abernethy to fill that news hour with expert reporting. And to get professionals who can handle the news the way it should be reported would cost seven big salaries, plus a bigger payroll for more camera crews and film editors to work with that many newsmen. Small wonder so much of local news is fluff, filler, and news conference folderol.

Not all news outlets are going the route of slicker and more demanding implements. Offset printing, which bypasses complicated typecasting in lead, costs less and is simpler than the vast publishing machinery a big letterpress enterprise needs. To go thoroughly basic, a considerable mimeograph enterprise can be set up for a few hundred dollars. Underground newspapers and papers for Blacks, Indians, and militant women have proliferated out of these cheaper alternatives. Similar news outlets could show up in cable TV, or even in the present broadcasting structure, if license challenges by some of the outside groups turn out to be successful.

The bigger and more traditional news outfits, however, will probably stay with trends to supertechnology, whatever the consequences for news standards. Their calculation is simple. Profit is on that route.

The Corporate Structure and Other Complexes

Printer and publisher William F. Schanen Jr. owned three small weekly newspapers in Wisconsin. One day in June, 1969, two kinds of notices came to him:[27]

1. He was notified that his *Ozaukee Press* had placed first for general excellence in the National Newspaper Association competition.
2. A parade of local businessmen cancelled their advertising.

In Schanen's home town of 9,000, the withdrawn ads were an imposing show of commercial muscle. A druggist pulled out his advertisement, then the owner of an appliance store, next the manager of a local five-and-ten, a car dealer, and a real estate broker. That was only the start. Schanen watched his advertising revenue dwindle from about $4,000 a week to $700.

Why? Because he had agreed to print a Milwaukee underground paper, *Kaleidoscope*, which a local machine-tool manufacturer judged obscene. The industrialist organized a boycott, sending out letters which said in part:

"I will not buy space in his newspapers, and I will not buy from anyone who advertises in his newspapers. Ladies and Gentlemen, I am looking for company."

In the next twelve months, Schanen estimated a loss of $300,000 in gross income. The *Ozaukee Press*—his largest paper, and the prize winner—dropped 2,500 in circulation, down to 4,000 copies a week. He merged his two other dailies, then put them up for sale, calculating that revenue had nose-dived 90 to 95 percent.

"Oh, yes, they've won," Schanen said of the boycotters. "I never was aware of what the boycott was about. We have a corporation here which operates a printing plant. I could never understand the depth of feeling. I'm 56 years old and I can't understand why I'm the only person here who approves of long hair and freedom of expression."

Whether your taste runs to long-haired status shakers or to conservative Wisconsin businessmen, one inescapable fact of the news business cuts through William Schanen's story. A news organization is an enterprise which must make money to survive.

Not even multimillionaires can take losses forever, as John Hay Whitney demonstrated in 1966 when he merged one of the finest newspapers in the country, the *New York Herald Tribune*, after sustaining an estimated $20 million in losses in eight years.[28] The *Herald Trib* became part of a three-headed mutation called the *World Journal Tribune*. The WJT, or "Widget" as it was derisively nicknamed, died less than a year later.

Most of the cost of printing news, and the entire cost of commercial broadcast news, is paid by advertisers, not by news consumers. What, then, happens when advertising and the news side conflict, as they often do? While seldom as obvious as the haymaker that hit publisher Schanen in Wisconsin, advertising clout is not rare. This use of dollar power can range from demands for favorable news stories as part of an advertising contract, to gentle suggestions over lunch from the head of the largest department store to the publisher.

Or what happens when influential advertisers decide they don't like the publisher's opinions? Or when the wire service teletype clatters out congressional testimony about empty calories in some of our packaged foods, and car bumpers that fail at speeds of more than five miles an hour?

Newspapers average 42 percent of their income from local sources, and a very considerable portion is food and auto advertising.[29] How the news outlet reacts to pressure will depend on the owner—the strength of his bank book, his competitive position, his other business interests, and his ethics. Rolfe Neill, editor of the *Philadelphia Daily News*, put it crisply: "The quality of journalism begins in an owner's soul."[30] News outlets with small advertising markets are especially vulnerable to soul-searching which decides in favor of the dollar; if the town's main advertisers pull out, the owner has nowhere else to look.

Schanen knew that, but decided to stick with his principles and publish a controversial disturber of the peace in his print shop. The record elsewhere is mixed. Along with the boycotters and the flexible ownerships can be found reasonable advertisers who would not try pressure and newsmen who would not give in to it. But the essential point still sticks out: as long as news operations depend mostly on advertising income, the *potential* for abusing the news process is severe, and the news consumer must be alert for it.

Economic pressures can build threateningly above the news in other ways. Through 1970 and 1971, a sagging economy diminished advertising revenue while inflation sent labor costs up. In one twelve-month span, more than 1,000 jobs vanished in just three of the largest news publishing companies.[31] McGraw-Hill trimmed 300 employees as its thirty-six trade and business publications became less profitable. Time, Inc. cut its staffs by 450 through layoffs and attrition. The *New York Times* left 300 jobs vacant as employees resigned or retired. The Times alone suffered a $14.5 million advertising decline in 1970, much of it because "help wanted" listings shrank as the job market tightened.

The pattern coursed through the entire print industry. Ten of the fifteen newspapers which print the greatest volume of advertising carried fewer pages of ads in 1970 than in the year before, and seventeen of the twenty top revenue producing magazines suffered declines.[32]

Congress banned cigarette advertising from radio and television beginning January 2, 1971. Immediately the broadcasters scrambled to recover from an annual $200 million loss in revenues, while the print media hastened to pick up the cigarette accounts—another problem of profit versus public interest.[33]

More than a year before cigarette commercials left the air, Andrew Heiskell,[34] chairman of Time, Inc., assured an inquisitive U.S. senator[35] that his company would continue to take cigarette advertising but would not accept any "overwhelming" additional amount. Yet writer Thomas Whiteside calculated that the first three issues of *Time* in 1971 carried almost twenty-one pages of cigarette ads, compared with eight pages during the same period of 1970. Its sister publication, *Life*, showed a similar increase in its first three issues, from twelve and a half pages of cigarette advertising to twenty-two.

Other publications also tapped into the new revenue. *Newsweek*, for example, scheduled fifty pages of cigarette ads for the first three months of 1971, against twenty-three in the first quarter of 1970. *Journalism Quarterly* reported a research study of increased cigarette advertising in fourteen major magazines. The number of ads and the amount of space devoted to cigarette advertising in the first three months of 1971 had doubled from the same period in 1970.[36]

When the television ban became law, Jack Kauffman, president of the newspaper publishers' Bureau of Advertising, promptly forecast that cigarette ads in papers would go up from an estimated $18 million in 1970 to some $60 million in 1971.[37]

"How can any publisher—anyone—make money out of selling advertisements for a product that is known to cause death on a disastrous national scale year after year?" asked reporter Whiteside. "The fact that *Life* and *Look* are in financial trouble can hardly be viewed as an acceptable excuse for their trying to prop up their corporate health at the expense of the health of their readers."

Whiteside charged that, with such honorable exceptions as *Mademoiselle* and *Glamour*, women's magazines also were handling an upsurge of added cigarette advertising after the broadcasting ban.

Management's ethics come into play in other problems of news versus dollars—for instance, in the matter of other interests linked to the ownership.

Group or chain journalism, where one owner controls two or more news enterprises, has been the long-term trend in the newspaper business. The electronic media tend toward an even more elaborate linkage, the conglomerates or super-corporations. Radio Corporation of America, for example, owns NBC, manufactures appliances and consumer goods, and is a leading defense and space research contractor.[38] CBS owns, among other holdings, the New York Yankees and Creative Playthings, and has invested millions in the credit affiliates of Ford, Chrysler, and General Motors.

In a study of twenty-nine conglomerates, *Broadcasting* magazine reported that electronic media were the most highly profitable of conglomerate operations, and cited gross annual incomes of up to $82 million for a single network to back up its conclusion: "There may be many trials and tribulations in the broadcasting business, but there still remains a buck to be made."[39]

That fat electronic buck bothers critics. Will the network which is one branch of a conglomerate dig hard for news about the industry which is another? Once again, the *potential* for profit to overwhelm public interest is obvious. Down in the trenches, some news organizations won't let their newsmen take part in activities which would even seem to compromise their fairness and integrity. The potential for conflicts of ethics is much bigger and more slippery within a conglomerate. It may be enough for a news executive or reporter simply to know that his newsroom is part of the larger financial framework, and therefore to avoid any investigative reporting into the master company's other nooks of business.

On the newspaper side, the trend has been towards less competition as owners string more and more dailies into their publishing corporations. Of 1,748 dailies in the U.S. in July, 1971, more than half—883—belonged to groups.[40] They ranged from the Gannett Company's forty-four newspapers to minimum chains of two. Group-owned newspapers accounted for more than 63 per cent of this country's weekday circulation of 62 million copies.

Group owners argue in favor of the economies which they say result from multiple ownership. Opponents bewail the passing of individually controlled newspapers and their diversity of voice in the local scene.

Whether or not the publisher who owns a chain of papers insists on his particular editorial viewpoint in each one—and many do not—the objection is familiar: the potential exists for undue influence by one person.

Clearly, diversity is lessened as papers go out of business or are bought out by competitors. Until 1956, Chicago had four big dailies under four separate ownerships.[41] Now it has four under a pair of ownerships, and two of the newspapers, Chicago Tribune Company's *Chicago Today* and Field Enterprises' *Chicago Daily News*, have lost up to an estimated $7 million and $5 million a year, respectively.[42] Although neither corporation wants to surrender the evening field to the other and each therefore subsidizes its loser, the odds are strong that Chicago eventually will be down to no more than three newspapers. It will be a sad day, for Chicago has been the last city in the U.S. with competing papers both morning and evening.

New York boasted fourteen dailies in 1920, which shrank to six by late 1963.[43] By 1967, the news consumer had his choice of the *Times* and the *Daily News* in the morning, and the *Post* at night—the three survivors. Complex reasons ran through the years of dying newspapers in our largest city, among them economics, technological backwardness enforced by union fears of automation, competition from electronic media, the population shift to the suburbs, and questionable management decisions.

The newspaper woes of Chicago and New York may seem harsh, yet those cities are two of only thirty-seven cities in the entire country which by 1971 still had two or more fully competitive newspapers.[44] In 1910, there were 689 cities with full competition; that is, competitive situations in which papers maintained separate ownerships and had no special arrangements to share the same printing plant or advertising force.

The news voices fade toward a single monotone in another way. In many cities today, the monopoly newspapers also own local radio or television outlets, and often both.

The careful news critic is wary of easy generalizations, however. Competition can yield better news products, but it can also degenerate into a contest to see who can offer the most sensational headlines. Lack of competition turns some news organizations lazy. Others use the financial security and less frantic pace to improve news coverage.

And while diversity may be scarcer, it is still on hand anywhere a news consumer is willing to read magazines and subscribe to a newspaper the caliber of the *Wall Street Journal, Philadelphia Inquirer, Washington Post, Des Moines Register, Boston Globe, Louisville Courier-Journal, New York Times,* or *Los Angeles Times*—that is, diversity of national and international coverage. In many communities, it is impossible to find more than one or two published versions of local news.

The concentration of ownership has drawn the attention of the Federal Communications Commission, which regulates the country's 7,100 radio and 900 television stations through licenses which must be renewed every three years.[45] The FCC announced it will no longer grant a broadcasting license to anyone owning another news outlet in the same market, and multiple ownerships within the same market would have to get rid of either broadcasting or print properties.[46]

Publishing executives at once began objecting that limiting their right to buy broadcast news outlets violates the First Amendment guarantee of freedom of the press.[47] As this book went to press, the issue was far from decided. On constitutional grounds, the cloak of the First Amendment is not yet clearly established for electronic media, and perhaps isn't relevant to this ownership issue anyway. Also unclear is current policy within the FCC itself, where the power balance has been swinging from holdover commissioners appointed by Lyndon Johnson to the new appointees of Richard Nixon.

The meanderings of the FCC over the last quarter century can't be summarized quickly; key changes occur as new commissioners are chosen for seven-year terms and the majority realigns. What remains constant is the crucial importance of FCC actions on the electronic media. For example, in 1969 the commission said it would quit rubber-stamping applications to renew broadcasting licenses and begin listening more closely to community complaints and competing applicants. On January 23 of that year, the FCC voted to strip WHDH-TV in Boston of its license, a landmark decision which the station appealed through the courts.[48]

The electronic media are government licensees on the theory that the airwaves are public property and must be overseen because of limited available wavelengths. Newspapers are under no such regulation. The possible total of printing presses, after all, is limited only by the economics of turning enough profit to sustain them, and freedom to print is a solidly established constitutional right. Even so, specific government policies do bear on publishers.

New postal rates which took effect in 1972, for example, hit magazines and newspapers with a 142 percent increase in mailing costs.[49] To cut the weight on which they have to pay postage, many magazines shifted to lighter paper, and some larger periodicals, such as *McCall's* and *Esquire*, shrank their page sizes. Subscription rates, already on an escalator, registered even sharper increases.

Even as other government agencies are citing the need for individual local ownership of newspapers, Internal Revenue Service tax regulations make the family-owned paper especially vulnerable. A father who establishes a newspaper can leave it to his offspring without the government taking a whopping tax bite. But when the offspring turns the ownership over to the third generation, a much higher tax rate applies. And ours is an era when many third generation heirs would be taking over. As was the case in the 1960s, many publishing families will find it more profitable to sell to a group or to buy other papers themselves.

Finally, newspaper competition was affected in 1970 when the Newspaper Preservation Act became law. It allows an antitrust exemption so that two or more newspapers can share printing, production, distribution, and the effort to sell advertising.[50]

Proponents say the legislative break for publishers enables papers to coexist in cities where one daily would otherwise be forced out of business or into outright sale to its rival.

Opponents say the law favors large papers and existing ownerships, guaranteeing them an unassailable advantage in operating efficiencies over anyone who might want to enter competition.

An Exaltation of Larks, A Conspiracy of Media

A pride of lions.   A school of fish.
A gaggle of geese on the ground, a skein of geese flying.

Author James Lipton once looked into our habit of naming creatures by the bunch and found back in English history other deft collective phrases, such as an exaltation of larks and a murmuration of starlings.[51] Similar play of the imagination is still with us, at least among folks who look at the news and see a conspiracy of media.

Many news consumers seem to think that the publisher or station owner rules all the stories at his news operation. Here's an incident which happened to the female half of this authorship.

A student mentioned to me that she was on the staff of Washington congressman Lloyd Meeds when he introduced a bill to cut the oil depletion allowance, that famed tax-break bonanza for the petroleum industry. She cited the case as one in which the congressman's hometown newspaper, the daily *Everett Herald*, kept the story out of print because management didn't want to offend major oil companies which were Herald advertisers.

An intriguing case of conspiracy—because although the student didn't know it, I was at the *Herald* editing teletype copy when this suppression supposedly happened.

Such plots just don't go on in the average day-to-day news operation.

First of all, if someone had told me to keep the story out, I would have spit in his right eye while my companion in the wire room spit in his left. Journalism isn't, to borrow a collective phrase, a host of angels. But it's a rare news office that doesn't have a number of personalities who will explode at a hint of doctoring the news.

For another thing, most publishers have virtually nothing to do with the hour-by-hour news operation. Many are businessmen, as writer Joseph Goulden once described them, being chauffeured off from the office every afternoon to mogul somewhere else for a while, and generally they see what's in their newspapers about the same time the news consumer does.[52]

What could have happened to the congressman's story, and in all likelihood did, is that it went into any of several crannies we've been talking about in this chapter. It may have been overlooked in the hurried winnowing of wire service stories. It may have been set in type for use, but left out of the paper because the day's bulk of advertising cut sharply into the space for news. Most likely of all, maybe it wasn't even transmitted by the wire services because bills aimed at the oil depletion allowance aren't uncommon.

Sometimes the consumer will suspect a national conspiracy working on the news. Circumstantial evidence looks plentiful. Early in 1971, to take one example of a news fad, a flurry of articles appeared about giant hot springs deep underground, a promising new source of steam power generation but probably not a major solution to this country's impending shortage of electricity. In one short span, stories appeared in *Saturday Review*, in at least nine West Coast newspapers, and on Los Angeles television stations.[53]

A conspiracy to promote the development of this geothermal energy? No—a junket some weeks earlier to the steam energy fields at Cerro Prieto, Mexico, sponsored by the University of California. Writers for all the news organizations which ran stories went on the Cerro Prieto trip.

Other times, coincidence accounts for similar coverage. For instance, *Life* and *Newsweek* had cover stories on the women's rights movement three days apart.[54] *Time* and *Newsweek* ran cover stories on welfare in simultaneous issues.[55] This points up another reason why different news outlets often have similar coverage. Newsmen share certain assumptions about the news.

The aspects of the news apparatus we've been talking about can affect the news in many ways, and the news consumer should be aware of them. But not all of these influences can be found in any single news outlet, and any that are there likely came on the tide of broad trends. The consumer should be aware, too, that these influences on the news mostly happen separately and maybe even haphazardly; that many a contortion within the news process may account for shortcomings, but the deliberate kink of conspiracy probably won't be one of them.

Chapter 4

Miss Peach by Mell Lazarus. Courtesy of Publishers-Hall Syndicate.

Stories Untold

"By jingo, there used to be a peg legged fellow lived up the road from us, name of Smokey Daggett, and one night old Smokey started out for town on foot . . ."

Back when the world had fewer years upon its shoulders, a story could unfold this way, idling leisurely in the company of its listeners. If today's news could be told in such winsome circumstances, we would be informed better and more agreeably than we are.

The storyteller's knack is to deftly tweak our curiosity, then to enrapture us. When performed with the full magic an expert can summon out of language, it is a high art. Even in an age of telecasts from the moon, one of the most wondrous devices of communications still is an Irishman fueled with ale.

But modern man's daily teller of tales, the news media, cannot win such easy rapport with the audience. That audience now sprawls by the million beyond the traditional storyteller's little circle, and its interests and needs are proportionately hard to know. Added to the task of today's newsman with a report about Smokey Daggett upon the darkened road are the mechanical complexities through which narrator now talks to his audience. And added yet again are the perplexities of making difficult topics understandable for the news consumer.

In such circumstances of our culture lie several reasons some stories go untold—reasons cerebral and reasons financial.

The View from Our Town

Somewhere in all of us the suspicion nags: we are not being told *everything*.

From a friend or relative or the informed source at the next desk, you learn in rich detail the town's current scandal—but hear not a breath about it on the news broadcasts. Or from what you know about the community, you judge that coverage in the daily paper sometimes doesn't jibe with the actuality.

No thrill is easier or cheaper than convincing ourselves some sinister plot keeps certain stories out of the news. But for the most part, the news media's delinquencies don't live up to our suspicions.

Discovering a conspiracy of newsmen is about as unlikely as finding a townful of news consumers who agree on every issue; the human species simply has too many mavericks to allow for such cahoots. We discussed in chapter three the fallacy of discerning a conspiracy of media whenever a story receives play from more than one news outlet. It's equally fallacious to cry conspiracy whenever a story isn't covered. News stories not told, or told ineptly or half-heartedly, are probably impeded not by deliberate plotting, but by frames of mind which inhibit their telling.

One is parochialism, the natural tendency to view the world in terms of one's own neighborhood. The charge of parochialism is usually lodged against the news operations headquartered in the most cosmopolitan region of the country, the Eastern Seaboard.

It is a fact of geography that many big communications enterprises are in the eastern U.S. Within an area of New York City, which on a continental scale counts for only a minuscule neighborhood, are main offices of the television and radio networks, ABC, CBS, and NBC; of many national magazines, including *Esquire, Fortune, Harper's, Life, National Review, Newsweek, New York, The Nation, The New Yorker,* and *Time;* of the two major wire services, Associated Press and United Press International; and of the *New York Daily News, New York Post, New York Times,* and *Wall Street Journal.*

The second address of the Eastern Establishment is Washington, D.C., which has the main news bureaus of most of the big newsgathering organizations; such national magazines as The *New Republic* and *U.S. News and World Report;* and the *Washington Post* and *Washington Star,* both influential newspapers whose dispatches appear in papers all over the country through national news syndicates.

Out of this high rent neighborhood of communicators can come some questionable visions of the rest of the country. One persistent notion of this sort seems to be that if the upper echelons in Washington and New York are transfixed by political speculation, hinterlands America must be, too. Accordingly, the national media provide us a nonstop presidential campaign, each inning four years long. The White House fixation overwhelms coverage of some events which have more useful angles. The annual conference of governors, for example, furnishes a grand chance for newsmen to dig into the perplexities of state government; instead, the meetings are reported by and large as a priming contest for presidential aspirants.[1]

And in more piquant ways, Eastern-based editors and writers sometimes see quaint mirages beyond the Appalachians. A photographer hired by National Geographic for an article about Alaska was instructed by his editor back in Washington, D.C., to head up the Yukon to find a certain Chilkoot woman "who knows all the old tales about the river."[2] He found her, but instead of tales of the Yukon, all she would talk about was the menace of longhaired hippies.

Yet whatever parochialism afflicts the East Coast news apparatus has been more nettlesome than serious. Potent correctives are at work—for instance, the competition between the national news operations. One newsgatherer's tunnel vision is another reporter's chance for a story. Also, most of the large news organizations have reporters stationed in other parts of the country, newsmen whose trade it is to know the local scene.

The more damaging parochialism in this country's newsgatherers is the small town, small city brand—the narrow view of the unEastern Establishment—which will not admit that the issues great in New York and Washington are vital elsewhere as well.

The news consumer can judge for himself whether his local media's views of the world beyond the municipal limits consist of a riot in a city halfway across the continent, an earthquake in Peru, and a hundred words about a famine in Pakistan. Here the national publications and networks are allies for the news consumer, providing coverage to measure the local version against. But for another common type of story, coverage of civic projects, he has to rely on his own insights to discern when parochialism is at work on the news.

The symptom he can watch for in the hometown media will be an immense swelling of local pride. Down through the years of proliferating freeways and multiplying skyscrapers, some of the best news enterprises lost their good sense and reported such projects with hurrahs instead of skeptical investigation. More recently, the great stadium binge has shown that local boosterism still is alive in the news media and doing well.[3]

Between 1960 and the end of 1971, at least twenty new sports stadiums were built or were on the way in this country's major metropolitan areas. The total cost amounts to about $800 million. This is an enormous outlay when cities are beset with needs for mass transit, pollution controls, better housing—and when all but a few of the building cities already had some type of sports stadium. Also, the new stadiums tend to be outside the urban core, away from the unsightliness of urban racism and poverty—one more example of fleeing a problem instead of doing something about it. Yet all across the country in the decade when the cities were lurching toward financial calamity, news outlets for the most part cheered on local stadium projects without asking *why* they should be built with public bond issues amid so many other needs.

The Currying of Sacred Cows

The critic quickest to damn East Coast journalists for parochialism probably does not mind at all a more general myopia of the news media: uncritical allegiance to country.

When he was Secretary of State, Dean Rusk told reporters pressing him with questions about the war in Southeast Asia that criticism gets to the point where "the question is, whose side are you on? Now, I'm Secretary of State of the United States, and I'm on our side."[4]

For all of Mr. Rusk's exasperation and the testy relationships between government leaders and newsmen in recent years, newsgatherers can be found too often on the side of the motherland when they should be on the side of inquiry.

Suppose that a news operation does break a story unflattering to this nation, as any diligent newsgatherer will at one time or another. Such news, heaven help this star-spangled chalice of liberty we so love, honor, revere, etc., is howled down as being against the "national interest."

But the definers of "national interest" in such a case will inevitably be public officials. Just as inevitably, a public official's version of the national interest will include the notion that his own mistakes should never be told. Yet what can be more in the ultimate interests of a democratic people than honesty? The highest form of patriotism is to serve as an unsparing critic, and the news media do too little service of this sort rather than too much.

Too little, for instance, in the decade or so when the news media generally treated the U.S. space program as a sacred cow. Faced with a story full of complex technology and imbued with the spirit of a race to the moon, many newsmen relied on the press handouts from the National Aeronautics and Space Administration. As long as the countdown to the moon went smoothly, all was well. Then when disaster hit—the fire in an Apollo test capsule which killed three astronauts on January 27, 1967—the news media discovered that there were no rescue plans for such an emergency, and that a report critical of workmanship in the building of the Apollo capsule had been made more than a year earlier.[5]

Other agencies have been the beneficiaries of uncritical reporting because their duties were regarded as so obviously good for the nation. The U.S. Army Corps of Engineers and the Peace Corps both enjoyed such treatment for different lengths of time. A current example to be watched, to see whether the news stories about it are toughminded instead of simpering, is the Environmental Protection Agency, created for the thankless job of cleansing pollution from our gargantuan system of enterprise.

Individuals as well as agencies may be accorded the kind of deference which leaves important stories untold. A President of the United States, for instance, gets enormous media attention from afar, but very little discomfiture up close, which is where answers usually are found.

When a politician is merely a presidential candidate, newsmen will question him ruthlessly. The instant he takes over the White House, however, awe sets in. News conferences and presidential interviews are, most of the time, saturated with deference—so saturated that a rare occasion when candor broke through should be cited as an example of what *could* be, if newsmen could occasionally bring themselves to utter the sentence: "But Mr. President, you didn't answer the question I asked."

The first week in May, 1971, police arrested more than 12,000 war protestors in Washington, D.C., in dragnet arrests without the customary legal procedure of booking, providing opportunity for counsel, and setting bail.[6] Midway through a presidential news conference on June 2, a reporter asked President Nixon whether he believed the Washington police had handled the situation properly. Although virtually all the arrests had been dismissed as illegal procedure on the part of the police, the President's reply glossed over this vital point and he confidently moved off to another question.

The story—the chief executive's stand on detention arrests without legal process—remained very much untold at this point. Before long, another question pressed the same topic; then two more in succession, including a followup which pointed out that the President still had not addressed himself to the issue of arrests without legal process. Mr. Nixon, plainly taken aback, quickly used a President's customary escape hatch by swiveling around to call next on a reporter noted for gadfly questions on less than vital topics.[7]

Where ideas rather than agencies or individuals are concerned—matters of government policy, for instance—the past decade has seen some movement away from overallegiance to the totem of "national security."[8] This is seen most clearly in the trend at the *New York Times*, which in the early 1960s learned about the Bay of Pigs invasion and about U–2 flights over the Soviet Union before the government made public any information about either, but held back the stories. Since then, because the leadership at the Times decided that the country should know about such matters, and that government officials' opinions about what to release are an untrustworthy guide, the newspaper has broken inside stories distasteful to government policy makers, most famously in the case of the classified Pentagon Papers.

Glance back over the list of topics: flaws in the space program, official policy on detention arrests, the U.S. role in the Caribbean and in Southeast Asia. In each case, the news consumer is better off knowing the story than not knowing it. The topics are major ones, certainly big enough that they could bear directly on any citizen. In each case, the news consumer may be called upon to provide part of his paycheck or his liberty or his life. But whenever a newsgatherer is too prone to allegiance in the name of flag and country, stories such as these will go untold.

The Practice of Sourcery

A particularly perplexing aspect of why stories may not get told lurks in the newsman's relationships with sources. Most reporters work some kind of beat system, from the man who covers the White House for a news network to the one who reports for a local daily on the doings at the court house. The people whom a newsman must see regularly can make his job easy or difficult, and both of them know it.

Frank Barnako, Jr. covers the Chicago city hall for WMAQ Radio–NBC News.[9] He and his colleagues spar with Mayor Richard J. Daley, one of the most powerful political bosses this country has ever seen. Listen to Barnako's blunt description of the contest:

> . . . We're trying to do an aggressive, professional job of covering the news, but there are practical considerations we can't ignore. We have to cover City Hall all year 'round, and if any one of us pushes the mayor too far, Daley is likely to be less available to that reporter in the future. . . . And without access to the Mayor, a City Hall reporter is worth very little indeed.
>
> An equally inhibiting factor is the force of the Mayor's own personality. My colleagues may not admit it, but I think deep in the subconscious of each of us is the fear that the mayor will blow up at one of us and say, "You punk kid . . ." Nobody likes to be dressed down by the most powerful urban politician in the country, least of all a reporter who must compete with other newsmen for public attention. So more often than not, we content ourselves with whatever crumbs the Mayor chooses to toss our way.[10]

What balance is achieved between newsman and source usually rests on the tacit knowledge that each needs the other. If the source is the newsman's pipeline to information, so is the newsman the source's conduit to the media audience. And fits of pique do have a way of subsiding. After Governor Edmund G. Brown won handily over his opponent in the 1962 gubernatorial race in California, Howard K. Smith anchored a television commentary which bade an unsentimental farewell to that opponent: *The Political Obituary of Richard M. Nixon.*[11] But early in the Nixon presidency, Smith, as an anchor man of ABC's evening news, was reported to be a White House favorite.

The flip side of the relationship, where a newsman and his sources get to be chummy with each other, can be even more invidious.

One of the potentially best reporters we ever knew fell into that trap. A personable fellow with wonderful ability, he'd been covering his city as a bureau correspondent only a few months when dinner invitations began arriving, along with tickets to country club dances and sports events. He accepted. Then he began spending even more time off the job with sources on his beat. He shared adjoining bar stools with councilmen regularly.

Before long he'd turned from a watchdog to a house pet. His value in that town was finished, so the managing editor transferred him to another beat, where the plot was recycled. Today he is no longer on that newspaper's staff.

Reporting, unfortunately, is no popularity contest. The best a reporter can hope for, if he's doing his job conscientiously, is respect from his sources. As he returns the Southern Comfort, he keeps his spirits up by reminding himself that he's still his own man—and the public's.

Backing into Tomorrow

Newsmen should be a bit better than most of us at the chancy job of looking ahead. Keeping abreast of events and knowing how to work with information are the skills involved, and these are news skills. But in spite of this, some of the notions governing areas of news coverage have been as backward as a driver who navigates by gazing into the rearview mirror instead of through the windshield.

So it is that in an era of mobility and leisure, newspapers by and large haven't gone beyond the brochure type of travel story which assures the reader "everything-is-jimdandy-in-scenic-Jimsonweed-City," while television and radio seldom do even that much. That in an era when virtually everyone below the very rich despairs of finding and financing decent housing, the real estate pages of most newspapers have been public relations puffery in praise of suburban sprawl and wafer-walled apartments. That news about women, in whatever medium, has been traditionally more confection than content, with women's rights, birth control, and genuine shoppers' information only recently thrusting through between the brides' photos and garden club notes.

There is no way to predict the future accurately. History is forever writhing off in directions we can't foretell. But perceiving social currents as they are happening is another matter, and here newsmen have frequently missed their calling.

May Ways of *Fortune* magazine cites this example:

> A relatively simple compound—automobile plus mass prosperity—brings mass ownership of automobiles, a phenomenon that can ruin cities, alter familial relations, and demand new forms and techniques of government. Adequate news analysis of this particular compound is about fifty years overdue and not yet in sight.[12]

Similarly, the move of rural residents to the great cities, a tremendous story across several decades, largely escaped the news media's attention until the cities were flooded with persons ill equipped to cope with urban living.

Nor have the news media grasped the significance of death control. While more and more of us live longer in this country, coverage of elder citizens has been largely the cliches of 100th birthdays and golden weddings. In the U.S. now, persons 100 years of age or older outnumber the total of industrial designers—about 15,000 to 10,000—yet no editor would run a formula story about a person solely because he is an industrial designer.[13] And golden weddings are no longer rare; one couple out of every five in the United States lives to celebrate a fiftieth wedding anniversary.[14]

In time, the news media may have gerontology reporters to write about the culture and doings of the elderly just as youth reporters in recent years have started to cover the younger scene. As the work week shrinks to four days and below, there may be leisure reporters, reporting on how people manage to fill their time. If the exploring thrust into outer space continues, there will be outer space correspondents. Perhaps it's fantasy to suggest there will be reporters in the general news media who will specialize in covering what computers are doing; perhaps not. As living styles change, reporters may specialize in reporting on communes, the way they now cover suburban beats.

Between the slacknesses of the past and the emerging future are recent developments in telling previously untold stories, and they are promising.

After some early hysteria and some haphazard retooling of outdoors editors into ecology specialists, many news enterprises now cover environmental topics continually and with expertise.[15]

Consumer reporters are appearing. Some of this trend is still stifled by reluctance to offend advertisers by naming them in critical stories, but some tough editors are showing you can do an honest job and still survive. Editor Thomas Pew of the Troy (Ohio) *Daily News* ran a series about Ralph Nader's 1965 book *Unsafe at Any Speed*, which significantly was subtitled *The designed-in dangers of the American automobile*. All local car dealers except one bound by a contract promptly pulled their advertising. But "you can't sell autos unless you advertise," Pew points out, and within a few weeks the car ads were back.[16]

A rebound of that sort is one way economic pressures sometimes help rather than hinder bold reporting. Another way is when news consumers show their willingness to pay for investigative reporting. When *New York Magazine* in its December 21, 1970, issue introduced its "Guerrilla Guide for the Consumer," a monthly pullout section of "strategy and tactics for the New York shopper," the issue was one of the largest sellers the magazine ever had.[17] That's the type of encouragement which hastens trends in news coverage.

Dollars versus Duty

The task of newsgathering is so difficult that the best of news operations cannot hope to report the world or even their home towns the way a diligent newsman knows it should be done. The worst never fret as long as the advertising revenue keeps tumbling in. The ordinary management which is neither the best nor the worst merely looks upon the news as a commercial product to be assembled with a minimum of strain.

Friction between newsmen and corporate leaders has erupted periodically in the television networks, colossal money-making enterprises whose news divisions customarily run in the red.[18] (The deficits come from special events coverage and public service documentaries; regularly scheduled news shows, such as the network evening news, have been financially successful.) Fred W. Friendly quit as President of CBS News in 1966 after the network overruled his decision to televise Senate hearings about Vietnam and opted for, as Friendly described it, "a fifth rerun of *Lucy*, then followed by an eighth rerun of *The Real McCoys.*"[19]

Friendly quoted the late Edward R. Murrow, the immensely respected commentator with whom he pioneered many broadcast news techniques:

> One of the basic troubles with radio and television news is that both instruments have grown up as an incompatible combination of show business, advertising, and news . . . The top management of the networks, with a few notable exceptions, has been trained in advertising, research, sales, or show business. But, by the nature of the corporate structure, they also make the final and crucial decisions having to do with news and public affairs . . . Upon occasion, economics and editorial judgment are in conflict. And there is no law which says dollars will be defeated by duty.[20]

The words are a tale monotonously told throughout the profession. Knock out the reference to the show business aspect, and Murrow's summary fits the print media as well. "The money men against the literary men," Willie Morris described the internecine struggle at Harper's which culminated when Morris resigned as editor-in-chief in March, 1971, and five of his key editors quit along with him. Such a dispute usually is more complex than a catchy phrase can imply—Harper's "money men," for instance, pointed out that the magazine under Morris's editorship was steadily *losing* money—but this well reported case is worth reading about as an example of how the dollars versus duty debate can wrack a publication.[21]

On the newspaper side, including all three where we've worked and the many where we know working reporters, the plaint runs much the same: "The trouble with that guy in the front office is that he just doesn't understand news."

Not all media management is guilty, just as not every newsman's complaint is justified. When profit and loss statements stand up to be counted, some news operations prove to be as generously funded as the business can afford. But the news consumer's bane is the publisher or station owner who behaves as if he had a license to print money. These are the ones who tolerate news only because it's useful to stuff in around the ads.

The way U.S. commercial news enterprises are structured, they must make money to continue to deliver the news. What should concern the consumer is whether the ownership returns enough investment to finance a good job of coverage. An increasing number of critics and journalism reviews have been striving to watch the performance records of the national media. We suggest that the news consumer get in the habit of sizing up his local news outlets to see whether the news gets shortchanged for the sake of the profit statement.

Radio: Is anything offered beyond the headlines—live hearings, depth interviews, special programs before elections? Is there a forum for unpopular causes as well as established views?

Television: Is the local newscast dominated by sports, weather, and clips from a parent network? Or, just as bad, is it visual radio with little more than a head shot of the anchorman and maybe a weather board? Does local coverage go beyond press conferences and ribbon cuttings? Is advertising held to no more than six or seven minutes during the half hour, including station breaks?

Magazines: If you live in a city with a local magazine which critically scans the community—beyond Chamber of Commerce boosterism and the calculation of advertising revenue—you are blessed beyond measure. Buy stock in the publication, advertise anything you can think of, write letters in the magazine's support, tell your friends, and above all, subscribe.

Newspapers: The implement for hard-hitting reporting of essential state and local issues. Does the staff include any full-time investigative reporters? Check your newspaper to see if it's topheavy with Associated Press (AP) or United Press International (UPI) wire copy and canned features from national syndicates. Or, at the other extreme, is it bulging with local public relations releases at the expense of telling you what's important in the world? How many bylined local stories can you find, and how many of those provide you with vital information? Make your own list of important general news at the moment; are the topics reported, and your questions about them answered?

These queries will suggest others to aim at the publisher who controls the purse strings. It's only fair to consider whether he can afford a better news product, and a clue about that lies in the percentage of news space. Many publishers, but few newsmen, happily settle for 70 percent advertising, then clutter the remaining 30 percent of the so-called news hole with crossword puzzles, bridge columns, garden sections and other possibly interesting but non-news items.

The First Amendment to the Constitution did not intend press freedom simply as a license to print money. It's not illegal for a newspaper to exist solely for advertising revenue. But if that's the case, the publisher should give it away labeled as a shopping throwaway and abjure pious mouthings about the people's right to know.

Of Time and the River of News

What any of us learns depends partly upon newsmen's views of news formats.

Television newsman Robert Abernethy provided an example of how the equipment and format of a news medium consumes a reporter's time. (See page 28.) But time works another major effect on the news. Almost to the point of iron habit, some media executives become accustomed to parcelling any news into brief units of time (or, in the published equivalent, short units of printed matter).

Magazines, with their more leisurely production schedules and the chance to run stories at length, can escape the mania of tell-it-all-in-a-dozen-sentences. The best newspapers are now providing column space for longer stories by their reporters. The medium most confounded about a comprehensible format is local television news, usually done in tidbits of film or videotape.

It is odd that a medium which has its viewers accustomed to watching half hour and hour shows would panic about running a news story more than a minute or two. But the concept that television news has to be a headline service is ingrained in many local stations. When he became news director of WOR-TV in New York in 1970, Lem Tucker remarked to an interviewer: "What was that example someone in our shop used—oh, that it's a good damn thing TV wasn't round during the Creation because *it* may have taken seven days and seven nights, but we could have *told* it in about a minute thirty."[22]

Tucker added that the "breathlessness" of television news can be both good and bad. Television cannot compete in terms of space. Walter Cronkite has pointed out that "one hour of TV news is roughly equal to just the front page of the New York Times"—and network news shows run just a *half* hour.[23] The medium's strong points are its pace and visual content. But how often does an anchorman come on the air and say, "Tonight we think this story from the state legislature is so important we're leaving out sports and weather to run it long"?

Radio, even more abrupt in its news, is properly a headline service, geared as it is to the mobility of commuters, housewives, and teenagers. Yet with its five- and ten-minute segments, radio has a flexibility not in the television news format, which seems uncomfortable anywhere between a two-minute squib and a half-hour documentary. Accordingly, radio news operations often do a more admirable job of providing commentary and background reports.

Newspapers have shared television's tendency toward abruptness, to some extent. Murray Kempton, a seasoned and trenchant columnist, quit the *New York Post* in 1969 after twenty years of column writing, remarking that "I have had less and less of a feeling that it was possible to be sensible in 800 words . . ."[24] In some newspaper offices, the insistence on brevity has softened. The *Los Angeles Times* is perhaps the most notable example, frequently allowing its reporters the space to write magazine length articles in the daily news columns.

In part, emasculated news may be over-reaction to the staggering deluge of events, for if the news consumer wades in words, the newsman paddles precariously on a flood of them. What this means, say, to a writer covering governmental affairs is outlined wryly by columnist John Roche, who admitted feeling swamped by voluminous reports from agencies and commissions. At the time, he had just finished the Fitzhugh recommendations for reorganizing the Pentagon.

> Feeling acute guilt that I was letting my readers down, I took my troubles to one of the proverbial wise men of journalism, Ken Crawford of *Newsweek*. "John, you actually read the Fitzhugh Report?" he asked. I admitted I had. "My God," said Crawford, "you should get a medal. I don't think even Fitzhugh has read the Fitzhugh Report."
>
> Then the light dawned. "You didn't get a potted handout?" Ken asked. "You missed the backgrounder?" I had not been in Washington when the report was released and, as a consequence, had obviously missed the backgrounder, the press conference at which it was passed out and the press was briefed on the contents. As for the handout—a summary prepared for the press highlighting a document's conclusions—I always threw them away . . .
>
> Ken thought about my reading hangup for a while, then thoughtfully he delivered his judgment: "You may miss a lot of scoops with this bad habit of yours, but in time things should break about even. About half the scoops are phony."[25]

At all levels and on almost all topics—governmental, technical, social—reporters organize their time, speed read, and do homework, but it's not enough. Astute managements have helped by freeing their professionals from the absurd assignment system which sends a newsman with a master's degree and several years' experience to cover the dedication of a bridge. Even so, most newspapers need to jettison entirely a number of dullard assignments being covered through force of habit. As for necessary but humdrum reports such as vital statistics and weather, a level of personnel below reporters has improved productivity and morale in the minority of newsrooms where it has been tried.

That still leaves plenty of unglamorous work for top newsmen, because the blunt fact is that important news work most often consists of patiently and tediously researching complex problems. If the management won't provide time and column space for reporters to do the difficult stories, that essential news stays in limbo.

Lois Wille of the *Chicago Daily News* is an example of a reporter who proves regularly that such assignments are worthwhile for a news organization and its readers. She has posed as a car buyer to uncover shady sales practices, visited high schools without official knowledge to tell of abysmal conditions that never appear in Board of Education releases, and reported abortion abuses years before the topic became a national fad. Again ahead of most other reporters, she researched a series on job and drug problems of returning Vietnam veterans.

Edgar May, who won a Pulitzer Prize for investigative reporting, was granted months to develop a series for the *Buffalo Evening News* on abuses of the social welfare system. He took a job as a caseworker and built enough information to later write a book, *The Wasted Americans*.

Such investigative reporting, found in the best of each news medium, is seldom glamorous, doesn't provide many inches of copy for the hours expended, and takes big investments of manpower and wages. But it is vital public service.

Each newspaper has a certain available news space which varies daily depending on the amount of advertising. Though eliminating non-news will help considerably in making room for enterprising reporting, management must also be willing to print "loose" rather than "tight" papers. In lay terminology, this simply means adding pages to accommodate the flow of news instead of restricting stories because the space can be filled with ads.

One of the most admirable balances in any of the media is demonstrated by the *Wall Street Journal*, a businessmen's publication whose depth and breadth of coverage sells more than 1,300,000 copies a day, the second largest daily circulation in the U.S. Many nonbusinessmen are also attracted to its special reports—three of them on every front page, ranging from press criticism to analysis of bikini sales—and to its brisk roundup of world news. As the result of an expanding general readership, the *Journal* is this country's best example of a national newspaper.

The *Journal* limits its daily advertising, turning its back on extra income to maintain the depth and quality of the news columns. The maximum number of pages the paper will print in any one day is forty. Typically, an issue of the *Journal* will be about seven to nine pages of news and features, about five pages of financial tables and charts, and what's left given over to advertising. This balance is what the *Journal* editors think their staff of about 140 reporters can fill with incisive reports.

Turn away ads? Pay reporters a minimum of $325 a week after five years experience? Why, we couldn't afford it, say some publishers. But the *Wall Street Journal* clinks impressively all the way to the bank. Far from making advertisers angry, the controlled quality draws business.

In 1971, for instance, the *Journal* carried the most expensive single ad ever placed in a newspaper. Goodyear paid $140,000 for an eight-page layout. That's for an ad which ran a single day. A writer from *Fortune* investigated the *Journal's* profitability, and came up with the "reasonable estimate" that the newspaper in 1970 made about $14 million after taxes, a profit margin of about 15.5 percent. This made the *Journal's* quality operation, according to the *Fortune* research, also "probably the most profitable newspaper in the country."[26]

On the television side, in-depth reports such as those seen on CBS's *60 Minutes* and NBC's *Chronolog* correspond in quality to some of the best work in print. As we watch our local evening reports, however, we conclude that camera crews' time would more wisely be spent showing the effects of soaring unemployment, environmental pollution and disintegration of the inner city than standing by for weeks in the hallway outside a grand jury chamber, recording for posterity the posteriors of reticent witnesses.

Indeed, while television news coverage is often accused of overdramatized action, studies indicate the opposite. Even Vietnam coverage has been preponderantly nonviolent, with news directors protesting that they have repeatedly chosen other aspects of the conflict over battle scenes.

If filmed conflict and violence occupy much less of television's news hole than generally believed, it's because such pictures have impact that far exceeds their length or frequency. Though television drama contains steady doses of violence, our senses have not been so dulled by shoot-em-ups that we yawn when Jack Ruby kills Lee Harvey Oswald live for the cameras, or Sen. Robert Kennedy lies bleeding and fatally wounded on the floor of a Los Angeles hotel kitchen. Those scenes are etched into us, whereas our memories ignore hundreds of eminently forgettable scenes.

That isn't merely a television phenomenon, of course. Among the photos distributed by the Associated Press and United Press International and withheld by most news desks, two stick with us.

One, taken in the aftermath of a fire at a pensioner's hotel, focused on the body of an old man, charred and crumpled into a toilet bowl, where in his terror he had sought escape.

The second showed the wrecked convertible in which Jayne Mansfield died in Louisiana, its top sheared off in the impact with a truck. The cutline explained that the white blob on the hood was what remained of the actress's blonde head.[27]

In Vietnam, the published pictures most remembered showed protesting Buddhists, burning like torches during self-immolations, and the series of stills as South Vietnam's security chief raised his revolver and shot, point blank, a suspected spy whose hands were tied.

Television news directors who defend their more typical product—lifeless film of routine occasions—say the cameras provide a sense of presence and credibility to the viewer, who sees a reporter on the scene and also gets a look at the participants. It's doubtful, however, that viewers are much more impressed after a few repeats of cliche film than news cameraman Dick Hutchings, who works out of NBC's Burbank, California, complex.[28]

"Ninety-eight percent of the stories are just like the ones we've done before," he observes.

Hutchings, who earns $313 a week, plus overtime, works with a sound man and a reporter. It costs roughly a thousand dollars a week in salaries for that three-man team, not counting the film, processing, editing and other studio expenses.

Local stations often economize by eliminating the sound man and having the reporter narrate the film back at the studio—a technique known as voice-over.

Although the expense would be much less, few stations employ Lem Tucker's idea of a photographer-journalist working alone. "A still camera in the right place can be a very probing instrument," Tucker remarks, "because of its mobility."[29] The idea could pay off in striking single pictures, series and montages.

The NBC *Nightly News* has done this brilliantly at times; a photo essay on the New Orleans funeral of jazz trumpeter Louis Armstrong in the summer of 1971 was remarkably evocative, with a succession of black faces in still shots. Also, the newsman's text can be more flexible when it's not tied to the time and action of film clips. When NBC used its segment of still photos in the funeral coverage, not a sound came over the air from reporter Jack Perkins, one of television's best at fitting his words to a scene; instead, jazz from the funeral procession was played as background.[30]

With less cost and equipment in routine assignments, news directors then could free the more elaborately equipped camera crews for in-depth investigations that might take several days.

The daily grind allows no such leisure now. Look at Dick Hutchings. At 7:30 A.M. he's sent for what the assignment editor describes as a nice easy feature, a lady truckdriver on her first day of work.

"Shouldn't be so bad," Hutch tells the sound man, Rod Gilmore. "It'll take half an hour to shoot, then we'll get some coffee." But at the union hall they find almost 200 teamsters, angry and restless after weeks of no work. For half an hour the two men work to calm the truckers' bruised egos and flaring tempers as they set up equipment to shoot a lady who's going to work.

When reporter Warren Wilson arrives he promises to get the truckers' unemployment story on the air and he does, two weeks later. Meanwhile, after an hour and a half of preliminaries, they get to the half hour of shooting. But they don't get their coffee.

The next assignment is the aftermath of the kidnaping of a banker's son. Although the kidnaper has been captured and the boy is safe, the editors want a follow-up, so Hutchings and Gilmore meet reporter David Horowitz, who has cased the kidnaper's route. To go with his narration, they film a doughnut shop, a phone booth, and a bank. Four and a half hours later, when the story is done, they've shot only 14 minutes of film. The rest of the effort went into checking maps, unloading equipment, loading film, and fighting traffic.

"We spend 85 percent of our time just driving and setting up equipment," Hutchings explains. At 2:40 P.M. they finally manage lunch hour while a motorcycle messenger hurries their exposed film to the studio.

When they pick up the two-way radio and call the office, the editor inquires, "Would you guys mind some overtime?" So they're off to a black-doll factory in Watts for another feature. But the reporter has forgotten to check the factory's closing time, and they just begin shooting when suddenly the plant goes silent for the night.

"I just took anything in that rush," a disgruntled Hutch tells the reporter. "I'm not handing this in." The day has ended without anything dramatic having happened, yet it's been almost nine hours of work.

"You go through so much to get film, then so many things can go wrong," says Hutchings. "Film may be defective. I can be off and expose it wrong. Or the projectionist can hit the switch wrong in the studio."

On the evening news the crew's work comes to just under five minutes of film: 2:31 for the lady truck driver and 2:27 on the kidnaping.

The consumer who realizes the effort that goes into each filmed minute can draw fair conclusions about his television news outlets by surveying their performance for a week or so. How many stories are accompanied by film? How many of these show action? How many of the action films show conflict? Was that footage necessary? How many stories might have been handled just as well with a still camera?

While staff, time, and space are constant problems for all media, newsmen sometimes are assigned to unnecessary mob reporting. The public caught on to this in a big way during Soviet Premier Nikita Khrushchev's visit to the United States in 1959. While visiting Iowa super-farmer Roswell Garst, Khrushchev was tracked by an army of more than 300 newsmen and photographers, and Garst reacted as if invaded by a plague of locusts. A memorable news picture shows him hurling ripe silage at the offenders.[31] The mob scenes have not improved.[32] In television, where the solution is merely a matter of sharing equipment, improvement is far overdue.

"The spectacle of a half dozen camera crews and a dozen microphones, several from the same organization, standing tripod to tripod at Andrews Air Force Base to witness the secretary of defense's routine departure for a NATO meeting, or to cover S. I. Hayakawa's, Abbie Hoffman's, or George Wallace's latest news conference, often says more about the news gatherers than it does about the news makers," says Fred Friendly, who became a Ford Foundation media consultant after his departure from CBS.[33]

Observing that the price of such overkill is often paid by missing truly significant stories, he proposed joint coverage of noncompetitive events. Such a pooled news service could connect the broadcast news organizations for one or two hours a day, with microwave and satellite circuits sending a daily schedule of film and electronic stories.

Of the three network news presidents only one—Richard Salant of CBS—responded favorably to the idea.

"What is required," Friendly believes, "are more voices, more stories covered comprehensively, not mountains of film magazines of virtually identical footage."

Chapter 5

'ABE, I GOT A GREAT IDEA FOR FOOLING
ALL OF THE PEOPLE ALL OF THE TIME...'

Lies, Half Truths, And Evasions

"The trouble with Adlai Stevenson," Harry Truman said, "is he has *never* understood the difference between real truth and political truth."

Political truth, it developed, can be the biggest and damnedest lie ever, but if motivated toward a pragmatic political goal, preferably for reasons of national interest, and stated with total belief and fervor, it becomes true.

And real truth?

"A boy *never* lies to his mother," Mr. Truman said.[1]

Robert Alan Aurthur, *Esquire*, August 1971

On May 5, 1960, the National Aeronautics and Space Administration announced that one of its weather research planes was missing on a "meteorological observation flight" in Turkey. It was conceivable, NASA suggested, that the pilot had blacked out from lack of oxygen and that the uncontrolled aircraft had drifted over Soviet territory. It seemed as if another Russian outrage had been perpetrated—especially since President Eisenhower had assured reporters at a news conference the year before that he had "personally" issued orders prohibiting provocative flights over the USSR. On May 6 the State Department's official spokesman, Lincoln White, declared that there was "absolutely no—N-O—deliberate attempt to violate Soviet air space . . ."

The next day Premier Nikita Khrushchev told the Supreme Soviet that the U-2 pilot, Francis Gary Powers, had been captured alive and had confessed his intelligence mission. Within a few hours the State Department was lamely admitting that "in endeavoring to obtain information now concealed behind the Iron Curtain, a flight over Soviet territory was probably undertaken by an unarmed civilian U-2 plane." Such flights, it quickly transpired, had been undertaken by pilots of the Central Intelligence Agency for the past four years.[2]

William McGaffin and Irwin Knoll, *Anything But the Truth*

From beginning to end, the Bay of Pigs was as humiliating for the American press as it was for the country as a whole. . . . The press had a right to be angry. It had been lied to, again and again, by President Kennedy, Allen W. Dulles, Dean Rusk, and everyone else in the hierarchy of blunderers responsible for the Bay of Pigs. But it also had the duty to be ashamed. No law required it to swallow uncritically everything that officialdom said. On the very day the American-planned, American-equipped expedition was landing at the Bay of Pigs, Secretary Rusk told a group of newsmen: "The American people are entitled to know whether we are intervening in Cuba or intend to do so in the future. The answer to that question is no."[3]

Victor Bernstein and Jesse Gordon, *Columbia University Forum*, Fall 1967

Mr. Johnson next strained the credulity of the press corps that fall (1965), when, after aluminum producers announced a price rise, the Administration said it would dump aluminum from government stockpiles on the market. This was an obvious (and successful) move to force a price rollback. But when reporters asked the obvious question, the White House told them there was "no connection" between the two moves. LBJ, they were asked to believe, had just decided to get rid of some old aluminum.

The list of outright prevarications, half truths, concealments and misleading denials by the Administration is almost as long as its impressive list of achievements.[4]

Charles Roberts, Newsweek, December 19, 1966

. . . As evidence that Americans are not directly involved in combat operations, (President Nixon) said that "no American stationed in Laos has ever been killed" by the enemy in the last six years.[5]

New York Times, March 7, 1970

. . . The White House said that under the new policy "any casualties that result from hostile enemy action" would be reported. Until yesterday, such casualties had been kept secret.

Over the weekend the White House had acknowledged that an army captain and 26 American civilians stationed in Laos had been killed or were missing as a result of enemy ground action over the last six years.[6]

New York Times, March 10, 1970

So Who Cares?

From the Office of the President to the office of the village clerk, the news consumer has been denied information, deceived, and just plain lied to.

This country has burgeoned beyond the town meeting where each qualified adult cast a direct vote in community policy. But the citizen of a representative democracy presumably retains his voice through the officials he elects, and he should get straight information from them as a way of measuring their performance.

If he does, he'll know when to re-elect officials and when to throw out the rascals and the inept. He'll know when to write angry letters and when to hoist his placard.

Most politicians naturally prefer to be liked, respected, and re-elected. Like the rest of us, they hate to be caught with their slips showing. Misjudgments, mistakes, and maneuvers in behalf of special interests seldom flow freely from their own public information officers who, after all, qualify as franchisers in the cosmetics industry. Their job is to cover the boss's blemishes and accentuate his best features.

The private citizen himself cannot check personally on every office of government and would probably not want to. Comprehensive newsgathering was already beyond the capabilities of a single man in London of the 1660s, which to our modern eye seems more like a village than a great city. With only a stale official gazette of foreign happenings to go by, naval bureaucrat Samuel Pepys spent hours each day checking into events. His circuit covered Westminster Hall, coffee houses, the Royal Exchange, and taverns, after which Pepys labored over the perplexities of separating fact from rumor.[7]

Today journalists function as the newsgatherers, and claim the protection of the First Amendment to the U.S. Constitution under the misleading phrase, freedom of the press. The news media have actually no claim to special privilege except as an extension of the citizen: to go where he cannot, summarize the important, explain the complex, uncover the dubious, and get the news to him. The newsman in these tasks acts as the citizen's proxy, his agent in doing the job of collecting the news.

If he is doing his job well, the newsman can be expected to make enemies whenever public officials aren't doing theirs.

Paradoxically, at a time when government and technology are growing increasingly complex and need watchdogging more than ever, the citizen has grown suspicious of the news media, and the natural alliance between him and the newsman has been weakened.

The stakes for spurning investigation-by-proxy are getting high. Say the Army announces in the morning that it plans to ship a trainload of nerve gas through your area. Is it safe? Of course, says the official statement. There's virtually no chance of a leak or a train wreck, and even if there were, an antidote is available.

The newsman digs deeper. What kind of antidote? Well, it's called atropine, itself a poison which happens to counteract the poison of the nerve gas. Be sure to inject it within thirty *seconds* or so after exposure to nerve gas. By stabbing yourself deep in the hip with a long needle. If you happen to have an atropine needle in your pocket.[8]

With that information in hand, you can make a more judicious decision about your willingness to have the gas moved through the neighborhood.

The example is not far-fetched. Nerve gas has been moved in this country under those same conditions. But the point holds for countless situations which may be less deadly but still are dangerous to the citizenry. Information which it is the media's job to provide can be the news consumer's antidote to officialdom's intentions.

Unhelpfully enough, the picture is not as simple as a television Western, with all the bureaucrats seedy and unshaven in dark hats and the reporters all cleancut in white Stetsons. For instance, take the five successive Presidents cited at the start of this chapter; historians haven't judged them as fiends who were strangers to the truth. Evaluations of their performance in office vary markedly and, in most cases where they covered up or deliberately misled the public—a situation which has fostered what is politely called the credibility gap—compassion might move observers to credit each of them for doing what he thought best for his country, his party, and himself. The trouble is, these categories don't always mesh.

Consider a case blended with three levels of concern: historical, political, and personal. Should a President admit fears about his health? In what he believes to be the long-range interests of the country, colored by his own emotions, he is apt not to.

Or, some loyalist on his staff may cover up for him. Near the end of World War II, President Franklin D. Roosevelt conferred with Russian Premier Joseph Stalin and British Prime Minister Winston Churchill at the Crimean city of Yalta. The meeting of Allied commanders-in-chief was just two months before the President's death in April, 1945.

Only the Army Signal Corps was allowed to take pictures, and Roosevelt's executive assistant suppressed the most honest photos of a haggard, dying president. Historians are still arguing about the wisdom of Roosevelt's decisions at Yalta, which included secret agreements in order to gain Russia's declaration of war against Japan.

The assistant was Jonathan Daniels, a respected newsman who later became editor of the *Raleigh News and Observer*. "I wanted FDR to look as well as anybody's boss," he later explained, adding that he should have known the President was dying, but instead had an illusion of his immortality.[9]

In recent years, deceiving or keeping information from the public has often been blamed on the necessities of national security. Is it wise to publicize peace negotiations? Foreign trade talks? Plans for nuclear de-escalation? Although such questions are thorny, a rule of thumb helps. If it turns out that the opposing governments were aware of the information, the case for hiding it from the American people is not persuasive.

U.S. news organizations agonized over what to report about the planned invasion of Cuba by CIA-trained exiles for months after details were reported on page one of the Guatemalan newspaper *La Hora* in the fall of 1960.[10]

Premier Fidel Castro obviously knew about it then, if not before, since the Guatemalan training base was reported to be common knowledge in Central America.

Yet the *Miami Herald*, which gleaned the major outlines of the plot by November, suppressed its story until January, 1961, when bits and pieces of the invasion plan began showing up in a few publications in this country. The Associated Press and United Press International, which most U.S. news outlets depend on for foreign news, repeatedly failed to follow up on signs suggesting a major story was yet to be uncovered. And the *New York Times,* just before the April invasion, played down reporter Tad Szulc's article on the U.S.-inspired venture against Cuba, eliminating the imminence of the invasion and the Central Intelligence Agency's involvement.

The result of this sorry chapter in the history of the Kennedy administration and the press was not that Premier Castro was caught unprepared. His troops cut down the exile landing force in three days at the Bay of Pigs. But because of the botched news policies, the American public had no chance to react to the plot, and public opinion was the one thing that might have aborted the misadventure.

President Kennedy, who had lectured newspaper executives about the pallid disclosures their publications did make, later changed his mind and told *New York Times* managing editor Turner Catledge:

"If you had printed more about the operation, you would have saved us from a colossal mistake."[11]

The newsman's job is to prod for answers, so that the citizen can look at the record and decide for himself. That's what the ethical, well-trained, hard-digging reporter, working for a news organization bent on public service, will do.

However, no one need submit to a lie detector or a test for tired blood before starting a news organization or going to work for one. The ranks are mixed with lazy newsmen who will use public relations handouts without asking the hard questions, those whose news judgments can be altered by a bottle of booze or an overseas junket, and those who mean well but are poorly trained. More insidious are those publishers and station owners whose interests revolve solely around profits.

So the news consumer must balance himself warily between gullibility and cynicism, continually evaluating the performances of both public officials and news outlets.

He must demand, too, that the news media keep him informed about more than government. When a strike by a single railroad union can tie up the country, threaten tens of thousands of other jobs, and keep food off tables, what that union does can hardly be considered private. When pilfering of stock certificates from brokerage firms reaches epidemic proportions, investors need to know. When unsafe cars are glamorously huckstered onto the market, someone needs to find the truth and tell it. That's not always easy for publications which depend on auto advertising unless they have, as some do, a barrier of unbreakable ethics between the advertising and editorial departments.

Consumers today are loudly unhappy about the news they are getting and the performance of the media. Television news executives say it's a case of blaming the messenger who brings bad news. We have been shattered by Vietnam, the first war brought to the nation's living rooms, thanks to television; by civil wars in our cities and on our campuses; by water, air, and ear pollution which threatens our health and our sanity; and by an unending list of other catastrophes. As a result, many a news consumer has quit, cold turkey. He now turns the television set off at news time, and he may read *Peanuts*, Ann Landers, and local sports before using the newspaper to carpet the canary cage.

But hear no evil, see no evil is far too dangerous for anyone who wants some control of his future, or his country's, or his children's. A more logical course is to try to keep the bureaucrats and businessmen honest, and to improve the performance of the nation's news outlets. The consumer who throws up his hands and quits usually does so because he can't find any effective buttons to push. He feels that he is not getting accurate information and, just as importantly, that he is not being heard.

The flow of information isn't supposed to be one way. Even in ancient China, ruled by autocratic emperors, wisdom dictated that "heaven listens through the voice of the people."[12] Imperial rule was supposed to take the people's wishes into account, according to Chinese political theory, if for no other reason than the practical. Otherwise town strikes would erupt, along with beating of the drum at the palace gates, or waylaying of an official's sedan chair.

In a twentieth century representative government, news organizations should be carrying citizens' messages to the governors as well as government policies to the people. Newsmen should be documenting unemployment and the hungry families which are caught in its wake, the plight of the elderly who cannot afford increased taxes and doctors' bills, the teenagers who cannot get job training which would give them a fair chance to escape poverty.

As Walter Lippmann, then the dean of U.S. columnists, explained to the International Press Institute in 1965:

"In my country we use a rough rule of thumb. It is that for controversial measures, the government should aim to rally a consensus, which in practical terms means a majority big enough to include from 60 to 75 percent of the voters. Only then will those who observe the law willingly and support the policy actively be numerous enough to persuade and induce the recalcitrant and dissident minority, leaving only a marginal minimum where legal coercion is needed."[13]

It may be, as British press historian Francis Williams claims, that a nation gets the news it deserves. "The press," he says, "is a mirror of the age because the degree of authority and independence it is permitted to exercise or is able to seize for itself, and the nature of its influence on public opinion, throw light on the real balance of power in society."[14]

Current legislative and executive efforts to shackle the press indicate that the citizens' right to information is in trouble.

The Spirit of 1787

It goes back farther than our parchment guarantee of freedom of the press.

When delegates met at Philadelphia in the summer of 1787 to draw up the federal constitution, their daily discussions were kept secret.[15] Sentries guarded the doors. And amid the disagreements which nearly wracked the assembly apart, a guileful leak appeared in the local Pennsylvania Packet:

"So great is the unanimity, we hear, that prevails in the Convention upon all great federal subjects, that it has been proposed to call the rooms in which they assemble—Unanimity Hall."[16]

Call it news management, or credibility gap, or some other euphemism. It's traveled under various names in our history, and will operate under a lot more.

The point is that if secrecy, force, and deceit all were present at so estimable a conclave as the birth of the constitution in 1787, then since that time they have attended more tawdry doings at every level of public life.

The news media themselves have flaws aplenty, all of which crimp the citizen's right to information. But newsmen are often more sinned against than sinning. As the citizen's proxy in searching out the news, they are up against a colossal amount of duplicity.

Some of these stratagems to suppress information are legal, or at least legalistic; some are devious; some are downright shady. Whatever the precise style of fetters the people of power put on newsgatherers, the media's ability to cope with this hampering is not so deft as our national mythology would have us believe. The First Amendment is all too easily gotten around.

At the local level, a standard problem for reporters has been the secret session so beloved by city councilmen and school board members. Mayors, too, have a way of going into closed session: they clam up. As tensions have built in the cities, mayors across the political spectrum have retreated into feuds with newsmen.[17]

Not only government figures bar the door. Corporations and labor unions have been known to ban reporters for doing their job too diligently.

Recently, some protest groups have refused to permit coverage by reporters of a different race or culture or sex.[18]

Other times, the duel between the newsman and those in authority is about sources who talk to the newsman in confidence. Some reporters have gone to jail rather than comply with court orders to reveal information gained from these essential people. Eighteen states have "shield" laws under which newsmen need not reveal their sources, but lack of a similar federal law still means that subpoenas can hit a newsman from almost any direction and on nearly any topic that happens to pop up in a courtroom.[19]

The cast in the subpoena drama has been remarkably mixed. Ramsey Clark, a spokesman for civil liberties, was U.S. Attorney General when the Department of Justice in 1968 subpoenaed newsmen's notes and film clips for the Chicago Seven political conspiracy trial.[20] *Fortune* magazine was subpoenaed by the Department of Justice in 1969, when the Nixon administration had come to power, for notes used in preparing an article about industrialist Jim Ling.[21] *The Chicago Tribune*, according to its counsel, Don H. Reuben, had to contend with subpoenas on the average of "at least once a year" throughout the 1950s and 1960s.[22] And *Broadcasting magazine* reported that 123 subpoenas were served on NBC, CBS, and the stations they own from January 1969 to July, 1971.[23]

Periodically a major case develops out of this matter of protecting sources, which affects many more news outlets than the few examples just cited. A landmark case resulted from a subpoena which summoned *New York Times* reporter Earl Caldwell to testify before a federal grand jury in an investigation of the Black Panther party. In November, 1970, a U.S. Court of Appeals upheld reporter Caldwell's refusal to testify.[24] Faced with resistance from major publications and the television networks, Attorney General John Mitchell said he would modify the Justice Department's vigorous attempts to command reporters' notebooks and film out-takes as evidence.[25]

Even yet, the issue is not resolved towards solid protection for newsmen. The Court of Appeals decision said the government must show a "compelling need" for such evidence,[26] and the Attorney General promised only to negotiate "to reach agreement on the scope of the subpoenas" in the future.[27]

One lesson of the "Pentagon Papers" is that the federal government is quick to offer the argument of overriding need in legal conflict with the news media. In that furor, the Justice Department obtained injunctions to prevent newspapers from publishing material about a study of U.S. policy on Vietnam.

The case was complicated by the fact that the forty-seven-volume study bore the official stamp of secrecy that is on millions of government documents, but the essential point of law for newsmen was restraint on what could be told. The Supreme Court upheld the right to reveal the contents of the Pentagon Papers, quoting earlier decisions on press freedom which said the government "carries a heavy burden of showing justification for the enforcement of such a restraint."[28] But the narrow basis of the decision left the newspapers open for prosecution for violating security classification of documents, a large loophole when so much government paperwork bears a label of secrecy.

Profound issues of disclosure versus the right to know have not shown up so dramatically in state laws, but newsman and legislator have skirmished there countless times.

Some of the most sharply honed measures to show up in state legislatures have included bills to punish newsmen for publishing inaccuracies,[29] to ban them from polling places,[30] to penalize them for broadcasting faulty information about riots,[31] and to keep them from the scenes of crime and disaster until a police official grants written permission.[32] In similar sentiment have been proposals to license newsmen, setting up a system similar to a bar association's governance of the legal profession.[33]

The motives behind such proposals may be mean or noble, but few state legislators have been as openly vengeful as state representative Harry R. J. Comer of Pennsylvania when he introduced a bill in 1971 to charge the news media $200,000 a year for use of the capitol news room.[34]

"To be truthful, this is a slap back at the lousy press," Comer said. His bill, amended down to $50,000 annual rent, lost by a single vote in the Pennsylvania House of Representatives.

Pique accounts for most measures of the above sort. The most drastic, such as the state law inspired by Senator Huey Long of Louisiana in 1934 to impose a license tax on newspapers critical of his political regime,[35] have been overruled in the courts. But spite legislation of this sort can be a threat whenever emotions run high against the news media.

Official reticence, courtroom maneuvers, and avenging legislators are open foes for the newsgatherer. Politics is the embezzler within the First Amendment.

Politics is a league of shared confidences, of broad winks at human failings for the sake of power. Secrets are honored or revealed or traded as the situation demands; they are not routinely reported, for power functions most smoothly out of sight. But the newsman deals in revelation.

The big-league contests where politics and news contend involve the Presidency, and the occupant of the oval office has a number of techniques to use on the news media.

One is plain old pressure, intense and direct. In the early 1960s, David Halberstam of the New York Times filed stories from Vietnam which showed that U.S. military plans there were going badly. (Along with Malcolm Browne of the Associated Press and Neil Sheehan of United Press International, Halberstam was far ahead of the U.S. government and the American public in realizing the tragedy of Vietnam; all three men won recognition for their blunt reporting from the field.) The Kennedy administration meanwhile was claiming that the war was being won.

Nettled by Halberstam's reports, President Kennedy suggested to *New York Times* publisher Arthur Ochs Sulzberger that Halberstam had become too involved with the Vietnam story, and perhaps should be transferred.[36] *The Times* refused to buckle, and instead canceled a forthcoming vacation for Halberstam to avoid even any appearance of having given in.

Another technique is to hide unfavorable news behind a load of other stories.[37] On September 26, 1969, President Nixon held his first news conference in more than three months. Naturally, White House stories hit the newspapers and broadcast media by the bunch. That same day, a routine news release at the Social Security Administration announced that persons receiving Medicare hospital benefits would have to pay the first $52 of their expenses, instead of the old figure of $44. This was pocketbook news, an added cost of 18 percent in deductible coverage, for the 5.9 million elder citizens using Medicare in a year's time. The President's office had been handling major news about the Social Security system—until this story, which was released as obscurely as possible.

A more acrobatic example of managing the news by distraction was provided by President Johnson in March, 1967.[38] Senator Robert F. Kennedy was scheduled to criticize the President's Vietnam policy in a Senate speech. A few hours before Kennedy stood up in the Senate, President Johnson suddenly called a news conference to announce a message from the Soviet Union about disarmament talks, then bustled off to Howard University to give a speech on civil rights, then dropped in on a ceremony at the Office of Education to talk about schools.

Ever since the technology of communications has enabled a speaker to talk directly to a national audience, the politician has had a strong trump over the newsman. Franklin D. Roosevelt, using the radio for periodic "fireside chats" with the American electorate from 1933 until 1945, was the first President to master persuasion through national broadcasts.[39] When television came along, Thomas E. Dewey was perhaps the first political campaigner to realize that TV was not merely radio with a camera looking on. Dewey, known as a very stiff personality and a loser in his lackluster runs for the Presidency in 1944 and 1948, adopted an impressively informal television style in his 1950 campaign for reelection as governor of New York.[40]

In 1952, regional telecasts were used in Dwight Eisenhower's successful presidential campaign.[41] In that same race, Eisenhower's running mate Richard M. Nixon was accused of unethical conduct in receiving $18,235 from a secret fund set up by California business interests.[42] Nixon's place on the electoral ticket was jeopardized until the vice presidential nominee went on national television for an emotional rebuttal which included references to his wife's "respectable Republican cloth coat"[43] and the family's spaniel, Checkers.

The Nixon career, in fact, is worth looking at as a case study of tensions between the working newsmen and the electronic politician. For one thing, from his 1952 Checkers speech to his election as President in 1968, Richard M. Nixon qualified as the country's most durable television politician. For another, his use of the broadcasting media to counterbalance questioning newsmen has been the most comprehensive plan to date.

The Checkers speech showed television's usefulness, as mentioned.[44] A ruder lesson in the medium's potency came for Nixon when the less experienced John F. Kennedy outshone him in the televised debates of the 1960 presidential campaign. In 1962, in his famous "last press conference" after being defeated in his race for the governorship of California, Nixon said bitterly:

". . . I can only say thank God for television and radio for keeping the newspapers a little more honest . . ."[45]

Came the 1968 presidential campaign, and a full strategy was evident. Candidate Nixon boxed out the working newsmen as much as possible and relied on carefully packaged television shows in which he answered questions from friendly audiences.[46]

As President, Nixon quickly put the same strategy to work, with some added flourishes. Addressing the country in television speeches, which President Nixon did while permitting news conferences more infrequently than any other modern President, maintained the buffer against questioning by newsmen.[47] But the networks followed these presidential addresses with analysis by commentators. Vice President Spiro T. Agnew's famous blast of November 13, 1969, against "a small band of network commentators and self-appointed analysts" was aimed at such commentary, and networks and individual affiliate stations both became more cautious.[48]

The White House news corps, meanwhile, was further bypassed as the President visited editors and publishers in meetings around the country.[49] Herbert G. Klein, in the new job of Director of Communications for the Executive Branch, in effect opened the first full-fledged presidential public relations office, telephoning television stations for copies of any editorial comment after a presidential speech, mailing out "fact kits" which supported the administration's stand on issues, arranging for the administration's top men to be interviewed and to appear on television.[50]

Whether the elaborate circuitry set up to bypass the working newsmen amounts to finesse or guile is a matter of phrasing. What's important for the news consumer is to realize just what the processing of presidential news really is.

The stoutest rein on the right to know is censorship, and for all our enshrinement of freedom of the press, this country has a considerable history of censorship.

In 1798, when the United States was just getting under way, a federal law made it illegal to publish "any false, scandalous or malicious writing" about the government. Federalist Attorney General Timothy Pickering flipped through pages of the opposition press to impose the Sedition Act whenever possible. At least 13 newsmen on Jeffersonian newspapers were indicted, and at least six of them served jail sentences for the criticism they printed.[51]

Dissenting journalists fared little better during the Civil War. "Must I shoot a simple-minded soldier boy who deserts, while I must not touch a hair of a wily agitator who induces him to desert . . . ?" President Lincoln asked rhetorically.[52] In some cases Lincoln approved the suppression, at other times he overruled military commanders when they shut down newspapers. In the turbulent course of the war, at least 28 Northern newspapers, most of them supporters of the peace wing of the Democratic party, were put under some form of government restraint.[53]

World War I brought a choice of censorship: mild or tough. The federal Committee on Public Information drew up a voluntary censorship code, which most of the nation's press abided by.[54] For those politically dissident journalists who wouldn't, there was the Espionage Act of 1917, under which the U.S. Postmaster General could ban from the mail any publications which displayed such anti-war sentiments as attempting to cause "insubordination, disloyalty, mutiny or refusal of duty" in the military.[55] Seventy-five papers are known to have been restricted this way, many of them foreign language or socialist journals.[56] In the case of the Milwaukee Leader, a socialist paper which opposed U.S. participation in the war, the Supreme Court upheld the Postmaster General's right to withdraw second class mailing privileges,[57] a decision which still stands.[58]

Even before the United States entered World War II, a new sedition law appeared—the 1940 Smith Act, which provides for prosecution of persons who put out "any written or printed matter advocating, advising, or teaching the duty, necessity, desirability or propriety of overthrowing or destroying any government in the United States by force or violence."[59] As with the Supreme Court decision on the government's power to take away mailing privileges, the law still remains on the books.

Voluntary censorship again was the general rule during World War II.[60] An intriguing exception was the territory of Hawaii, where military censorship descended five days after Pearl Harbor was bombed on December 7, 1941. Publications from the major Honolulu dailies down to high school newspapers were censored throughout most of the war, and radio stations were monitored constantly by military intelligence personnel.[61]

The Vietnam war, longest in America's history, also produced the longest running conflict between our news media and military censorship. Official censorship, complete with general orders and sharp scissors, was not invoked, but unofficial varieties were tried by government and military authorities almost any time unfavorable news was imminent. Correspondents were hampered by travel restrictions and the refusal by commanders to let their men talk.

Some notable instances were the military refusal to permit correspondents to cover the besieged U.S. forces at Khe Sanh in 1968,[62] and the "embargo" on coverage of the South Vietnamese military thrust into Laos in 1971.[63]

Newsmen and military brass clashed in countless other instances as well; at times, official efforts were made to discredit reporters who broke unfavorable stories. Perhaps one sign that television news came of age in Vietnam is that the broadcasters faced the same harassment which print newsmen have long undergone in combat theatres. Two memorable cases provide the reminder that official anger is bipartisan.

In 1965, at least two high officials of the Johnson administration phoned CBS to question the motives of reporter Morley Safer after his filmed report on Marines burning a village during a military sweep.[64]

In 1970, the Nixon White House tried to write off as a fraud the story CBS reporter Don Webster did about a South Vietnamese sergeant stabbing a wounded prisoner to death—an attempt CBS rebutted with careful proof on its evening national news show.[65]

Censor, irate official, politician; courtroom, battalion headquarters, television studio; the citizen's right to information knows many checkpoints. If the citizen, the news consumer, sides with those who try to use the media for their own ends, he is cutting himself off from whatever quantity of truth the newsgatherer could provide him.

The Mirror Breakers

When former President Harry Truman imparted the distinction between real truth and political truth, he gave out more candor and insight than the news consumer is likely to hear very often.

Rarer even than a politician who will confess publicly to categories of "truth" was two-time presidential candidate Adlai Stevenson, who didn't know there was a difference to confess. The news consumer cannot count on an Adlai Stevenson being available to talk the common brand of truth instead of the bogus variety. And while serving as U.S. ambassador to the United Nations, even the candid Stevenson was trapped into using faked photographs from the CIA to deny that American-trained pilots were flying air support for the unsuccessful Bay of Pigs invasion.[66]

What the news consumer can count on, in the gathering of information, is a lot of deception and diversion being tried on his proxy—the newsman. Persons who make and administer policy have viewpoints and vested interests. They are not dispassionate about their own programs and records.

Columnist Murray Kempton once made the useful suggestion that reporters should scrutinize politicians and businessmen as if they were the Mafia.[67] He had a point. The most upright of public men as well as the most lowly have to deal in alliances and influence, enforced loyalties and potent command—a sanitized gang war without the tommyguns and, if we're lucky, without the corruption. The exercise of power, after all, is to bend others to your own will, to achieve the triumph of your side over others.

Men of power, then, are partisans, for their own interests and for themselves. The news consumer forgets this at his peril.

The citizen must be a critic, and a good one, because he's up against professionals in the game of power. Consider U.S. Senator Hugh Scott, who blasted off in September, 1970, with a statement that it's time for the television networks to "pull up their socks and realize they're making people angry."[68]

He expressed outrage at a television newsman who, in reporting President Nixon's warm reception by college students at Kansas State University, remarked that the President, after all, had picked a friendly campus.[69] Scott said the President would have been equally welcome anywhere, and rejected "the idea that the President of the United States has to be frightened off by a handful of contemptibles."

The news consumer has to juggle Scott's remarks into perspective. The first item up is Scott's job as Senate Republican leader, a position which required him to make outraged political noises when his party's leader asked it, or when he himself believed some political advantage might be summoned.

Next the news consumer might note the expanse of Scott's generalization. His gripe in this case was against one newsman—Dan Rather of CBS, whose irreverent coverage of White House maneuvers has irked both Democratic and Republican administrations—but the Senator's comment broadened to include the television networks.

Then the news consumer should flick back through his mind to what he knows about Presidents in public. Since President Kennedy's murder in the streets of Dallas, many an expert has said a President cannot be adequately protected in an open crowd, no matter how many Secret Service men are around. President Johnson seldom ventured out during his last few years in office, and largely stuck to military bases and banquets when he did make a "public" appearance. His Cabinet officers met hostile receptions on campuses when they defended the administration's Vietnam policy.

President Nixon, to the time Scott made his remark in late 1970, had traveled somewhat more freely, but usually to sports and civic events which could, indeed, be said to have provided friendly crowds. Presidential appearances are carefully orchestrated; that's nothing new. And remember candidate Nixon's 1960 and 1968 campaigns, in which his "spontaneous" demonstrations —balloons, confetti, and all—were most carefully arranged.

Couple the record of presidential care in selecting public platforms with the fact that many campuses erupted into anti-Nixon protests less than six months before the Nixon speech at Kansas State, during the military thrust into Cambodia and in the aftermath of the Kent State shootings.

The television reporter's remark adds up to honest reporting. Senator Scott's noises, like those of others in diverse political camps, seem to have been calculated along a dark new line in American life: public unhappiness with the news media.

Reporters, editors, publishers, station owners, and news organizations need quantities of criticism. A strong case can be made for saying that, overall, most are not doing an adequate job.

But the dangerous national error is that the news media have been taking the most severe criticism for what they've been doing best, such as prying the people's business out of closed files and deflating persons in public life who are addicted to "facts" that just aren't so.

Indeed, many of the news media's severest problems are sins of omission, the stories that newsmen are not getting, for a variety of reasons we'll suggest as we go along.

Much of the criticism, then, has itself been unfair, inadequate, and politically motivated—reeking of all the duplicity which the political shock troopers accuse the media of.

Never has there been a better chance to blame the messenger for the messages, for we are awash in the news these days. A people has never before had so much access to so huge a total wordage in printed and broadcast reports.

The amount and diversity of news coverage has within it a source of great strength, for the news consumer who proceeds wisely can listen to many different voices in his quest for a balanced view. But it can also be frustrating and disheartening, as he turns on his radio or television or picks up his newspaper, to be constantly bombarded with catastrophe.

So, when a political leader pushes forward to say, as some have done stridently, that our woes are the fault of the news media which distort the world, things seem suddenly simpler and less dismaying. Reform the news media and save the world. Break the mirrors and make us all beautiful. The news consumer, in his frustration, nods in agreement.

However, the world isn't that simple, and the news consumer, if he is going to sort out the trickery of both messenger and messages, must train himself as a critic. It can be done, through an understanding of how the news media work, their limitations and possibilities—and by asking warily of any other critic, "What are you peddling?"

Chapter 6

Background Story

Who Says So?

A "slight cold" compelled President Kennedy to return to Washington, the White House press secretary told reporters in Chicago the morning of October 20, 1962.[1]

The official diagnosis did not add up for some members of the national press corps. With congressional elections two weeks ahead, the President had just begun an extensive campaign tour. ". . . It didn't seem logical to us, as political as he is and as tough as he is, for him to come waltzing back here because of a little cold," James Reston of the New York Times explained several months later.[2] Washington reporters began digging for other reasons for the President's abrupt return to the White House.

As a starting point, newsmen knew that Russian power and American power were faced off over two current trouble spots:

1. The island of Cuba had been receiving technical and military aid from the Soviet Union for two and a half years.
2. West Berlin, a political island within the Soviet Union's power bloc, was garrisoned with U.S. troops.

Rumors abounded, fed by reports that some U.S. military units were on the move. But all day of October 20, news sources within the Kennedy administration denied that the President had come back to the capital for any reason except his cold. When one reporter asked presidential press secretary Pierre Salinger if there was any other motive for President Kennedy's sudden swerve from the campaign trip, Salinger replied: "Absolutely none."[3]

Skeptical newsmen kept pressing. At the Washington Post that night, managing editor Alfred Friendly told several of his reporters to check with potential sources. Murray Marder zeroed in on the Department of State:

> I started calling some of the people I knew at State, but before I could ask them what was happening, they told me they couldn't say anything. Well, needless to say, this was strange.
>
> Then I went roaming around the State Department to see who was in the offices. I had noticed that two people from the CIA had signed in on the duty roster, which was later, as you know, removed. The executive offices were lighted, and so were the offices for the Alliance for Progress and Inter-American Affairs.

This made it pretty evident that the situation had nothing to do with Berlin. There were no lights and no activity in the European Affairs offices.

Then I ran into an official, whom I can't name or identify; I didn't ask him but told him we had a Cuban crisis on our hands. He apparently didn't know what to say, so he said nothing. We talked in vague terms. He didn't tell me anything tangible at all, but it was enough to convince me that I was on the right track, that it was Cuba, that it would involve the U.N., and that it was a crisis of great magnitude.[4]

The next morning, October 21, the *Post* broke its story: **Marine Moves in South Linked to Cuban Crisis.**[5]

On nationwide television the evening of October 22, President Kennedy told the country that Russian missiles were in Cuba. In the face of this "clandestine, reckless, and provocative threat to world peace," he said, U.S. military strength was being deployed to force the dismantling of the Cuban missile sites.[6]

Until the President went on the air, government officials were silent about the Cuban missile crisis. Despite that silence, the staff of the *Washington Post* (and several other news organizations a day later) assembled a story which alerted readers to the dangerous grapple that ensued between the United States and the Soviet Union.

By What Authority?

The *Washington Post's* disclosure of the Cuban missile crisis, despite official refusals to confirm the story, points up one of the newsman's major dilemmas.

On one hand, a basic journalistic rule is that every news story must make clear to consumers the source from which the information came. Newsmen term this the authority or attribution for a story, and if a report does not contain the attributed comments of the persons involved, the news consumers have every right to be skeptical.

On the other hand, when no one in authority will comment, the newsman must turn to other methods if he believes the story is critical to the public's right to know. Reporter Marder, backed by his managing editor, believed that the Cuban missile story fell into that classification. He investigated, the *Post* printed his unattributed story, and it was proved right by later developments.

True, the news consumer might have had a better documented version of the situation if officials of the Kennedy administration had talked frankly and honestly. But a case of this sort teaches him the lesson a reporter learns early: the more critical and vital the story, the more likely is the "no comment" response or even actual deception.

So Alfred Friendly sent his reporter investigating, and printed the story based on those investigations, even though it was an exception to his own preferred method of operation, expressed in a staff memo:

> Direct attribution is the best way of handling news and information about an event or conditions or situations of which we do not have direct, eye-witness knowledge ourselves. This is always the best way, inasmuch as it provides the reader with a knowledge of the source, enabling him to evaluate its credibility for himself. It involves no pretense of having direct knowledge which we do not have. It avoids the risk of having the newspaper used to disseminate material for which the author is unwilling to take public responsibility.[7]

However, working in Washington, D.C., where unattributed statements begin at the top and are part of a long tradition, Friendly knew that his staff would not always be able to reach the ideal. In decades of dealing with the news media, U.S. Presidents have set the tone by classifying their remarks to reporters—stipulating the kind of "identification" they want—in one of several ways:

1. Direct quotation allowed. The President's televised news conferences are the best example of the type, and the danger is clearly recorded in President Nixon's comment about accused murderer Charles Manson, described later in this chapter.
2. Not directly attributed to the President, but a vague attribution such as "a high administration source" or "an unimpeachable source in the White House." This takes the heat off the President but, since other officials also encourage this use of hidden attribution, it confuses the news audience.
3. No attribution. The reporter can use the information on his own authority, but may not quote anyone:

   The President plans to consider possible avenues towards peace
   in the Mideast in a meeting tomorrow with his top advisors.

4. Off-the-record. The information is given as explanation for a reporter and his editors, but is not to be used, either with or without attribution, in any immediate story.[8]

Legitimate reasons exist for occasionally using less than direct quotation, especially in informal conversation between newsmen and high officials. A President deep in diplomatic discussions to end a war or some other crisis may not want to take the chance of inadvertently bobbling a phrase or a fact and thereby spoiling months or years of work. In January, 1964, a dispute between the United States and Panama centered on the use of a single word.

The United States would agree only to "discuss" a new Canal Zone treaty; Panama wanted to "negotiate."[9]

Background sessions under the tricky rules of less than full attribution can help the newsmen get perspective on complicated events, but there are dangers involved. Such sessions can be used subtly by a President to shape the way a newsman sees an event, while hemming the newsman away from directly reporting the President's words. Backgrounders can also be used for "trial balloons," at little risk to the President.

A noteworthy case occurred when President-elect John F. Kennedy wanted to name his brother as U.S. attorney general, but was not sure whether a storm of nepotism charges would be raised. To find out, he leaked the story, without attribution, then sat back to assess the results. Had the public outcry been severe, he could have decided against naming Robert Kennedy to the cabinet without the embarrassment of having to reverse himself publicly. No storm resulted. At most, it was a mild shower which the trial balloon easily survived, and about a month after the story first appeared in the news, Robert Kennedy was duly nominated by the President.[10]

Instances such as this are far from rare. Critics term them "using the press"; supporters term them "smart diplomacy."

While other officials have not generally used as elaborate a system of classifying remarks as have Presidents, the disease of you-can-use-the-information-but-don't-print-my-name has run rampant in the Capitol.

Ford Foundation President McGeorge Bundy, an aide to Presidents Kennedy and Johnson, described the results to the American Society of Newspaper Editors: "The politicians know what's going on, the reporters know what's going on. Only the poor public is left confused, ill-informed and increasingly mad about the practice."[11]

Wall Street Journal reporter Alan Otten, writing of President Lyndon Johnson's fondness for the background session, called it "a device that perhaps more than any other lends itself to government news management." And, he added, "the more remote the degree of attribution, the more danger to the reporter."[12]

Though Washington reporters have occasionally staged mild rebellions against unattributed remarks, the practice continues.

The newsmen have been somewhat more successful in fending off sources who try to trap them into silence by passing along information off-the-record, that fourth category of remarks which means that the information is not to be reported at all. A smart reporter often refuses to agree to off-the-record remarks and stops the informant. If a source offers information, then follows up with a statement that it was off the record—Congressmen have done this even at public hearings—the reporter points out that such an agreement can only be made in advance.

Adding up the practices on the giving and receiving sides of official statements, the news consumer comes to this total: reporters and their regular sources of information develop working relationships that frequently are useful, often are comfortable, and sometimes inhibit the public's right to know.

At the local level as well as at the national, reporters walk a fine line between having the confidence of their sources and being overwhelmed by them.

A reporter who accepts newsmaker Joe's invitations to exclusive parties, finds free tickets to ballgames waiting in his mailbox, and has the run of privileged circles, may wake up to find that he is no longer being candid with the public about Joe's financial dealings. If his managing editor finds out before he does, he may lose his job. Sooner or later, every reporter can expect to learn that reporting is not a popularity contest. The good ones learn fast.

If pinning sources on stories is difficult at home, it is almost impossible in some areas of international reporting. Consider the potential frustrations of a reporter in a foreign culture, at a language disadvantage, in a country where governments are changed regularly by coups d'etat rather than elections, and where "news" is what the government decrees. Consider the problems in Russia, where the foreign press corps was once warned to stop quoting "dregs of society," including Nobel Prize-winning novelist Aleksandr I. Solzhenitsyn.[13]

An even more extreme problem existed for years in trying to get news out of Communist China, which allowed so few Western newsmen to visit that the ones who got in became instant celebrities to other newsmen. The China watchers in Hong Kong sifted every shred of rumor, watched mainland television, crops, and weather. The resulting reporting was spotty, speculative, and lacking in authority.

The newsman's problems of authority, domestic and foreign, come in endless varieties. Sometimes they can be blamed on reporters who are not tough enough on their sources; sometimes on a lazy reporter whose "authoritative source" may be the guy on the next bar stool. Sometimes the lack of authority is unavoidable and legitimate.

If a reporter has investigated thoroughly and can present his evidence, his story will be credible even if the logical sources won't talk.

The sign-ins in the State Department register, the lights burning in the Latin American section, and the nonstatements from regular sources made a strong case for Marder's story.

Among each spring's Pulitzer Prize announcements are awards for investigative reporting, which in many cases have involved deducing the facts of a story when sources were clamped tight. When a vital story is broken this way, the true winner is the public, whose right to know is being served faithfully and skilfully.

The working rules, then, are these:

1. The consumer has every right to expect a clear source for every statement in every news story, except where a reporter witnesses the event himself and except for statements of common knowledge.

What's common knowledge? That's tricky, and depends on the audience being written for. This example, one of countless good stories attributed to Mark Twain, shows the danger of qualifying *everything*:

> A woman giving the name of Mrs. James Jones, who is reported to be one of the society leaders of the city, is said to have given what purported to be a party yesterday to a number of alleged ladies. The hostess claims to be wife of a reputed attorney.[14]

Somewhere between that level of overkill and not providing any sources at all is the area of common knowledge—and common sense. Perhaps we can say common knowledge is a body of facts established by prior reporting and in all likelihood known by most of the news audience—or, better yet, which can be found out by the news audience from reference works or other routine inquiry.

2. If the source won't talk, but the story is vital to the public's right to know, the reporter's job is to investigate and present his evidence. If a source was queried and would not comment, the story should say so; it'll help the consumer to know what effort was made to dig out information.
3. If the reporter presents no source and no credible evidence, the story moves from the category of news to speculation, and the reporter's reputation— and his news organization's—is squarely on the line.

In no way can a consumer be even reasonably sure about such a story. But one thing he can do is to check bylines and newsgathering organizations carefully, keeping track of speculative stories to see if they eventually turn out to be true. That will give him something of a track record for accuracy, but it's still subject, in any particular case, to the whim of the anonymous source or the reporter's hunch.

A reader who follows these guidelines will gain skill in separating speculative reports from straight, attributed news. But that's only half the battle.

Talking about the best of the nonattributed statements, those that turn out to be true, Stan Opotowsky, managing editor of the *New York Post*, outlined the reader's other problem:

"My concern is not over publishing anonymous statements which are true, but rather in publishing attributable statements which we know damn well are lies—maybe white lies, maybe half lies, but lies."[15]

Who Is Worth Listening To?

The next sentry duty for the consumer, then, is to watch out for those white lies, half lies, plain old 100% lies—and for mistake, misunderstanding, and mischief as well.

If the voice on a tape recorder tells you the earth is a trapezoid, you receive both accuracy and inaccuracy. The voice is transmitted faithfully, but what the voice *says* is false.

That's the fix you are in when sham—and as we will see, it may be falsehood or merely insignificance—lodges itself in news stories despite the most scrupulous efforts by newsmen to be accurate. You have to go beyond the media's faithful transmission of a quote or other piece of information, and consider whether the source may be feeding sham into the media.

Two techniques help the consumer to make his judgments:

1. He must be aware of whom he is listening to, and why.
2. No matter what the source, he must listen skeptically.

We listen to some sources because of the positions they occupy. Whoever is President at the moment, we pay attention to what he says because the power of the Presidency can mean a policy decision we applaud or one we fear, a law we favor or a law we dislike, war or peace.

A presidential news conference may produce several different news stories, all keyed to some comment by the President. Every turn of a phrase is scrutinized by newsmen for hints of what the President may do next.

There is almost no chance that a President will be quoted inaccurately when he talks at a public news conference. Tape recorders, a printed transcript from a complete shorthand record, and television cameras will show exactly what he said. So, what the reporters pass along to their audience is not a struggle for attribution and accuracy, but a contest to pry comment from the President about various issues.

Presidents take this duel seriously. Those who've been in office since live telecasting of presidential news conferences began—Kennedy, Johnson, Nixon —[16] have rehearsed with their aides beforehand, going over questions they think are likely to be asked.[17]

Others we listen to because of their positions include government officials, senators, congressmen, governors, mayors—up or down the line as far as the consumer's individual interests take him.

At a noon news conference, the Secretary of State addresses himself to a trade agreement signed with Indonesia, the appointment of a new cultural affairs aide, and other matters which don't immediately bear on us. The same afternoon, a local city councilman introduces a curfew law which would keep everyone under eighteen off the streets after eight P.M.

The city councilman gets listened to most keenly this day. The consumer considers whom he is listening to, and knows he listens because the person's remarks can affect his life some way.

Next question: is he listening skeptically?

An officeholder is a politician as well as a human being. What he says may be slanted to help his party or himself, or to cover up the failings of either.

When Lyndon Johnson was President, he sometimes played word games with reporters to conceal his plans until he could personally announce them. In March, 1967, President Johnson was asked about a report that he was searching for a successor to Henry Cabot Lodge as the U.S. ambassador to South Vietnam. The President responded: "No, there is no truth that I am looking for a successor."[18] Less than a week later, Ellsworth Bunker was named to replace Lodge at the Saigon embassy. White House news secretary George Christian maintained that the President's original remark had been "absolutely accurate"; he had not been *searching* for a successor to Lodge because he already had *found* one.

The next administration carried on the tradition of playing word games about U.S. actions in Southeast Asia. U.S. and South Vietnamese military units went into Cambodia in May, 1970. Sources in the Nixon administration, including President Nixon and Secretary of Defense Laird, explained that the purpose was to capture a Viet Cong headquarters in the Cambodian jungle near the boundary of South Vietnam. When no Viet Cong headquarters was found, the same officials, including Secretary Laird and President Nixon, explained that the real purpose of the raid had been to capture enemy weapons and food supplies.

Even when an officeholder speaks on television and the camera transmits every working of his vocal cords, he will occasionally try to cover an obvious boner by protesting that he didn't really say what he said. A famous example occurred when President Nixon spoke to law enforcement officials in Denver on August 3, 1970, and television recorded his flat statement about the Charles Manson case being tried in Los Angeles: "Here is a man who was guilty, directly or indirectly, of eight murders without reason."[19]

A cardinal rule is that "guilty" is a decision produced by our process of trial, and until that decision is pronounced, the accused is suspected of or charged with committing a crime. After President Nixon forgot to qualify his remark this way, the presidential press secretary tried to unsay the President's prejudicial comment: "His obvious intention was to refer to the alleged charges against Mr. Manson."[20] Later that day, the President himself had to try further to unsay: "My remarks were in the context of my expression of a tendency on the part of some to glamorize those identified with a crime. The last thing I would do is prejudice the legal rights of any person in any circumstance."[21]

The news consumer should remember that we all try to put the best face on what we do. It started in the Garden of Eden, James Reston once suggested. That story Adam and Eve put out about the apple; actually, "she tempted him with something else."[22]

Is a person worth listening to simply because he is in office? Put it this way: we sift from the news media the remarks of those public officials whose words or actions can affect us in some way that we care about. We examine those remarks to see what motives may be behind them.

We listen to some persons because of their special knowledge about a topic.

This is uncertain territory. It's hard for a layman to know which experts deserve to be listened to, and to know how accurate they are if we do listen.

The sheer number of experts available to us through modern communications is befuddling. Three hundred years ago, nearly every person in England with any scientific skills at all could be found at a meeting of The Royal Society, and the Society's journal was the country's sole regular report of scientific knowledge.[23] Today, as Alvin Toffler estimates in *Future Shock*, "90 percent of all the scientists who ever lived are now alive,"[24] and the news consumer hardly needs to be told that their works and comments flood around us from many news outlets.

Nor are scientists the only experts who abound today. In the 1920s, syndicated newspaper columnists began writing regular "expert" evaluations of the political scene; by now, several hundred commentators give us their opinions regularly by print, radio, and television.[25]

We also hear all the time from those who claim to be expert in telling us what we think about issues—the pollsters.

And there are countless organizations rallying around countless causes, each providing information, misinformation, or a smooth blend of the two—the pressure group as expert.

What is the reader to do when he encounters someone else's words about deoxyribonucleic acid, about the Gallup Poll percentages of the public who approved the shooting of students at Kent State University, about the "findings" of groups lined up for and against nuclear power plants?

The expert's credentials probably will not be as well known as a political leader's. And the consequences of what he says may be harder to grasp, too.

But the consumer still can be a skeptic. For one thing, he can weigh the expert's words to see whether what is said is a prediction or a definite result. He can keep reminding himself that a prediction is not a reality until after it happens.

For example, a prediction by a scientist that a gene, the basic chemical unit of heredity, can someday be analyzed is one thing; actual isolation of a gene from the complex chain of life, as was achieved at Harvard Medical

School in 1969, is something different.[26] The difference, you might say, between a fellow talking about taking a step for mankind on the moon and actually doing it.

A political commentator is very often dealing in predictions or interpretations. This is chancy business, and the consumer should keep it in mind. William McGaffin, a respected political analyst who reports for the *Chicago Daily News*, soon after the 1968 presidential election provided his readers the names of six men who would fill certain posts in the Nixon cabinet.[27] Three were chosen for the cabinet, but not for the jobs McGaffin predicted, and the others weren't named to anything. Earlier in 1968, political commentators assumed that President Johnson would be an automatic candidate for reelection, and discussed the presidential picture with that in mind. Bill Lawrence of ABC television was one of the very few who suggested correctly that Johnson might not run.

Bearing in mind that predictions are only predictions, however expertly made, the consumer can keep himself from banking too heavily on words which glisten with news of the future. When heart transplants were first achieved and all manner of predictions were being heard, anyone who assumed the medical breakthrough would change his own life was hoping in haste.[28] An organ transplant may affect him, if he becomes one of the very small percentage of citizens who will have such surgery, but the problems of tissue rejection and the expense and difficulty of the surgery leave the odds, so far, very much against the chance that many of us will undergo such transplants.

Scientists have laboratory results to back up their words. Commentators have their own experience and the opinions of other persons who have been around politics. Public opinion pollsters have a problem: the raw material of their expertise is what their interviewees tell them, truthful or not.

Polling has come into our public life somewhat the way the forward pass came into football. Instead of grinding along step by step to see what actually develops, we use this fast shortcut to the end of the field. In theory, we get to know the score that much more quickly. But as some coaches point out, throwing the ball can lead to three things and two of them, an incomplete pass or an interception, are bad. When a polling crew asks its questions of the sample segment of our population, three things can happen, and two of them aren't very good for accurate prediction:

1. An interviewee will tell the truth;
2. An interviewee will not tell the truth;
3. An interviewee will say he is undecided.

The reader should take poll results with caution. He should be sure, for instance, how many persons were polled, when, and precisely what the wording of the questions was.

The use of poll results can be ridiculous. On October 30, 1961, the

Burlington (Vermont) *Free Press* provided a classic example. The headline said: **Vermonters Favor Barry Goldwater.** This was based on the story's third paragraph, which read:

> Of the 24 delegates and alternates from Vermont, eight responded to the poll. Goldwater received four votes, Gov. Nelson A. Rockefeller of New York received three votes and former Vice President Richard M. Nixon received one vote.[29]

In short, Senator Goldwater was landsliding through Vermont on the basis of four votes out of a possible twenty-four.

Contrast such slippery use of a poll with this paragraph from a 1968 *Wall Street Journal* story, which provides numbers *and* analysis:

> . . . A *Wall Street Journal* survey of over 50 top executives indicates that, having once brought themselves to oppose a Republican presidential candidate, a surprising number of executives are taking a far more critical view of the GOP's national ticket than they once did. Indeed, among Mr. Johnson's 1964 business supporters who are willing to discuss their current political learnings, slightly less than half are supporting Mr. Nixon. The rest are split about evenly between Humphrey men and executives who are undecided whether to vote at all because they don't like either candidate much.[30]

So far, we have been talking about misuse or overuse of techniques, most of them having to do with prediction or interpretation. Next is a brand of sham news put out not for the sake of the information itself, but for the sake of a cause—the "expert" testimony of pressure groups.

It's wise not to take the word of any organization until you know something of its membership and aims. Look beyond the name of the organization, because a resounding title may be merely a false front.

During World War II, 112,000 American citizens of Japanese ancestry were interned in guarded camps, although no acts of disloyalty were reported before the Nisei were rounded up and taken from their homes.[31] For several decades, racial prejudice had spawned a number of organizations which opposed full rights of citizenship for the Japanese. Which of the following organizations would you single out as anti-Japanese?

The Americanism Educational League.
The California Citizens Council.
Home Front Commandos.
The Pacific Coast Japanese Problem League.
The American Foundation for the Exclusion of the Japanese.
No Japs, Inc.

The answer: all of them. Some were blatant in the names they chose, some preferred a bit more disguise—and the point is that the name alone may not be a very accurate guide to an organization's purpose.

Once a reader or viewer warily goes behind an organization's name, he should pause to consider just what sort of information the group is offering. If it adds up to diatribe and argument, it should be used with the greatest of care. On the other hand, if the organization has compiled voting records on an issue or reliable cost estimates no one else has provided, the information may be extremely helpful.

As for a generalization about experts, individual and corporate? Perhaps it's this: the news consumer can protect himself somewhat by sorting prediction from actuality and hard information from propaganda.

The words of some persons show up in the news media because they are celebrities.

Historian Daniel Boorstin made this distinction: "The hero was a big man; the celebrity is a big name."[32]

Boorstin also noted the shift in personages whose names we think are big:

> Of the subjects of biographical articles appearing in the *Saturday Evening Post* and the now-defunct *Collier's* in five sample years between 1901 and 1914, 74 per cent came from politics, business, and the professions. But after about 1922 well over half of them came from the world of entertainment.[33]

Our era has its own celebrities, from rock musicians to astronauts. Perhaps the true importance of celebrities, beyond the skills that bring them to our attention, is that they are an expression of a society's values at a certain moment.

Politicians surely believe so. They attempt to transfer glamor from famous supporters to themselves.[34]

In 1968, Aretha Franklin, Ben Gazzara, Andy Warhol, Truman Capote, Hank Aaron, Rod McKuen, and several dozen other well-known persons announced they preferred Robert Kennedy for President.

Alan Arkin, Edward Albee, Jules Feiffer, Dustin Hoffman, Paul Newman, Eartha Kitt, and several dozen others announced they preferred Eugene McCarthy.

Richard Nixon's roster of celebrities included John Wayne, Bart Starr, Ray Bolger, Rudy Vallee, Joe Louis, and Ginger Rogers.

When the consumer comes across the words of a celebrity, the skeptic in him should ask this: is this source talking about something he knows about? Or is he offering an opinion merely because his big name gives him entry to the media?

In January, 1964, astronaut John Glenn announced he was running for the Democratic nomination for a U.S. Senate seat from Ohio. "I feel that it provides the best opportunity to make use of the experience I have gained in twenty-two years of government service," Glenn said.[35]

A question forms automatically in the mind of the careful news consumer: what did John Glenn do in those "twenty-two years of government service?"

The answer: he was a Marine flier and the first American astronaut to orbit the earth.

Neither accomplishment certified any special talent for the American process of government, but they didn't disqualify Colonel Glenn either. Every public official is an amateur back at the point where he enters politics.

The careful citizen's next question: what does John Glenn say about public issues?

The answer: nothing—nothing at all. Because he still was in the Marine Corps, Colonel Glenn explained, he couldn't enter into any manner of political discussion until his discharge, six weeks away.[36]

Colonel Glenn eventually withdrew from the Senate race because of an injury suffered when he slipped in the bathtub, but his luck rather than his celebrityhood let him down. Yet, when Glenn was listened to skeptically, he had little to offer as a candidate except celebrityhood.

Learning to look skeptically at big names may tell us, then, that a beauty contest winner may not know much about swindles which rob American consumers of millions of dollars each year. A famous lawyer may not know much about automobile safety beyond habitually buckling his seat belt.

Unless the beauty contest winner is Bess Myerson, a former Miss America who went on to become New York City's Commissioner of Consumer Affairs.

Unless the lawyer is Ralph Nader, a crusader for auto safety and author of *Unsafe at Any Speed*.

How does the consumer separate these two from other beauty queens and lawyers, any number of whom may also have opinions to offer? By asking if the celebrity is talking about something he knows; by checking to see that he can back up his remarks with something besides an inflated name.

An approximate guide through this question of who is worth listening to comes down to this:

1. The consumer should consider whether the source of a statement is someone who can affect his life, by something done or said.
2. Everyone's credentials are open to suspicion. Any comment should be looked over for its basis. What evidence does the source offer to prove what he says? What's his record?
3. An utterance is not a reality. That is, just because something is said does not make it true, or even likely to happen.
4. Many times a consumer cannot know for certain whether a statement is sham. But he can hedge his bets and not rely too heavily on the statement being true.

Whose Side Is Told?

"Never trust a cop," Professor Jacob Scher was fond of barking at his reporting students at Northwestern University.

Scher's point was one of accuracy: don't expect a policeman to do your job for you. Maybe he'll have all the names, addresses, and other information right; maybe he won't. You'd better doublecheck.

Scher's admonition reflected no dislike of police. It was simply his way of getting students to sit up and take notice of their own responsibilities. But the significance of his remark has broadened in recent years with the surge of student unrest, racial disorder, and environmental disorientation.

"Never trust a cop" now means to the knowledgeable reporter, don't settle for the side of the story that's easiest to get or most traditional. Find out who else is involved, and see what they have to say.

A reporter is sent out to cover a racial disorder. If he gets there in time, he reports what he sees. Then who does he talk to?

The old answer would most often have been the police and the mayor. They furnish the "authoritative" statements.

But that's only the establishment side, and newsmen labored to overcome that bias. So they broadened their view to include not only the police and the mayor, but also a responsible spokesman of the Black community.

Unhappily, that raises another problem, which a Washington State study on race and violence expresses like this:

> If a white man wrote a letter to a newspaper or magazine or went on radio or television and announced, "I speak for all white people when I say . . .", he would be hooted down. We have realized for a long time that no individual is the spokesman for the white community. And yet there has been a traditional tendency to view the black community as a monolith. Instead of knowledgeable coverage of events in the black areas of this state, reporters have been sent out to find "their leaders" and the media audience has been led to believe a select group with one point of view can represent the overall thinking of the black community.[37]

In Cleveland, whites and Negroes from racially troubled areas complained about the reporting. The city's community relations office stepped forward with a list of "responsible" sources from both areas, which the news media declined to use. The Wall Street Journal quoted one Cleveland news executive as explaining: "I think what we were given was a list of people who represent the establishment."[38]

To try to overcome the establishment-only bias, reporters and editors have worked to enlarge their views by including diverse elements of the Black community.

One of the key questions is whether only "responsible" leaders, if indeed they can be identified, should be included; or should the news media also report on those leaders who are most militant, most violence-prone, and perhaps most involved in the confrontations?

Also, can the importance of a leader be judged from his noise level? Are the news media, when they report his statements, merely reporting, or are they promoting his cause? And who speaks for the Black community's silent majority?

Such questions indicate the perplexities these situations spill forth for the newsman.

Adequate coverage of the Black community, newsmen and their critics now concede, depends on knowing a great deal about the area on a continuing basis.

Washington State's race and violence report of 1969 continues:

> The media are in the midst of reorganizing their coverage of what is going on in the black community. At this time, while motives seem sincere and in the best tradition of honest reporting, the results are still spotty. . . . In this time of specialization, we have police reporters, city hall reporters, religion editors, and full-time movie reporters. But too often the man covering the ghetto has to split his time on freeway openings, flower shows and county fairs.[39]

The point has been hammered home in reports by violence commissions across the country. The voluminous U.S. Riot Commission report spends a full chapter on media coverage, in which it makes this corroborating point:

> The Commission's major concern with the news media is not riot reporting as such, but in the failure to report adequately on race relations and ghetto problems and to bring more Negroes into journalism. . . . In defining, explaining and reporting this broader, more complex and ultimately far more fundamental subject, the communications media, ironically, have failed to communicate.
>
> They have not communicated to the majority of their audience, which is white, a sense of the degradation, misery and hopelessness in living in the ghetto. They have not communicated to whites a feeling for the difficulties and frustrations of being a Negro in the United States. They have not shown understanding or appreciation of—and thus have not communicated—a sense of Negro culture, thought or history.[40]

The pages of the commission reports come alive when a student from Staten Island sits in a college classroom where the instructor is talking about *New York Magazine's* expose of furniture fraud in Harlem.[41] The instructor has just quoted a case in which a man on welfare was charged $649 for merchandise on credit that he could have purchased for $360 with cash.

"I never heard that before," says the student. "It sure helps explain the riots in the city, doesn't it?"

It sure does, but New York Magazine, months after the burning and looting in the city, was the first place he had been introduced to that perspective.

The news media's coverage of race and violence makes a handy example, but remember that the principles apply to any story where there are likely to be contending points of view.

The CBS Evening News with Walter Cronkite has tackled the immense, complex environmental story on such a continuing basis, using a pictorial lead-in that symbolically shows the world in man's hand. NBC has done much the same thing without the symbolic picture. The perspective of the birdwatchers, the conservationists, is being told along with those of industry and government.

The differences between the youth culture and the older generation; the other side of a war; both sides of a religious conflict; labor and management; the Pentagon and the GI; in every case, the story has to stand up to that question of whose side is being told.

The consumer, in taking stock of both national and local news media, will find it helpful to ask himself about each newspaper, radio and television news organization, and magazine news operation:

1. Is it covering the major issues?
2. Does it give only crisis coverage, or is there continuing coverage which attempts to anticipate, pinpoint, and put into perspective the major issues?
3. Whose side is reported?

When a crisis erupts, it's too late to begin the reporting.

Chapter 7

Robert Osborn for Fortune Magazine.

Hoaxing and Hornblowing

Truth, elusive truth.

Truth unvarnished and truth thick with layers of gloss. Truth lost in the swamps and truth unknown at the pinnacles.

The statistical truth of a tense White House announcement in 1964 that the U.S. force of destroyers off the coast of South Vietnam had been doubled.[1] The numerical truth that instead of one destroyer on station, now—two.

My half truth, your white lie, his malicious falsehood.

The truth dog-eared from use on the unconcerned. The truth in mint condition, rolled out only for rare visits to the conscience.

Plainly, truth knows many garbs. Poets and preachers have chased it through the mind of man for centuries. Jurists and scholars ritually pursue it into other fields. One way or another, this book so far has been mostly about the nature of truth in the news flow. Time now for a look at those who bend truth, for a living or for the kick of it. Their work too is an important part of the news process. Whatever portions of truth the news consumer can gather from his sources of information, he'll have to sort out hoaxes and public relations ploys that come along.

Aladdin's Treasure and Other Dross

Lincoln the Lover, proclaimed the cover of *The Atlantic Monthly*. Inside, the introductory note by Editor Ellery Sedgwick waxed ecstatic: "Picture an orderly and prosaic office when Aladdin's treasure was dumped on the editor's desk!"[2]

What a trove it was. With this long-lost correspondence from the young romance between Abraham Lincoln and Ann Rutledge, a legend leapt to life in Lincoln's own penmanship. Besides these priceless endearments, the finder furnished the magazine other letters written by Lincoln during his early manhood and books with marginal comments in his handwriting.

The array of the collection and the tests which proved the writing paper to be the proper age convinced Editor Sedgwick his historical scoop was authentic. Beginning in the issue of December, 1928, *The Atlantic* blazoned Abe and Ann in a three-part series.

One problem: the editorial staff in the cultured confines of *The Atlantic's* Boston offices had missed a clue the simplest country lad would have spotted. One of the letters from Lincoln to a surveyor he had worked for in the early 1830s included the line: "There seems some controversy between him and Green concerning that North East quarter of Section 40—you remember?"

There is no such thing as a Section 40 in the American land system. Ever since the rectangular survey came into being with the Ordinance of 1785, the American landscape west of the Ohio River has been divided into townships of 36 sections each—that is, tracts of land uniformly six miles by six.[3] So, a country dweller might refer to Section 6, or Section 19, or any number up to 36—but never any higher. It was inconceivable that a man who had worked as an assistant surveyor could make such a reference. As a legion of readers and scholars promptly informed *The Atlantic*, the prized Lincoln letters were a hoax.

Hoaxes infiltrate the news fairly often.[4] Many are not as flimsy as the faked letters which fooled Editor Sedgwick. Often a hoax has that most superb and untrackable of joint authorships—rumor. Other times, deliberate concoctions spread the hoaxer's message, whether it be deadly political or simply funny. Either way, newsgatherers swallow falsehood, and reports which are supposed to convey information as accurately as possible to the consumer become larded with phony stories.

Some hoaxes live on and on. Here's one which will probably show up again sometime in new guise. From an Associated Press dispatch in September, 1966:

> SAIGON (AP) The ups and downs in the life of Nguyen Van Teo—repairman employed by the U.S. military—have landed him in a Saigon hospital.
>
> He submitted this accident report to his superior:
>
> "When I arrived at the military aid command building to fix it, I found that the rains had dislodged a large number of tile from the roof. So I rigged up a beam with a pulley at the top of the building and hoisted up a couple of barrels full of tile.
>
> "When I fixed the building, there was a lot of tile left over. I hoisted the barrel back up again and secured the line at the bottom, and then went up and filled the barrel with the extra tile. Then I went down to the bottom and cast off the line.
>
> "Unfortunately, the barrel of tile was heavier than I was and before I knew what was happening, the barrel started down, jerking me off the ground. I decided to hang on and half way up I met the barrel coming down and received a severe blow on the shoulder.
>
> "I then continued to the top, banging my head against the beam and getting my fingers jammed in the pulley. When the barrel hit the ground, it burst its bottom, allowing all the tile to spill out. I was now heavier than the barrel and I started down again at high speed.

"Halfway down I met the barrel coming up, and received severe injuries to my chin. When I hit the ground, I landed on the tile, getting several painful cuts from the sharp edges.

"At this point I must have lost my presence of mind because I let go the line. The barrel then came down, giving me another heavy blow on the head and putting me in the hospital.

"I respectfully request sick leave."

Nguyen Van Teo's request was granted.[5]

The *Columbia Journalism Review* noted that at least five earlier versions of this barreling calamity could be found, all the way back to a skit by the late radio comedian Fred Allen. Every time it comes around, a number of editors seem not to see the unlikelihood of the workman's mishaps, nor even wonder how probable it is that a barrel would burst its bottom when dropped to the ground. Barrels normally are as stout as the skull of a gullible editor.

Anyway, the much-traveled workman does not make his rounds alone. Among other perennials who bob into the news every so often:

1. The baby sitter who gets stuck on a freshly painted toilet seat her evening's employers neglected to warn her about. In 1959, an elaborate version written by a reporter for the *St. Paul Dispatch* was picked up by the Associated Press and appeared in papers all across the country. Edward M. Miller, a *Portland Oregonian* editor who had exposed a similar story as a fraud a quarter century before, wired the AP: THAT GAL MUST BE GETTING AS TIRED AS SOME OF THE REST OF US.[6]
2. The woman driver who stops to help a stalled motorist. He asks for a push to get his car started, explaining that because of the automatic transmission she'll have to get up to thirty-five miles an hour before the engine will start. The lady backs off and rams his car at thirty-five m.p.h.
3. The truck driver who, according to the variant you prefer, finds another man with his wife or has a feud with a neighbor. He has his revenge by dumping his truckload of cement, garbage or fertilizer—again, take your pick—in the lover/neighbor's convertible.

Some hoaxes thrive as regional favorites. In our part of the country, the Pacific Northwest, the sasquatch is a frequent newsmaker. Folks keep spotting this ape-like creature in the boondocks, but oddly enough in an era when man is crowding in so heavily on other wildlife that some species are threatened with extinction, no one has ever bagged a sasquatch. Perhaps it's because the "evidence" frequently comes back to someone such as the gentleman a few winters ago who cut big footprints out of plywood, nailed them to his boots, and made sasquatch tracks all over the countryside and on into the headlines.[7]

For a short span in the spring of 1969, newspapers in the Northwest caught what might be called elephantsitis. This story relates that a baby elephant at the city zoo has been taught the stunt of sitting on a red chair. Somehow, and this part is never quite clear, the elephant galumphs into the zoo's parking lot, spies a red Volkswagen, and plops down on it with crushing effect. Newspapers in Portland, Seattle and Tacoma all carried some manner of report on the sitting elephant—each version happening in their own cities.[8]

In a Southern California classic, the hoaxed put their faith in the automotive instead of the animal world. Editor William Bronson of the conservationist quarterly *Cry California* spoofed the cult of the auto by concocting a motoring couple he called Frank and Marilee Farrier. According to Bronson, they were the ultimate Los Angelenos. Deep in debt on the installment plan, the Farriers had sold their house and were living on the L.A. freeways in a motor home, constantly on the go to and from their jobs and spending nights in a parking garage. Other reporters persistently tried to find the mobile pair, despite Bronson's prompt explanation that they didn't exist.[9]

"I named her Marilee for 'merrily we roll along,'" he later recounted. "Farrier means a blacksmith who shoes horses, and I thought that was a tip-off. Besides, I'm from Northern California and I had no idea people would take (the Farriers) seriously."[10]

In the Midwest in 1906, City Editor John Meyer of the *Appleton* (Wisconsin) *Crescent* spread to countless other newspapers an intriguing tale he had been duped with. A soft-hearted farmer couldn't bear to shoot his faithful old horse. Instead he put a stick of dynamite in the horse's mouth, and the steed was blown to bits in mid-gallop around the pasture.[11] Hoax connoisseur Curtis D. MacDougall, who tracked this one down, reports that Meyer sold the story to every newspaper he queried.

Some humorous hoaxes have required considerable calculation and enterprise. The rivalry between Joseph Pulitzer's *New York World* and William Randolph Hearst's *New York Journal* brewed an intramural hoax during the Spanish-American War. Both newspapers tried to tap into each other's war news, so one day the *Journal* included in a casualty list the name of Colonel Reflipe W. Thenuz. Turn the first part of the name around, pronounce the last name phonetically, and you have the admission the *Journal* tricked its rival into printing: *We pilfer the news.*[12]

Colonel Thenuz, the elephantsitis virus, and the case of the exploding nag are all harmless enough. Better than that, they furnish a laugh or two. But more poisonous hoaxes seep into the news just as easily. The worst of these feed prejudice and rancor on a nationwide scale. Usually they spring from the habit of backing up a belief with impressive quotations, citations, or examples. The ideal specimens, naturally, would be those you make up yourself to cover all angles. The difficult decade of the 1960s ended with the right and the left in America each trumpeting a major piece of phony propaganda.

The entry from the right came, according to the lore of the believers, by the way of Dusseldorf, Germany, where in the dark of a spring night in 1919 Allied occupation soldiers raided a communist headquarters and found "Rules for Bringing About a Revolution." They read:

A. Corrupt the young, get them away from religion. Get them interested in sex. Make them superficial; destroy their ruggedness.

B. Get control of all means of publicity and thereby:

1. Get people's minds off their government by focusing their attention on athletics, sexy books and plays and other trivialities.

2. Divide the people into hostile groups by constantly harping on controversial matters of no importance.

3. Destroy the people's faith in their natural leaders by holding the latter up to contempt, ridicule and obloquy.

4. Always preach true democracy but seize power as fast and as ruthlessly as possible.

5. By encouraging government extravagance, destroy its credit, produce fear of inflation with rising prices and general discontent.

6. Foment unnecessary strikes in vital industries, encourage civil disorders and foster a lenient and soft attitude on the part of government toward such disorders.

7. By specious argument, cause the breakdown of the old moral virtues: honesty, sobriety, continence, faith in the pledged word, ruggedness.

C. Cause the registration of all firearms on some pretext, with a view to confiscating them and leaving the population helpless.[13]

The Rules are revealing on several counts. The language is contemporary Middle American—"get them away from," "get them interested in," "destroy their ruggedness"—instead of the distinctive Marxist jargon. "Always preach true democracy" has an oddly American ring, coming from a point in European history when the radical byword of the day would more likely have been "socialism." Registration of firearms is also a modern American topic, coming into public debate in the early 1960s.

And most intriguing of all is the revelation that interest in sex is a communist plot.

Nonetheless, the Dusseldorf Rules have been endlessly reprinted in U.S. papers and newsletters, inevitably with a tag line suggesting this is precisely what's happening to us this very moment. Singer Pat Boone touted the rules to a rally at the Cotton Bowl in Dallas in May, 1970.[14] At least three U.S. Representatives read them into the Congressional Record.[15]

Conservative columnist James J. Kilpatrick responded to readers who mailed in copies of the Dusseldorf Rules by branding the communist commandments a hoax, and not a very deft one at that. He pointed out that a skeptical Congressman, Frank Bow of Ohio, "smelled a fake and asked J. Edgar Hoover about the paper. Hoover's conclusion: 'The document is spurious.'"[16]

When his debunking brought in even more mail avowing belief in the Rules, Kilpatrick lambasted both the fraud and the gullibles who swallowed it. He concluded:

> My right-wing friends, I say, will not be moved. The FBI, and the Senate Internal Security subcommittee dismiss the Dusseldorf Rules as spurious. Staff members of the Library of Congress Slavic and Central European Division searched the papers of Henry T. Allen, commander in Germany in the spring of 1919, as well as contemporary American, British and German newspapers, without finding a trace of the document. Archives of the Chief of Military History disclose nothing. . . . Yet credulity persists; and so long as men and women are willing to be Dusseldorfed, new hoaxes will come along.[17]

While the right-wingers were being Dusseldorfed, Americans farther left along the political spectrum were being Hamburged. Their scripture purportedly was from a speech by Nazi leader Adolf Hitler in Hamburg in 1932. This famous excerpt read:

> The streets of our country are in turmoil. The universities are filled with students rebelling and rioting.
>
> Communists are seeking to destroy our country. Russia is threatening us with her might and the republic is in danger. Yes, danger from within and without.
>
> We need law and order. Yes, without law and order our nation cannot survive. Elect us and we shall restore law and order.[18]

So, while some citizens were drawing a parallel from contemporary America back to a diabolical communist plot, others were sketching one from the Nixon administration, which came into office with a record of law-and-order campaign vows, back to a diabolical Nazi preachment. And again, the innuendo traveled far and wide via the news media.

Fortunately the lineage of the "law and order" quote is clearer than that of the Dusseldorf Rules, at least for a ways, and it's worth a look as a case study of a hoax on the move.

The quote made its national debut when Jerome Beatty Jr. read it in a California newsletter and reprinted it in his "Trade Winds" column in *Saturday Review* on May 17, 1969.

After that, Hitler's homily indeed was on the trade winds—repeated on talk shows, printed in Berkeley on a leaflet adorned with a photo of California's Governor Ronald Reagan, quoted to a congressional committee.[19] A scant two weeks after the quote appeared in *Saturday Review*, Senator Edmund Muskie used it in a speech to the National Council on Crime and Delinquency.

The Progressive magazine reprinted it from Muskie's speech. Supreme Court Justice William O. Douglas apparently picked it up from *The Progressive* and included it in his manuscript for *Points of Rebellion*.[20]

Then came the retreat. *Newsweek* and CBS asked Beatty about the quote.[21] Beatty traced it from the publication where he first read it to "a professor at California State College, Long Beach, who said he had gotten it from a university professor.[22] For a while it was assumed that the latter had found it in some original research in Germany. It turned out that he had seen it posted on a bulletin board somewhere, he couldn't remember where. Hardly the kind of research one would expect from a professor."

Other research meanwhile drew a blank. The Library of Congress couldn't verify the quote, and reported that William L. Shirer, a painstaking historian of the Third Reich, couldn't either.[23]

Beatty ran a followup report in his column in the December 20, 1969 issue of *Saturday Review*, advising that the quote seemed to be a phony.[24] The first printing of Justice Douglas's *Points of Rebellion* contains the quote on page 58, but it's been deleted in subsequent printings.[25]

Despite such efforts to backtrack, the Hitler declaration will probably live on. For one thing, as Beatty points out, "when researchers try to disprove it, they always repeat it in full."[26]

Repetition is the life's pulse of a hoax. We lapse into the habit of accepting a story when it is imprinted frequently enough in our consciousness. A hoax merely is a bogus shipment in the brain's system of handling information.

Some indefatigable hoaxes are cruel in their fraudulence. The recurrent reports that a large number of bands from cigarette packs or pieces of foil from packages of chewing gum will buy needed health equipment for a sick person have worked their painful deceit countless times. Fortunately, this particular hoax seems to have passed from the news, although it still lives on as spoken rumor.

Other chronic reports stir hatred against some target groups within society. Early in this century, members of the Russian Czar's secret police launched *The Protocols of the Elders of Zion*, a hoax which appeared in various forms before and since.[27] The *Protocols* in that refurbished version purportedly were a verbatim account of a Zionist meeting at Basel, Switzerland, in 1897, which set forth plans to bring down Christianity. Instead, they were a plagiarism from an 1864 pamphlet written by a French liberal to ridicule Napoleon III, who hardly qualifies as a Zionist secret agent.

Even when thoroughly disproved, the *Protocols* lived on. In this country, they were an inspiration for automobile mogul Henry Ford when his newspaper, *The Dearborn Independent*, waged an anti-Semitic campaign for ninety-one straight weeks in 1920 and 1921.[28]

More recently, a hoax going the rounds suggests that the peace symbol, commonly used by many protest groups, was a mark of medieval foes of Christianity. This story will inevitably follow much the same route as the Dusseldorf Rules, despite the careful explanation by the man who designed the symbol for a British organization called Campaign for Nuclear Disarmament in 1958.

Hoaxes with such heavy political overtones can perhaps be singled out more readily than any except the thoroughly ludicrous, such as the workman battered up and down by the barrel. More difficult are hoaxes done for good motive, sometimes with a quantity of sympathy helping them along.

In 1968, the Pennsylvania State Commissioner for the Blind announced that six college students had been blinded from staring into the sun while entranced by the influence of the drug LSD.[29] The story made national headlines, and in the face of skeptics who noted there had been no verifiable information about the students, the commissioner stuck by his story and Gov. Raymond Shafer and other state officials backed him up. Within a week the hoax collapsed. Gov. Shafer announced that the commissioner was a "distraught and sick" man whose apparent motivation "was his concern over illegal use of LSD by children."[30]

How can the consumer deal with hoaxes? Sometimes he can't, at least when a new phony story makes its first appearance. The number of hoaxes which slip into print and broadcasts prove that even veteran editors who have handled stories by the thousand can all too often be fooled. But the consumer can do himself some good with a few basic defenses:

1. Look at the internal evidence of a story. The tale of the workman belabored by the barrel quickly breaks down into a phony when you examine it bit by bit. The eternally sitting babysitter, the elephant in the parking lot, and the lady who drives into another car at disastrous speed don't hold up well under scrutiny, either. Since when is paint *that* strong an adhesive? How does that elephant get loose into the parking lot, and does a Volkswagen really resemble a red chair? And how likely is (a) any plan to push one modern car rapidly with another, given the current frail design of bumpers, grills, and headlights, or (b) a driver who innocently will ram a car at thirty-five miles an hour, quite possibly a killing impact?

   In the more serious realm of political hoaxes, where real harm can be done to your beliefs, see whether the story simply seems too pat. The Hitler law and order quote is in this category. It is suspiciously exact to sentiments prominent forty years after it was supposedly spoken, and sentiments expressed in a different language and out of a different political heritage besides. The Dusseldorf Rules are even more obviously carpentered to fit the current discontents of some citizens; the language and issues within the Rules show they are a modern concoction instead of a 1919 Marxist committee report.

2. Watch for followup reports. Here again, having different news sources available is a valuable advantage for the consumer. The competition to tell the story directs a lot of pressures against fraud. The hoax of the LSD blindings, for instance, simply could not stand up against the continual inquiry from competing newsmen, and not many days after the initial report, the consumer had the exposé as well.

3. The eternal advice: be skeptical. This doesn't mean living the cliché that you can't believe anything you read or hear. The knack is to be as careful

as possible before making up your mind—and even then leaving the way open for a change of mind if new evidence warrants it.

The news media are the creations of the personalities and intelligences of mortal beings. With the ganglia of humanness strung through their mechanical apparatus this way, news enterprises are bound to fall for phoniness at times. The consumer's safeguard is to use as much logic and data as he possesses to judge whether the information in the news package is verifiable.

Horns of Plenty and Plenty of Horns

The date was Monday, November 9, and all the producers and middlemen who work the ingredients of Thanksgiving dinner onto American tables were in high gear when the Secretary of Health, Education and Welfare took a swipe at the sauce.[31]

Some of the cranberry crop had been contaminated through the use of the weed-killer aminotriazole, Secretary Arthur S. Flemming said, which had produced cancer in rats during laboratory tests. He did not ban the sale of berries or sauce because no evidence existed that the weed-killer also produced cancer in humans, so he said the public must use its own discretion. Nervous grocers immediately cleared their shelves, and news headlines unsettled shoppers.

Executive Vice President Ambrose Stevens of Ocean Spray, colossus of the cranberry industry, had been warned of the announcement a day in advance by a friendly newspaperman. Stevens raced for Washington to be instantly available for rebuttal, and meanwhile enlisted the public relations staff at Batten, Barton, Durstine & Osborn, one of the nation's largest advertising and public relations firms, headquartered in New York.

By Monday noon a counterattack was under way. The Ocean Spray executive issued a statement denying the secretary's charges and affirming the purity of the cranberry crop. Seven people were mobilized by BBDO, including a vice president and the manager of product publicity; all questions about cranberries were answered from their offices so they could make sure no misinformation was released. A news conference was called for the next day, Tuesday, November 10.

Other wheels whirred into motion. Stevens was interviewed Tuesday morning on NBC's *Today* show. The Grocery Manufacturers Association, meeting in New York, let him speak at their luncheon after BBDO explained the urgency.

In a telegram to the HEW secretary, Stevens asked for "immediate steps to rectify the incalculable damages caused by your ill-informed and ill-advised press statement."

"You are killing a thoroughbred in order to destroy a single flea," he added. Stevens also held a news conference on Tuesday.

Came Wednesday, and Ocean Spray's president sent two telegrams. The first went to the President of the United States, asking that all cranberry growing districts be classified as disaster areas. The other, to Secretary Flemming, told him that a $100 million damage suit was being filed against the government.

BBDO's staff continued its rapid programming, arranging television, newspaper and radio interviews which drummed on the theme: the government cranberry announcement was "unfair, ill-informed and ill-advised."

The chief of the public relations effort explained that Ocean Spray did not concede any of the crop was contaminated. The weed killer had been used "under procedures approved by the Department of Agriculture and then banned September 18 because of a difference of opinion between Agriculture and the Food and Drug Administration.

"Because our client did not believe and still does not believe there was any contamination at all, there was no need for us to tell retailers to remove cranberries from their shelves. They did that under their own volition and in response to the news stories (of the HEW announcement)."

The public relations staff labored to provide the food industry and the press with "scientific facts." The matter of political science figured in their efforts, too. The year was 1959, and presidential hopefuls were jockeying for position. Dwight D. Eisenhower, at the end of his second term, was prohibited by law from seeking reelection in the coming year, so Vice President Richard M. Nixon was aiming for the top spot. The vice president ate four portions of cranberry sauce.

The junior senator from Massachusetts, headquarters of Ocean Spray and a major cranberry producing state, also listened to reason. Sen. John F. Kennedy drank a toast with cranberry juice.

By Friday, November 13, the HEW secretary had invited the president of Ocean Spray to Washington "to try to arrive at a conclusion."

Over the weekend Ocean Spray and BBDO set up public relations headquarters in the capital. The staff was supplemented by secretaries provided by both Massachusetts senators and one of its congressmen.

HEW's top public information officers also helped the BBDO staff, which spent all night Monday drafting and mimeographing press statements to be handed out at HEW before the conference. The principal statement came from Stevens, who proposed a four-step testing plan.

Late Wednesday, now nine days after the cranberry caper began, Ocean Spray looked over the HEW secretary's amendments to the proposal and accepted them. The plan provided tests of fresh and processed berries in all stages of marketing and labels assuring housewives that no aminotriazole lurked in the cranberries.

The announcement was made public Thursday, November 19. Ten days later, *Editor & Publisher* magazine ran the story of the public relations campaign under the headline, **PR Puts Cranberries Back in Thanksgiving.**

In addition to all the pro-cranberry news stories generated, *Editor & Publisher* noted that some food editors had resumed cranberry sauce recipes in the week before Thanksgiving. Although cranberry sales didn't match previous years, the disaster of a total public boycott was avoided, and the industry weathered the crisis.

The executive in charge of the BBDO staff was modest. "Our role was mainly that of professional technicians making sure that the facts from our client, Ocean Spray Cranberries, Inc., got through as speedily as possible to all channels of communication," he said. "Now the real job begins of restoring public confidence in cranberries."

Channels of communication. Public confidence. Although this type of classic campaign isn't often laid open to the general consumer, all of the techniques of the Ocean Spray effort are common enough in public relations work. The news consumer must be aware that much of the daily run of news finds its way to him through some kind of public relations system.

Almost all offices of government from the White House to city hall have people working at public relations, though their titles vary widely. So do most businesses. The American cornucopia of goods and services is also a horn on which countless trills of publicity are played.

Who are the hornblowers? They can range from the clerk at the counter to the top executive at the telephone. All businesses, branches of government, and well-known figures have publics to which they must relate, so even if no one in an organization holds the precise job description or title, somebody there is dealing with public relations.[32]

The cranberry story suggests some of the ways a public relations campaign can help change minds. More routinely, however, public relations specialists provide news releases to the media, entertain important guests, write speeches for executives, get answers to newsmen's questions, produce annual reports, and work in many other ways to funnel favorable information about their employer to stockholders, employees, customers, and the public at large.

What a newcomer to journalism must quickly adjust to, and what the news consumer must keep in mind, is that public relations people are biased in a way that newsmen are not. They're devoted to telling how Sunshine College, or American Biscuits, or the Warmsville town clerk's office, is succeeding. Or, upon rarer occasion, why they need higher prices, higher profits, a tax break, or all of those.

A newsman, given the same story, will strive for balance, digging out strengths *and* weaknesses, successes *and* failures, reasons why higher prices, profits, and a tax break might not be a good idea. The way public relations has developed, however, the consumer can expect no exposés, and little balance, from PR departments.

On the other hand, public relations people occasionally are subject to fits of candor about their jobs. Alan Harrington, writing in Esquire, described his this way:

> There are a million definitions of public relations. From my own experience in the business, I have found it to be the craft of arranging the truth so that people will like you. Public relations specialists make flower arrangements of the facts, placing them so that the wilted and less attractive petals are hidden by sturdy blooms. Public relations almost invariably involves altering the truth in a nice way, if only by withholding unpleasant news. The PR man may tell the truth and nothing but the truth, but he seldom aims at telling the whole truth. . . . This could, severely, be called the art, science, skill, dodge or trade of lying.[33]

A key to the problem is that public relations deals in rearranging reality with words. A government statement may reasonably be countered by BBDO if the cranberries are actually safe. But if they aren't, no amount of glistening words will make them so.

The pollution of your bright brown sky won't go away because a public relations man explains that it's not as bad as it looks, and neither will its effects on your lungs. Nevertheless, some PR practitioners see their trade simply as an arranging of attitudes or a re-defining of reality. Merely convince the townspeople of the autumnal beauty of crisp, brown skies.

One of the pioneers in public relations, who practiced at the beginning of this century as modern PR got its start, counseled against such shenanigans.

During the heyday of industrial robber barons in the late 1800s, big business operated with great scorn for the consumer's right to know about its doings. The public be damned. By the turn of the century, the industrial giants were hit with predictable responses: muckrakers who published investigative reports of corporate sins; angry consumers; and a trend toward regulatory legislation.

What companies must do, Ivy Lee told the unsettled businessmen, was to make their operations public, and to change what the public didn't like. In their own self-interest, he said, they must have the public interest at heart.[34]

His most spectacular demonstration of what he meant came when he was hired by the Rockefeller family to turn around its negative image. The name "Rockefeller" had long been tarnished by the business practices of the original John D. in forging the Standard Oil monopoly, and was more recently smirched because National Guard troops had killed eleven women and two children during a strike at the Rockefeller-owned Colorado Fuel and Iron Company—the infamous Ludlow Massacre.[35]

Ivy Lee urged the Rockefellers to provide concrete examples of other

ideals besides their historic business ethic. Following his counsel, the Rocke-
fellers paid for the reconstruction of Williamsburg, Virginia, the building of
Rockefeller Center, and the founding of the Riverside Memorial Church in New
York City.[36]

Today, some public relations specialists follow Ivy Lee's ethical footsteps.
But many do not have the power within their organizations to build their own
Williamsburgs. Instead, many are mere clerks or messenger boys. In the most
truthful of all possible worlds, even the clerkly PR practitioner would be absent
from the information process.

The most famous maverick in recent business history has been Robert
Townsend, who headed the Avis rent-a-car firm in its "We try harder because
we're No. 2" period. Townsend's policy on a public relations staff:

> Fire this whole department. . . . If you have an outside P.R. firm, fire them too.
> Most businesses have a normal P.R. operation: press releases, clipping services,
> attempts to get interviewed; all being handled, as usual, by people who are
> embarrassingly uninformed about the company's plans and objectives. We made
> many mistakes at Avis, but we were at least smart enough to realize that the
> professional P.R. operation was as dead as the button-hook industry. . . . We
> called in the top ten or so people in the company and the telephone operators
> and told them they were the P.R. department. The telephone operators were
> given the home phones of the ten people and asked to find one of them if any
> of the working press called with a question. . . .[37]

The Wall Street Journal, which does this country's top job in business
news, works toward the Townsend formula in its own way. *The Journal* customarily refuses to rely on information from a public relations firm, and instead
insists on checking directly with the company.[38] The newspaper has also done
scathing reporting on dubious PR practices.

Yet, plenty of PR effort still goes into trying to tiptoe around embarrassing facts. If working conditions on the assembly line are so tiring, monoto-
nous, and dehumanizing that absentee rates skyrocket, the hornblowers won't
deal with that. Instead, they'll enthuse about how much money the workers
make, and the retirement plan.

Such slanting of news happens before the newsman gets to the story
which should center on absenteeism. If he follows up the PR release—or as
PR folks prefer to say, the news release—by talking with workers, he will probably discover that focus. And sometimes he'll be helped by competing PR.
At contract time, for instance, both union and management may provide position papers, releases, and off-the-cuff statements that will be challenged from
the other side.

Consumer advocates, too, have lately been using public relations techniques with increasing skill.

When Dr. Herbert Denenberg was plucked from a campus in January,

1971, to become Pennsylvania's insurance commissioner, Gov. Milton Shapp told him to "transform the insurance department . . . into a consumer-protection agency."[39]

The first thing Denenberg did was hire a press secretary, and at his first news conference he declared: "I'll be accused of being a publicity hound, and I don't deny that. I know that until insurance becomes a matter of breakfast-table conversation throughout Pennsylvania, nothing will get done."

Denenberg drafted legislation for no-fault automobile insurance. Then when some Philadelphia lawyers sponsored a radio commercial to denounce no-fault, he fired back with a release that called the commercial fraudulent.

"The trial lawyers are intent upon clinging to a legal system for auto accidents that produces delay, waste, inefficiency, fraud, inequity, and disaster for virtually every group in our society—except trial lawyers," he charged.

Next Denenberg turned to health insurance. Blue Cross filed its annual rate increase request, which in the past had been approved almost automatically. This time, Blue Cross was told it would have to cancel its contracts with ninety hospitals and negotiate agreements more favorable to its subscribers.

Denenberg also urged the public to shop for insurance, because costs sometimes vary widely for similar coverage.

Coming from a prestigious insurance professorship at the Wharton School of Finance and Commerce at the University of Pennsylvania, Denenberg is knowledgeable. But what has made his work so effective is that he is also eminently quotable. The message he puts out to the public is hard to forget:

"The motto of this office, which I am going to have translated into Latin and hung over the door, is 'The Consumer Has Been Screwed Long Enough!' "

Are consumers benefiting? Apparently so. Rules invoked during his first year in office, says the insurance department, will save Pennsylvania $10 million a year on life, accident, health, and credit insurance.

If the battle of words continues to build support for his policies, the public may benefit in other ways from Denenberg's publicity seeking, but he himself thinks his days are numbered.

"I'm just accumulating a lot of enemies," he explains, "and eventually they'll catch up with me. I'll get in trouble and I'll be through. But I don't give a damn."

Denenberg is forthright about his methods and goals, and the news consumer can decide whose public relations he wants to believe, as long as he knows that's what he's hearing or reading.

As long as he *knows*. That's where we get back to news organizations. It's their job always to provide fair and balanced coverage. Therefore, when a news outlet uses public relations releases it should:

1. Prominently indicate the source of the material.
2. In controversial stories, get comments from spokesmen for other points of

view, and dig further into the questions that may not be answered in the PR release.

3. In the case of an elaborate campaign such as The Great Cranberry Rescue, let the public know that the moves are being programmed by a major public relations agency.

4. Always clearly label advertising—that space which someone buys to sell his goods or promote his cause—and never allow it to look like news. Public relations people flood broadcasters with tapes and film, and the print media with written material and excellent photographs. The stories are described as "in the public interest," but also just happen to be of benefit to a particular client or employer.

   Travel, real estate, garden and food sections of newspapers have been particularly suspect. Some publications even promise "news" stories as a bonus to a prospective advertiser. The news consumer can do some checking. Are stories about vacation paradises accompanied by ads for the same places? Do stories contain balanced reports, warts and all?

5. Refuse to let anyone in its organization accept gifts or favors from anyone with whom he deals professionally. Put the ban on freebies in writing and make it adamant company policy.

The influencing of reporters and editors is a sophisticated and widespread game, especially when targeting those specialized writers who cover business and industry.

How many readers of men's fashion news, for example, know about the annual Men's Fashion Association press week? Readers of *The National Observer* found out in a front page report.

The week supposedly is a business event which allows fashion writers to see, in one place, all the major showings for a new fashion season. Diane K. Shah explained the reality:

> The first bag of loot was awaiting each reporter in his or her room at the Marriott Motor Hotel. The bag itself was a green herringbone cloth tote bag, compliments of Revira and Burlington Industries, Inc. J. P. Stevens and Co. thoughtfully had provided a white vinyl fold-over clipboard complete with calendar and writing paper. There was a zippered notebook from Deering Milliken, Inc., cleverly made out of its latest polyester fabric. Aramis, the men's cosmetics branch of Estee Lauder, had sent along a brown leather liquor carrier brimming with men's and women's cosmetics. But one could easily replace these items with the bottle of I. W. Harper bourbon which, though no note was attached, probably came from the MFA. There were little cellophane packets of nuts, cookies, crackers and pretzels in the extraordinary event that one got hungry between feasts. But the prize package had to be the offering from Christian Dior: a gold choker necklace.
>
> "I guess business must be bad," moaned one reporter. "There was so much more last year."[40]

Then Reporter Shah zeroed in on the Sears Roebuck and Co. party:

> Sears may not have the image of a sophisticated fashion house, but it is trying hard. Its party insures that all reporters will give it due consideration.
>
> No sooner has one shed his coat than he is handed a large black plastic bag, which contains nothing more than an envelope filled with small colored-paper circles. Each circle means booty.
>
> One quickly races to the tables stacked with Sears clothing and begins trading circles for garments. If one can survive the mob scene, one makes off with a pair of men's knit slacks, two cotton sports shirts, a pull-over, a vest, a leather belt, and a tie.
>
> "It's like Christmas here. I haven't had so much fun in years!" exclaimed one woman.
>
> But the fun was just beginning. Preceding the filet mignon dinner (with appropriate wine) was the "fashion show"—nothing less than a New York musical. Sears had brought in four Broadway actors and actresses and a couple of dozen models to entertain with song, dance, and a bit of couture slipped in. The tab for the evening, it is reported, was $47,000.[41]

The week also contained fourteen other Roman-banquet sized meals, a free hotel room for each reporter and, reported Diane Shah, "enough liquor to float a barge."

A highlight was the Lulu Awards dinner, sponsored by Burlington Industries, at which outstanding fashion writers were honored. The judges were recruited from the menswear industry.

Norman Carr, executive director of the Men's Fashion Association, which is the public relations wing of the Menswear Retailers Association, explained the innocence of the week's festivities.

"There's nothing hucksterish about it," he said. "There's a general sensation that this is part of the total package. And there's something nice about giving. It has created a nice relationship between the industry and the press. There are no strings attached. Nobody's nose goes out of joint if a reporter writes an unfavorable story."[42]

Despite such disclaimers, anyone who wants to is well within his rights to try to influence news organizations. Indeed, one hoary definition of public relations is "free advertising."

The responsibility for being influenced, or for using any material in their reports which is less than news, must be borne by the news outlets themselves. "That (drink) (trip) (favor) won't influence me," goes the old refrain. Or, "Everybody does it." Bunk.

Such favors are insidious, and no ironclad evidence has ever been offered to prove that they don't influence news. Unless proof is offered, the news consumer has every right to be skeptical. Just why should a reporter accept free drinks, meals, jaunts? What *is* the point of those freebies? Are they simply endless charity with no strings attached? Why do the givers keep giving, some of them lavishly, if the payola doesn't have any effect on newsmen?

And despite the other refrain, not everyone does it. An editor's note at the end of Diane Shah's story explains:

> Tough luck—but this newspaper devoutly believes its own staff members should not reap the benefits of significant tokens of affection bestowed by firms or folk they write about. Writer Diane Shah, as usual, paid her own hotel bill and will turn in an expense slip to *The Observer*. The loot she brought back to the office at the editors' suggestion, for photographic evidence, will soon be in the hands of worthy charities.

At any one time in forums where newsmen discuss problems with each other, ethical examples such as these will appear:

1. The Associated Press will not allow any member to accept money, gifts, expense paid trips or other favors.[13] Neither will the *New York Times*.
2. Employes at the *Wall Street Journal* are warned not to use their access to unpublished information for their own gain, nor to go on expense-paid trips.
3. The *Philadelphia Inquirer* breaks tradition by paying for its phone bill in the state capitol newsroom, and it refuses to allow reporters to accept any gratuities or travel.
4. At the *Louisville Courier-Journal*, everything sent in as a gift or a sample is contributed to charity.

Other news organizations have also tackled the many problems forthrightly. Of course, any codes of ethics or ground rules can be subverted, so in the end it comes back to the integrity of individual newsmen.

"Ethics and morals can't be legislated, can't be achieved by edict, although sometimes they help," said the *Philadelphia Inquirer's* Executive Editor, John McMullan. "What might be considered a favor influential on one person might just have the opposite effect on another person. But you do develop a feeling for ethics and this, I hope, is what we have achieved."

Chapter 8

Miss Peach by Mell Lazarus. Courtesy of Publishers-Hall Syndicate.

The Reporter:
Messenger? Advocate?

"Umm, well, you know," grumbles the news consumer. "More *objective*. Newsmen need to be more *objective*."

Steel-gray eyes aglint, the model newsgatherer this very moment is processing information for a story.

"Ought to tell only the facts," the news consumer chides.

Amid the newsroom clatter, facts are checked out, sources are contacted for their feedback.

"Shouldn't slant the news," urges the news consumer.

Now, brain whirring, the newsgatherer channels data into story form. The typewriter blurts into action and . . .

So much for the utopian newsroom. And so much, unfortunately, for any news consumer's fantasy that objectivity is possible if the newsman would simply gear his mind to it. This expectation has the same warp as the language describing the model newsgatherer at work. It supposes that a person can have the precision of a machine.

Check out, feedback, data; either in coinage or current usage, the words are products of the electronic age. *Process, contact, channel;* their casual use as verbs instead of in their birthright as nouns is likewise jargon from modern science and technology. The graceless shadows which mass production casts into our language slant across our ideas as well. A citizen of 1905 would have been as puzzled by the notion of pure objectivity in the news as by the robotlike words depicting the model newsgatherer.

As the following sampler of quotes illustrates, newsmen themselves debate this matter of objectivity. It serves as the sort of intramural controversy which medieval scholars found in the question of how many angels could dance on the head of a pin. The arguments are impossible to prove or disprove, but nuances of logic can play there nimbly all night long.

If I'm any good as an analyst, I have a right to an opinion.[1] *The late H. V. Kaltenborn, radio commentator.*

A person presumably is expected to go on the air and be objective, which is to say that he's to go on the air and to have no likes, no dislikes, no feelings, no views, no values, no standards—to be a machine. If I were objective . . . (I) would have to be put away somewhere in an institution, because (I'd) be some sort of vegetable . . . I make no pretense at being objective . . . Objectivity is impossible to a normal human being. Fairness, however, is attainable, and that's what we strive for.[2] *David Brinkley, NBC television news commentator.*

I don't see that it's my job to oppose or support a President. My job is to tell what's going on. I'm a historian, a current historian.[3] *Howard K. Smith, ABC television news anchor man.*

A staff member cannot arrange *news stories* to fit his own beliefs and preferences. Give the other side a voice—even if you think they are wrong.[4] *Memo to the staff of the Buffalo Evening News.*

Being a reporter, as I understood the term, did not imply ideological teetotalism; it merely required holding one's ideology like a gentleman.[5] *Edmond Taylor, former European correspondent for The Chicago Tribune.*

(Objectivity) produces something like a symmetrical pile of clam shells with all the succulent goodness carefully removed.[6] *Stanley Walker, managing editor of the late New York Herald Tribune.*

Objectivity is the determination to write and edit with the elimination of as much personal bias as humanly possible, to present facts and situations as close to reality as possible, to avoid our own pejorative phrases or comments, to give accused people or institutions the right of immediate reply, to present all shadings of opinion and counter-argument, and most of all, to keep examining ourselves day by day and story by story to see if we are being as objective as we can.[7] *A. M. Rosenthal, managing editor, New York Times.*

Actually, the debate is not about objectivity, but about opinion. So is the news consumer's complaint, properly put.

Objectivity, in its dictionary sense, is the state, quality, or relation of being objective. In turn, the meaning listed for objective is: "uninfluenced by emotion, surmise, or personal prejudice."[8]

Well and good; but who among us goes through life uninfluenced by how we happen to feel at the moment, by the habit of wondering, by whims we have about persons of different skin or tongue? Objectivity, pure as a liquid distilled into a laboratory flask, is not in us.

Critics complain that newsmen do not stick to the facts. But facts are mercurial. When a person says, "I see this fact," he is really saying, "This is what a chain of events in my nervous system, triggered by an image in my eye and modulated by my emotional apparatus, tells me is a fact."

It may not be someone else's fact. The news consumer might remind himself about the Japanese movie *Rashomon*.[9] On the screen comes the same story told four times from the viewpoints of four different participants. The set of facts remains the same, but the view of them through each different set of eyes changes kaleidoscopically.

In any news report, the consumer is getting one *Rashomon* segment. He has the right to demand that whatever version the newsman does for him be done as honestly and fairly as possible.

To add a complication, facts can change because the newsman is there viewing them. People will or will not say certain things, they will or will not do certain things—all because the news-gathering process is focused on them.

The news conference, for instance, is a verbal event created by someone with a message to convey. But the newsman's questions or perceptions may bring about a story different from what the source had in mind. The same may happen at a demonstration, the anti-establishment's brand of news conference.

Probably because it was propounded in the name of science, this sequence of unintentional cause and effect carries a grand name: the Uncertainty Principle.[10] Its theorist, physicist Werner Heisenberg, pointed out to his "objective" colleagues that mere observation of a phenomenon affects that phenomenon. Heisenberg was working in the realm of particulate matter, but any scientist is more than an invisible presence at an experiment. It is he who turns up the Bunsen burner a few degrees, who handles the test tubes, who times the experimental process.

Any observer, consciously or not, sets terms on what he observes—the newsman no less than the scientist.

Some valuable curmudgeon in our past once said that most men are perpendicular, but only a few are upright. Newsmen need to come from all too sparse ranks of the upright. But then the question submits itself: upright in what role?

"Messenger," the imaginary news consumer at the start of this chapter would say.

"Advocate," a growing number of newsmen now say.

The Ghost From the Glass Cage

He was a thin, earnest figure inside the bulletproof glass box which shielded him momentarily from death.[11] Four months passed in the Jerusalem courtroom, the defendant in his capsule quietly listening day after day. When it came time to testify in his own defense, Adolf Eichmann, head of Hitler's Department of Jewish Affairs, stood and mildly described himself as "a man of average character."

He was a good German, he said, who could not stand the sight of blood and who merely followed orders to ferret out Jews and ship them to the gas ovens.

"The trouble with Eichmann," Hannah Arendt explained in *Eichmann in Jerusalem*, "was precisely that so many were like him, and that the many were neither perverted nor sadistic, that they were, and still are, terribly and terrifyingly normal." They were doing their patriotic duty, following orders stolidly.[12]

Though Eichmann was hanged in 1962 for crimes against humanity, he haunts consciences across the years. Agonized about the tragedy of Vietnam and social malfunctions within the U.S., many Americans who can only hazily recall the Nazi bureaucrat himself are shunning the methodical obedience he personified. Within the news media, this resolve not to be servant to the system has become a call for advocacy reporting.

Nor will they be the servants of blustering quotes, the advocates say. The late Sen. Joseph McCarthy occurs in their nightmares, too, waving "documents" and declaiming that the names on his lists are a swarm of Communists and fellow travelers working for the State Department, hauling private citizens and government officials before his one-man subcommittee and subjecting them to trial by Congress and press, as news outlets carried his charges and laid bare his victims day after day, month after month, without proof, without protest.[13]

The newsmen were doing their job, weren't they? They were quoting accurately what the senator said.

Words repeated mechanically and orders followed dutifully are the sins of the past, some reporters now insist. These men and women of the media demand the right to report from a personal viewpoint and a moral stance that goes far beyond the observing of events.

Although they don't emerge in identical ideological tones, most of the voices come from newspaper ranks, and here are some of their concerns.

Nicholas von Hoffman, *Washington Post* columnist: "What editors and politicians call objective journalism is the present moment, the isolated incident, without any secondary or qualifying information. . . . By these standards objectivity consists of limiting oneself to accurate quotation."[14]

Von Hoffman, differing from some other advocates, does not see himself as a reformer. His distinguished career covers many of the era's toughest stories, including the Mississippi freedom marches, but he says, "I think you're mad if you come into journalism with the idea that you're going to change things for the better. I write because I enjoy it. I sincerely believe in what I write and I get a kick out of getting those Washington mossbacks angry."[15]

J. Anthony Lukas, staff writer for the *New York Times Magazine*: Trying to describe the behavior of Federal District Court Judge Julius J. Hoffman during the conspiracy trial of the Chicago Seven, "I could not even say 'he snapped.' I could always say 'lawyers charged' he was doing these things, but I couldn't say that I saw it myself."[16] Lukas believes that "von Hoffman has caught the tone and flavor of the trial in a way that has been almost impossible for those of us operating under tighter editorial restrictions."[17]

Stephen Levine, who at age 17 was already a columnist for the *Des Moines Register* and *Tribune Syndicate*: He deplores "the ready capacity of reporters and editors and publishers to hide behind a kind of cool detachment and abdicating their responsibility in society. No matter who you are and what your business is, your business is living in this country at this time, and therefore I really think if you want to continue to live in this country . . . and want this country to continue to live, you will have to become involved in its problems."[18]

Ron Dorfman, editor of the *Chicago Journalism Review*: "Every news story that you write is advocacy of something, even if it is only neutrality."[19] He says reporters copped out during the civil rights campaigns in the 1960s by not making a choice between such protagonists as protest leader Martin Luther King and Birmingham public safety commissioner Eugene "Bull" Connor.

These and other newsmen have fed debate recently in the country's newsrooms and among our ablest reporters, yet the New Journalism, as advocacy sometimes is called, has its roots firmly into history.

The first small newspapers hatched in colonial America were advocates in disagreements between royal governors and disgruntled businessmen who denounced tax and trade restrictions. When the colonists broke with England, editors avidly committed their news columns for—and some against—the Revolution. Then in the young nation, many became mouthpieces of political parties.

Hurrah and harangue rang through the reports, with even George Washington allowed no pedestal while he presided over the government. "If ever a nation was debauched by a man, the American nation has been debauched by Washington," Benjamin Franklin Bache wrote in 1796.[20] His rhetoric was not unusual.

Our own century began during the excesses of yellow journalism, which soared blithely beyond accuracy. The fare in William Randolph Hearst's *New York Journal* can be judged from the headlines: **One Mad Blow Kills Child, Startling Confession of a Wholesale Murderer Who Begs to be Hanged, Why Young Girls Kill Themselves,** and **Strange Things Women Do for Love.**[21]

At the same time, Adolph Ochs was expanding the responsible reputation that the smaller *New York Times* had enjoyed since its founding in 1851.[22] He and like-minded editors would finally prevail with accuracy, fairness, and the doctrine of objectivity that grew to be accepted throughout the news industry. Compartmentalization of news developed, too, roughly along these lines:

> *Straight news*—concise reports of timely events, without the writer's opinions.
> *News in perspective*—an attempt to background the news so readers will understand *why*. A military coup has failed in Morocco. What led to it? Back-

ground, as the term usually is used, is not supposed to include reportorial opinion, but the selection of information often indicates how the reporter feels as well as how much he knows.

News analysis—background which customarily includes the writer's opinions and predictions.

Investigative reporting—depth reporting; the press as watchdog. Are television repairmen bilking the public? Is the tax collector lining his own pockets? Is the factory at the edge of town ignoring air quality standards?

Columns—opinion by local or national writers such as James Reston, William F. Buckley, and Art Buchwald, who usually have regular spots within each newspaper that buys their output. Editors often try for a diversity of voices, though most have shunned radicals. The electronic media have been less successful with the format. ABC television, for example, tried hiring a stable of opinionmakers for its evening news in 1968, but their reports were not as provocative as hoped for, and the effort fizzled.[23]

Editorials—the official opinion of the newspaper. Incisive, hard-hitting local editorials with some balance of wit are hard to find. Many papers suffer from a malady called Afghanistanism—a willingness to take a critical stand on anything which doesn't touch their readers and advertisers. Others pack the space with ready-made editorials on standard topics—*The Carnage On Our Highways* is a favorite—which some national syndicates sell the same way they merchandise columns and features.

The steps from straight news through editorial opinion are not always clear even to reporters and editors, and they have been lost on all but the most analytical news consumers. Distinctive formats customarily identify editorials and columnists, but few newspapers consistently label anything else.

Some television stations, roundly criticized for mixing straight news and opinion, have developed "commentary" or "news analysis" overprints which come on screen as their editorial voices are heard. Others, in the radio tradition, provide standard introductions that "the following is the opinion of this station's management." Because of seesaw rulings by the Federal Communications Commission, some do no editorializing at all.

The problem of unopinionated versus advocacy reporting is further muddled by the honorable tradition of contests which reward advocacy. Each year, for instance, the Scripps-Howard Foundation awards $5,000 for superior work in *promoting* conservation. A Robert F. Kennedy award recognizes outstanding coverage of the *problems* of poverty and discrimination.

Less highmindedly, pots of cash are frequently set up by trade associations or industries to encourage favorable stories. All in all, more than 130 prize contests for newsmen hold out their attractions for almost every conceivable angle of favorable coverage.[24]

Perhaps the classic contest is the one wreathed in cigar smoke. The *Columbia Journalism Review* offered a tongue-in-cheek Bribe Award to the Cigar Institute of America for coming up with this ultimate bonanza: $4,200 in prizes offered to press photographers for published news photographs that show "a cigar presented in an interesting and favorable manner."[25] The *Review* extended its award to include *National Press Photographer* and *Editor & Publisher* magazines, which accepted ads for the contest.

Another nagging problem of the "straight" approach is that the news format can be easily subverted. "Just quote your sources," orders the managing editor. "Sure," says the advocate, then searches the boondocks for someone whose ideas are a carbon copy of his own. Unethical reporters, and there are some, have been known to invent quotes, a practice which any competent editor will reward with unemployment.

Advocacy, then, in one form or another, has been around for a long time, but the current debate threatens to go giant steps beyond anything previously known in U.S. journalism.

In the first place, the current crop of advocates wants an end to compartmentalized opinion. They say straight news without opinion is an impossible ideal which leads only to sanitizing and emasculating reality. They would shift the standard from straight news, with its emphasis on information, to viewpoint reporting with emphasis on opinion and reform.

In the second place, many advocates believe that such a shift also demands changes in control of the news. If reporters are qualified to report and express opinion, the argument goes, then editors should not be allowed to alter copy significantly, and publishers should be obliged to print their reporters' work. In the last few years, reporters have protested in several cases by fighting to remove their bylines from stories changed substantially during editing.

The question of who owns a newsman's copy is thorny. Until the late 1960s the assumption of reporters and publishers alike was that, in hiring a reporter, the publisher became owner of everything produced on the job. Many American Newspaper Guild contracts agree. But going beyond the old assumptions, newsmen have been asking: who owns a reporter's story if his news organization refuses to use it?

The *Chicago Journalism Review* caused management protests in 1969 and 1970 when it printed two rejected stories.[26] The *Chicago Daily News* had killed an article about housewives angry at supermarkets, and the *Chicago Sun-Times* had decided not to print an investigative report of suspicious business dealings by a city housing official.

"Our contract with the guild says that anything done on company time is company property," editor James Hoge of the *Sun-Times* pointed out.[27]

"When a reporter has a valid gripe," replied Dan Rottenberg of the *Review*, "the public interest demands that he tell his story in print, as honestly and completely as possible—including, wherever pertinent, the reprinting of the material in question so that readers are not forced to rely only on the judgment of the journalism review."[28]

This question of what should be printed can be tortuous. In Syracuse, an article about a rock festival was spindled.[29] The story ultimately showed up not in another publication, but in the newspaper which had rejected it in the first place. A make-up editor on the *Syracuse Herald Journal* inserted the article after the higher ranking city editor decided against using it. The make-up editor was fired, along with the reporter.

The case went to a New York State Department of Labor referee, who ruled that the offending editor and reporter "in effect made the owner publish something against his will. They substituted their concept of fairness for that of the owner of the newspaper. In so doing, they were subverting the owner's freedom of the press. The action . . . was not merely insubordination, it was an infringement of the publisher's constitutional rights."

An owner's freedom of the press, retort the activists, does not exist in solitary splendor. It is constitutionally bound to the people's right to know, which depends on reporters' rights to get their stories printed. An increasing number of reporters believe they have identified an essential conflict: the publisher owes his ultimate allegiance to the advertiser, while the newsman owes his to the reader.

Seeing news operations as unique in the business world, reporters have called for more voice in newsroom policy, have established journalism reviews to scrutinize their news enterprises, are calling for ownership of papers by the people who produce them, and are experimenting with changes in newswriting techniques.

Many reporters would gladly dump the story form known as the inverted pyramid, which tries to summarize the news in the first sentences, then gives additional information in decreasing order of importance, sticking to bare bone facts without much description. Where managements will allow it, writers are experimenting with new adaptations of old forms such as chronological and anecdotal styles, and some are influenced by the personal, free-flowing prose of Tom Wolfe and Norman Mailer, who sluice into their reportage a niagara of thoughts and sensations. Inspiration along these lines has also come from long reporting pieces in *Harper's* and *The Atlantic* which have accentuated the writer's state of mind and have included long sections of earthy dialogue.

Here's an example of the gap between an event and a report done in traditional style. Associated Press stringer Tim Reiterman first describes the scene he tried to report on in Berkeley, then presents the story written from information he phoned hurriedly to the wire service:[30]

BERKELEY—Monday, February 16. Today there was a riot, a mass action that involved hundreds of young people, police and me.

The leaflets on power poles announced, "Rally at Provo Park 4 P.M. Try the Government of Amerika in the streets." It was a TDA demonstration, the Day After the "Chicago Seven" and their lawyers were given two decades of contempt sentences by Judge Julius Hoffman.

At 3:50 a few hundred of us milled around the muddy park waiting. The rain let up and big dummies of Hoffman appeared. One was complete with its own gallows. Firecrackers popped as evangelist Hubert Lindsey admonished: "You miserable souls, there isn't a man on earth that I hate." A hippie girl squirted lighter fluid on a nine foot effigy with a pig's face.

I stood on a bench with Kathy, a *Berkeley Tribe* photographer. She told me her baby had come last week, a seven pound girl. We laughed as a garbage can was hoisted up the flag pole. Police photographers took pictures from rooftops. A burning dummy went up the pole.

The crackle of loudspeakers drew us to the tiny concourse. Paul Glusman, a local activist, was talking. I tried to listen, but was fascinated by a plainclothes-man perched in a tree busy panning the crowd and Glusman with a movie camera. He was dressed like me and had a goatee.

It was a small crowd, maybe a thousand packed tight in the rain. Glusman raised his voice: ". . . and we have to bring the conspiracy everywhere—to Berkeley, to every school, church and home." Loud applause and cries of "right on!" A man down front yelled, "Let's take to the streets."

"No," came angry shouts. I was disappointed so few people showed. It shattered strange elitist feelings you get living in Berkeley—feelings of somehow being a part of concerned, active people. Besides, I made a living from riot coverage last year.

"What is the verdict of the people," the next speaker cried.

"Guilty, guilty," roared the people, and some shouted: "Take to the streets. The streets are ours."

The crowd milled in place, leaderless and without direction. The effigy of Hoffman appeared on their shoulders and a line formed in Center Street. I ran to the front as the first window crashed to the sidewalk.

Cops at Center and Milvia. I ran past a cop who yelled to stop. I didn't want to be caught in any crush between "pigs" and "people." As usual, Lieutenant Schillinger ordered them to break up because "you have no permit to march." The front ranks surged toward police. One little cop grabbed the Hoffman doll and things happened. The doll fell apart; cops rushed in swinging. A bearded man punched a cop; another kid finished him with a stick. More hand to hand fighting, then demonstrators ran over the cops yelling "Shattuck Avenue, close downtown." They jostled me as they poured past, breaking windows and hoot-ing. Kathy snapped pictures furiously from one knee.

"You O.K.?" I asked.

"Sure, this is outa sight. We're overdue for a riot." (It was her first photo assignment since her baby had come . . .)

Should I call in the story? No. Stick with the march. I ran but couldn't catch the front ranks. Cops cut me off at Shattuck. They clubbed some kid across the back and neck as he scrambled by. Motorists honked. I slipped as I dodged rocks with cops.

It was safer with the rioters. We ripped through the last blocks of Center Street leaving a wake of glass and frightened merchants. A construction bar-ricade exploded through the last unbroken window at Bank of America. A cheer went up. Glass rained down behind me. A rock smacked a kid to my right. "Fuckers, why don't they learn not to hit their own people?" he cried holding his cheek.

Call AP. How many arrests? How many injuries? How did it start? Who started it? All questions I couldn't possibly answer. I decided to make a quick phone call. The action would move to Telegraph Avenue or the campus.

"We've got a small riot here," I began, then gave AP the story in organized form as best I could. Running for Telegraph and Bancroft, I asked myself what really happened. Already I was trying to sort out faces. Were they young? Mostly university students? Street people? And I recalled rumors that S.D.S. Weathermen would take over the rally. The media and almost everyone else credited Weathermen with any violent street action. But street fighting wasn't new to Berkeley, and S.D.S. here was at best a brand of rhetoric. What does a Weatherman look like?

Longhairs were halting traffic at Telegraph and Bancroft. One man shattered the windshield of a moving car with his umbrella. Another sat on the wet street in front of cars. "This isn't a fucking peace march," one girl snapped at him. Human chains finally did the job. "Power to the people," they shouted as traffic backed up.

Thirty cops in flak jackets cleared the streets. A helicopter circled overhead— a reminder that police requested two helicopters to help with crime fighting. "You pigs get rid of that copter, and we'll be real peaceful," a straight-looking student type shouted. Chunks of ice from an ice cream cart sailed into the street. Cheers as a cop was hit. Embarrassed he turned to another cop, talking, pretending nothing happened.

"Pigs look silly, don't they," commented my friend Allan from the Radical Students Union.

"Whose thing is this?"

"Can't tell you," he laughed; but he really didn't know.

Back to the telephone. AP was hustling. Jim White took my first call just ten minutes before. Paul Lee typed the first add as fast as I could tell it. "How many windows now?," he asked.

"Dozens."

"Any injuries?"

"None serious enough to note," and so on. The clatter of typewriters and the crowd were distractions. I left the booth sensing I had forgotten something. The cops had pulled on gas masks and grouped. "Back to Shattuck," someone shouted. A smart move. We doubletimed downtown again smashing parking meters and windows overlooked earlier. A hip teenager drove a twelve foot board through plate glass at the bank. I ducked into a phone booth. Jim and Paul were busy on the story. I gave Earl a play by play:

"Police scattered demonstrators along Fulton. A kid was clubbed badly, but not arrested. Small packs are breaking through an auto roadblock and getting to more windows. No injuries. Gotta go; they're past me now."

I threw my notes in the street. They were uselessly wet, and I had a dry pad. I ran to Shattuck checking damage en route. Stores were locked and merchandise removed from the windows.

Sales people hung back in fear as I ran by. They thought I was a rioter, but the rioters were further downtown roaming in small groups. Cops lumbered after the "people," ratpacking the slowest. One kid went down in broken glass at American Savings and Loan. Three cops jabbed him as he looked up at me frightened and bleeding from the mouth. "What's your name?" I called.

"Dave Baker." They dragged him to the car then sped off under a hail of bricks and things. Sirens, breaking glass, screams, red lights. It was hit and run by both sides.

Another arrest. Al Juke was his name. "What's your occupation?" I yelled. A cop shoved his club in my gut. "Get out of the way," he ordered. I waved last year's press pass, but Juke was in the car and gone.

Only two arrests? There had to be more I told myself. "Two arrests," I told AP. "Check with the cops."

Susan, the beat reporter for the EXAMINER, was scared. Her first riot. She hadn't seen any arrests, so I filled her in as we walked close to the buildings. Then more sirens and red flashes shot across the slick streets.

A cop pushed me away, but inside the barber shop I glimpsed a man on his back with blood running from his mouth and nose.

"What happened? I'm with the AP."

"Talk to Lieutenant Sanders at the station. Now move."

A butcher in his stained smock muttered, "Dirty hoodlums." He told me: "This young cop was chasing a pack of hoodlums. Twenty or thirty of them turned and beat him. Knocked him to the curb and hit him with fists and something. We come out and pulled him. Looked half dead. Would have killed them if they come back." He slipped an automatic pistol halfway out of his pocket.

A CHRONICLE reporter ran up gasping, "What happened?" As usual he showed up winded and firing questions. As usual he disappeared before you could grill him.

AP sucked up details of the cop beating. "Hear anything about looting a Safeway?" Jim White asked.

"No, which Safeway?"

"Ashby Avenue. A new kid with Photography said checkers at Safeway threw cans back at rioters who had disrupted the shelves."

I started for Safeway but overheard a police radio: "Sniper at College and Bancroft confirmed."

A reserve cop at College refused to talk. When I told him I wouldn't use his name, he related: "Sniper took two shots at me from a building. A bullet hit the barricade that was here." I coaxed him to give his name, then called in again.

Was he lying? A phony name? "Check with the cops," I told AP.

More than nine blocks of store windows were gone. Jagged glass framed display cases. Repairmen laughed about overtime as they worked under the street lights. The bookstore owner complained about insurance rates as wet rioters crunched along the glass-strewn sidewalk. Cops, four to a car, stopped all young people, frisking, asking questions—harassing. I kept a press card ready.

The following morning I was handed an AP dispatch with my byline.

BY TIM REITERMAN

Associated Press Writer

BERKELEY (AP)—Six policemen were injured and 13 persons were arrested Monday night as yelling demonstrators surged through downtown Berkeley protesting Judge Julius Hoffman's contempt sentences against the Chicago Seven.

Hundreds of windows were smashed with rocks and clubs as the demonstrators roamed through a nine-block area for a total of four hours.

In San Francisco, an earlier demonstration at the Federal Building attracted 2,000 demonstrators and was orderly.

In Berkeley, a brief rally was under way at Provo Park near City Hall when someone shouted "Take to the streets—the streets are ours." The crowd moved up Center Street toward Shattuck Avenue, and a block away police tried to explain that a parade was illegal without a permit.

Police pulled down a nine-foot effigy of Hoffman the crowd was carrying and a scuffle broke out. Then the crowd surged eastward toward the University of California, breaking windows as they went.

Earlier, a speaker under the effigy shouted: "What is the verdict of the people?"

"Guilty," roared the estimated 1,000 demonstrators.

The crowd crossed Shattuck and moved along Oxford Street until it came to the entrance of the University of California where the throng blocked the road and stopped rush hour traffic.

Police arrived with gas masks but no gas was used immediately and officers worked deliberately to unsnarl traffic and keep it moving.

The demonstrators moved into the street and surrounded the police, then headed toward the downtown area, breaking windows and parking meter posts along the way.

The San Francisco demonstration, sponsored by the National Lawyers Guild, ignored some 35 police officers who stood nearby.

Marvin Stender, president of the Guild, told the crowd that Hoffman had sentenced the seven defendants and their attorneys while the jury was still out and asked:

"What will be next—elimination of the jury entirely?"

Activist reporters are also challenging a traditional management argument that, for the sake of the publication's reputation for fairness, reporters must abstain from involvement in politics, social issues, and protest demonstrations. Many reporters flout what they believe is a double standard.

"I have as much right to picket the White House as my boss has to eat lunch there with the President," goes the current attitude.

In their search for basic changes, activist newsmen have looked to Europe, and particularly to *Le Monde*, the internationally admired French newspaper.

Leslie R. Colitt of Reuters News Service explains *Le Monde's* operation this way:

Unlike the American practice, there is no copy desk and no division of function between copy editing and reporting. Each staff member is a "journalist" in charge of a specialty. He may cover a story directly or rewrite or edit the news agency reports on his subject. Department chiefs check headlines and make space allotments but do not change copy.

As is the rule in European journalism, there is no clear line between reporting and opinion. "We are proud," said an editor, "not of our objectivity but of our independence." The assumption is that the reader knows the viewpoint of the reporter and expects it to be reflected in his copy.[31]

As a result, the readers seem ready to argue with the writers, but seldom with the newspaper, and the context and nuance of the news are treated as essential to understanding the facts. Le Monde, furthermore, is controlled by its staff. Says Jean Schwoebel, the newspaper's diplomatic editor and a leader in Le Monde's governing structure:

"If you want to exert influence in a capitalist country there is only one way and that is to have part of the ownership; the rest is without value."[32]

No single American newspaper has produced that blend. The Kansas City Star and the Milwaukee Journal are employee owned, but neither is a hotbed of advocacy.[33] Several newspapers have employee stock plans which will eventually result in staff control. Others have agreed to newsmen's participation in limited policymaking, while a few allow or encourage advocacy. So far the potential is great, but the inroads are small, the steps tentative, and the movement often disparaged or misunderstood.

Advocacy can easily be abused by ill-trained or lazy newsmen. Significantly, however, some of the best news minds in the country favor it, and they know its success depends on a greater number of highly skilled newsmen.

"The next thing you know," grumbles a less than enchanted journalist, "they'll want to elect the managing editor." Yes, that's likely, and whether they succeed with that and other changes will tell a great deal about the product the news consumer will see in the years ahead.

Robert J. Donovan, associate editor of the Los Angeles Times and a news executive sympathetic to advocacy, sums it up:

Should the press be merely a chronicler, a mirror of yesterday's affairs? Or, through advocacy journalism, as it is called, and through the kind of investigative and crusading reporting that moves public opinion, should we, too, try to shape events?

The gravitational pull of the times, it seems to me, is dragging . . . the press in the latter direction. In some ways this is a good thing, if it is not carried too far . . . The danger to newspapers is that they might lose the reasonable objectivity that tradition rightly requires and that they might sacrifice their role of consistently providing day-to-day information for the people.[34]

"Well, folks, I was had."

One summer night when the town of Alick, Louisiana, was sloshing with humidity, A. J. Liebling watched Governor Earl Long work for re-election. For fifty-seven sweltering minutes as Long fondled every issue in the campaign and some no one else had thought of, his audience hung entranced on every curlicue of word and thought.

A steamy little campaign rally doesn't amount to much in the full chronicle of mankind, but muss and hubbub of this sort are what a reporter has to deal with all the time. The role the reporter sees himself in as he handles life's dishevelment will affect the story passed along to the news consumer.

The newsman who considers himself a dutiful messenger would likely quote the governor at length, pick out the highlights of the speech, give structure to the rambling performance.

Depending upon the caliber of Long's opposition, the newsman who sees himself as an active reformer might come down for or against the governor: if *AGAINST*, pointing out in his story the humbug in Long's oratory; if *FOR*, citing its gusty appeal to the small town voters.

Liebling, however, wrote of the evening in Alick:

"It is difficult to report a speech by Uncle Earl chronologically, listing the thought in order of appearance. They chased one another on and off the stage like characters in a Shakespearean battle scene, full of alarums and sorties."[35]

Rarely will the news consumer be lucky enough to have on hand a Joe Liebling, who until his death in 1963 was an aggressive staff writer for *The New Yorker*. As in this blunt underlining of the governor's stump style, Liebling liked to ignore the customary reporting forms to focus instead on barricades to truth which were liable to trip reporter and reported alike. But unless forthrightness announces itself in a style something like Liebling's, the news consumer will have to judge by details of the story whether the reporter may be too far into the role of messenger or the role of advocate.

As quotes from several newsmen indicated earlier in the chapter, messenger and advocate each will commit their excesses in the name of a different loyalty. But the bilks worked on the news consumer will be similar; in either case, the consumer will be getting news reported without careful measuring of its proportions. From the advocate, the story may come in lopsided toward his own beliefs; from the messenger may come a narrow report trimmed away from valuable background information.

Either one, for instance, is likely to place too much faith in The Statement. This is the cult of the news conference—and of its street cousin, the demonstration.

Senator Joseph McCarthy's use of phony statements has already been mentioned. The assumption that the news media should be a messenger service never looked shabbier than in the era of McCarthyism. But so adept was the senator in the technique of the big lie issued as a sensational statement that newsmen were baffled about how to handle his venom.

As radio commentator Elmer Davis remarked at the time, no newspaper is comfortable with the notion of printing the sort of disclaimer needed: "For the truth about what you read below, see tomorrow's editorial page."[36]

In the face of the puzzlement and fear, Edward R. Murrow of CBS fought back at McCarthy with a television documentary about the senator's smear-and-run technique, a piece of advocacy reporting which is one of the most admired feats of modern journalism.[37]

The more conscientious workers in the news media learned from the McCarthy episode that faithful parroting of words can be treacherous, if the original words themselves are treacherous. Even so nasty a lesson can fade, however, as a reporter covers news conference after news conference, statement upon statement, with deadlines choking the effort to check for accuracy.

A necessary doublecheck must come from the consumer. He'll have to judge by the story whether the newsman has fallen into the habit of merely reciting messages, or whether he also is doing his job as a reporter out beyond the news conference microphones.

Although the advocate offers as one reason for his activism the need to debunk reckless charges, he too may fall for The Statement if it happens to bear out his own beliefs.

The charge that police assassinated twenty-eight members of the Black Panther party in several months of systematic raids was used unabashedly by some advocate newsmen, and in some "objective" reports as well, until it was disproved early in 1971 as a concoction by the party's lawyer.[38] Surely the history of the Panthers versus the police is open to many interpretations, but myth, whatever its origin, is not going to help us approach truth.

In like manner, boasts from protest leaders about shutting down a city, or putting enormous crowds of demonstrators into the streets, sometimes have been parroted in advocacy reporting as abjectly as any of Joe McCarthy's lies were repeated.

The consumer must ask: does the coverage go beyond what a spokesman is saying through a microphone or a bullhorn? Or does the reporter let the statement speak for itself? If so, does it contain its own proof and evidence? Is there another side to be searched out? Does the reporter offer any perspective—add, for instance, that Super Senator X is running for the presidency, which may explain his sudden interest in foreign policy, or that a power struggle is occurring within a protest movement and Maximum Leader Y may be making the loudest noise to draw attention to himself?

While looking at how a newsman handles The Statement, the news consumer also should note what sources the newsman is keeping steady company with.

The messenger's standard sources may be the government, school authorities, political party spokesmen—officialdom of whatever pedigree. So far, the advocate's taste has run more to social critics and leaders of protest groups.

Yet, life is not the exclusive province of hierarchies, whether those in power or those who would like to be in.

The messenger forgets that a title on the door does not mean an official spokesman is infallible, important or, for that matter, even in touch with reality. Institutions quickly get left behind the times; the reporter's habitual source may know very little about what is actually happening.

The advocate forgets that the ragtag group with a mimeograph machine may be no less an institution than the most grasping of congressional lobbies, with its own vested interests and party line to promote.

No camp has a monopoly on deceit. The long record of official falsehoods includes covering up everything from an H-bomb lost in Spain[39] to American invasion forces in Southeast Asia. Unfortunately for the news consumer, the anti-establishment is no less capable of duplicity.

Occasionally readers of the *Village Voice*, whose pages feature vividly personal journalism, will find a story in which the writer ruefully admits having been duped.

Shortly after a mass march on the Pentagon in 1967, *Voice* columnist Nat Hentoff cited a report in *New Left Notes*, a weekly newspaper published by Students for a Democratic Society.[40] According to that report, Washington police played down the Pentagon protest by issuing a crowd estimate of 55,000, although the police actually figured the number of marchers at about 318,000. Crowd estimating is a sport which becomes almost manic during election campaigns and seasons of mass protest, so Hentoff passed along the story and remarked that *New Left Notes* credited the information to "a reporter for the *Los Angeles Times*, Keith Wisely."

Two weeks later, Hentoff's column began: "Well, folks, I was had."[41]

Laying the error before his readers, he reported that "the editor of the *Los Angeles Times* has no knowledge of Mr. Wisely," and that a subsequent issue of *New Left Notes* ran on page 3 an item admitting the story was "a figment of someone's imagination." Going beyond the correction of his own error, Hentoff pointed out the lame effort by *New Left Notes*:

". . . It just won't do to bury a retraction the way those old bourgeois papers do."[42]

Another Voice columnist, Howard Smith, has written about having been deceived by a group he was politically sympathetic to. His comment:

"It seems my source and I both fell into the mistake, very common today, of assuming that the side with the most radical credentials is always right, and that in any hassles, legal or otherwise, it is always the side being victimized and ripped off."[43]

The news consumer must also watch both messenger and advocate for any display of small but flashy facts which can prejudice a story.

Time magazine in years past was famous for decorative facts of this sort.[44] Remember, a fact is not necessarily news. That a certain number of housewives went grocery shopping in Los Angeles this morning is a fact, but it is not news. *Time* stories often glittered with non-news facts such as a senator's shoe size or what he ate for breakfast. The idea, of course, is to impress the reader so with trivia that he will think the story just as informed in its important elements.

The news magazines are less flashy now than in the days when presidential candidate Adlai Stevenson could do little right in *Time* and little wrong in *Newsweek*, but the consumer must still watch out. Either a messenger or an advocate can create an illusion of truth with decorative facts.

The messenger may dutifully report the number of times a speech was interrupted by applause. But was the handclapping fervent, or merely polite? Or was it planted applause, swelling from the speaker's staff members and their families or some other coterie of imported enthusiasts? And did the reporter ask members of the audience for comment afterward?

Does the advocate slip into his story details which will hurt an opponent? An advocate reporter who would be outraged to hear the phrase "longhaired hippie" may use "crewcut Legionnaire" or "Rotarian mentality" or some other sneering description of his own object of scorn.

Be careful to distinguish between coloration and illumination, however. Wallace Carroll, now editor and publisher of the *Winston-Salem Journal* and *Sentinel*, recalls this example:

> . . . When I was with the Washington bureau of *The New York Times*, our Supreme Court reporter, Anthony Lewis, came in with a story that he thought would require an unusual touch. The "story," as he saw it, lay not in the majority opinion but in an unusual dissent by Justice Black. So after we had talked it over, he wrote a story which, after recording the majority opinion in the first paragraph, went on something like this:
>
> "In a passionate and despairing dissent, Justice Hugo Black rejected the majority opinion."
>
> Somehow or other this sentence escaped the copy desk gnomes in New York but it did not escape a reader in Seattle, and he wrote to the editors of the *Times*.

"I worked for the A.P. in the 1930's and I know that 'passionate' and 'despairing' are editorial words and you can't use them in a news story. Shame on the *Times* for letting adjectives like these get into its news columns."

This letter was forwarded to me with a succinct note from two of my betters in New York saying: "We agree."

It never pays to argue with your masters, but in this case I wrote back:

"It is possible that this alumnus of the A.P. in Seattle has a better 'feel' for the story than we had in Washington.

"But before I cleared the offending passage, I read Justice Black's dissent —all 16,000 words of it. And what impressed me from beginning to end was the passionate and despairing tone. And because passion and despair are seldom encountered in a judicial opinion, I thought this was news and worthy of noting in the *Times*."[45]

A lot of sound and some fury will go on between the messenger and the advocate through many a working shift yet to come. The dispute has the look of an issue which will mark an entire period of American journalism. For the duration, the news consumer can use what defensive techniques are available:

He can remind himself that there is no pure objectivity, and he is wasting wishes if he expects it.

He can learn to identify the kinds of news, and judge accordingly whether opinion unduly affects an item of information.

Herbert Brucker, former editor of the *Hartford Courant* and long a thoughtful writer about the news media, suggests a "journalistic litmus paper" the consumer can apply. It consists of this question:

"Is the writer, by the internal evidence of what he writes, trying to explain the news or plug a cause?"[46]

Chapter 9

"First, I want to thank the network for giving me this opportunity for rebuttal."

What's Missing?

Mystery lurked in the foggy moors, and the great sleuth was instructing his companions in the available clues. In response to what seemed a pontifical hint, one of the group asked the detective:

"Is there any point to which you would wish to draw my attention?"

"To the curious incident of the dog in the night-time."

"The dog did nothing in the night-time."

"That was the curious incident," remarked Sherlock Holmes.[1]

This chapter is about deduction. Which means it is about two topics. Deduction is a dual purpose word, the result of the separate verbs *deduce* and *deduct*. We'll be talking here about what is deducted from full information—data left out of news stories, somehow subtracted from the full account—and also about how the consumer can deduce—figure out what's missing. Sometimes what's missing will be perspective, sometimes the other side of a story, sometimes key facts or statements. Whatever it happens to be, the news is less trustworthy without it, and the news consumer's fund of information is the poorer.

Yesterday and Those Other Foreign Places

News is the new, the recent. The word itself automatically reminds the consumer of this on its every trip into his head, and he knows without having to think about it that the report he is absorbing from newsprint or wavelength is an item with newness.

Yet news stories deal with happenings which have been the contents of mankind as far back as our records of civilization go: struggle, drama, faith, sex, politics, community living. Life isn't reborn each day. It extends into our present moment through all those yesterdays. Because of this, the news is new, all right, but also old; the behavior that makes today's headlines has parentage back in the elapsed time we call the past.

The news is like a Shakespearean play, in a way. Each performance is a current event. The interpretation and setting are both new, products of our present culture. The automated theater in which we view the play is a modern creation. But the elements of the play and the roles performed by the cry of players go back through history with a sameness which communicates across the centuries.

The consumer can't expect all of the day's news to be freighted with hefty perspective. A report about a bank robbery needn't be told with a recital of the entire history of robbery. But some stories make much better sense if the topic is sketched against a historical background.

As an example of how background can be used to clarify facts which generally wisp around in the foreground haze, political reporter David Broder cites the trio of writers for the *Sunday Times* of London who wrote a book about our 1968 presidential election. The three—Lewis Chester, Godfrey Hodgson, and Bruce Page—titled their work *An American Melodrama.* "The quality their book has that is lacking in most of our own reporting about politics is scholarship," Broder said in his review.[2]

Take their reporting on the speech writers and advisors and assorted major-domos of the campaign entourages. Election year news is always fringed with articles about the candidates' political aides. "The best staff on Capitol Hill" and "the men around So-and-so" are standard topics and, because modern politics is an intricate exercise in image-making and scheduling, the staffers who do all the detail work behind a candidate's facade are legitimate news. But the *Times* men headed not toward the customary personality sketches, but back to medieval times and an eddy of history called "bastard feudalism."

An Oxford don named K. B. McFarlane had explained it a quarter of a century earlier. In the 14th century, some vassals began paying allegiance to their feudal lords not on the ancient basis of landholdings, but for the sake of money and power. McFarlane's summary:

> When a man asked another to be his 'good lord,' he was acquiring a temporary patron. In that loosely-knit and shamelessly competitive society, it was the ambition of every thrusting young gentleman—and also of everyone who aspired to gentility—to attach himself for as long as suited him to such as were in a position to further his interests. For those who wanted to rise in the world, "good lordship" was essential.[3]

What does a detail of medieval history have to do with American politics of the computer and TV camera? Here's the use in *An American Melodrama:*

> The serious point of the analogy is that the old, automatic allegiances of American politics, based on geography and on ethnic identification, have been largely replaced by a new kind of loyalty very much like "bastard feudalism." No longer does a clever and idealistic young man gravitate automatically into the sphere of a local leader such as William Jennings Bryan or Robert La Follette. He can join "the Kennedys," or he can attach himself to the retinue of some other "good lord" who can promise high adventure and reward. In the "loosely-knit and shamelessly competitive society" of contemporary America,

just as in England of Chaucer's day, the straightest road to fortune for a "thrusting young gentleman" lies not in self-help, but in joining the retinue of a great man and hoping to rise with his "good lord's" fortunes.[4]

With this bit of history, the authors give the reader new knowledge of old behavior. Their analogy to "bastard feudalism" closely fits this one aspect of our modern presidential politics, and tells a lot about allegiance and political power. The reader gains an insight he wouldn't otherwise have.

Again, not every story requires historical perspective of this sort. The pace of reporting needed to cover breaking news means that many of a day's stories won't have it. Notice that the political analysis by the authors from the *Sunday Times* of London showed up in the most leisurely reporting form of all, a book—although it could have appeared in a newspaper background story not governed by the pace of the day's events. The consumer can watch these interpretive stories to see what perspective is offered, if any is.

Any news consumer can compile his own list of missing backdrops for the news. Briefly, here are a few which have occurred to us in the course of watching coverage in the past few years:

1. Stories we saw about draft resistance during the high tide of protest against the Vietnam war seldom included the perspective that such resistance was nothing new in the American tradition. Countless U.S. families are descended from immigrants who came to this country to escape military conscription in their European homelands. And even here, there were enormous riots against the draft during the Civil War,[5] while in World War I, 20,873 men reported to military camps as conscientious objectors and another 337,649 men were on the War Department records as draft evaders of one kind or another.[6]
2. Communes have been reported as a recent phenomenon, although they are a long theme in U.S. history. At least 170 communes can be found in our history between 1663 and 1900.[7]
3. One assumption behind much reporting about government policies at home and abroad is that the U.S. is a young country, still a bold newcomer on the world scene. But ours is one of the world's oldest nations in terms of type of government. The Soviet Union, France, the People's Republic of China, the nations of Europe—the U.S. by now has an older form of government than nearly all other nations.

Sometimes the missing perspective is simply a matter of recent knowledge which could be filled in even as the event is happening. If the media aren't alert enough, a newsmaker may get away with an attempt to slant the record by concealing the perspective. One of the first big television news events, the Kefauver Committee's hearings on organized crime in mid-March, 1951, was a staged performance. For all the colossal coverage, that item of pertinence was not passed along to the national audience by either the broadcasters or the print media or, naturally enough, the committee itself.

A novelty in the early days of TV, the New York hearings of the anti-crime committee under the chairmanship of Sen. Estes Kefauver of Tennessee were broadcast live over a twenty-station hookup.[8] An unprecedented audience watched as gambler Frank Costello was grilled day after day in the witness chair. Newspapers and magazines, focusing on the TV drama of the underworld chieftain with the nervous hands, added to the coverage.

But the Costello testimony was a repeat melodrama, rigged up before the cameras to fix public attention on the committee's inquiry into organized crime. The Kefauver Committee had already questioned Costello fully in closed session a month earlier. Hauled in again, this time before the television cameras, Costello had to give the same answers he uttered in private, or lay himself open to charges of perjury. As two of Kefauver's counsel admitted later, Costello was set up to look like an underworld kingpin.

"He was, in fact, over the hill at the time of the hearings," attorney Downey Rice conceded, "and we had extreme difficulty in trying to demonstrate that he had been active at all in the years just prior to the hearings."[9]

Rufus King, who had been the committee's legislative counsel, recalled that the staff had a saying about how to insure maximum effect from its hoodlum grilling: "The way to make a sensation is to knock over some big ones."[10]

Even yet, the evidence of the job the Kefauver Committee did on Costello —and the whole country—is to be found not in the voluminous coverage by the news media, but buried deep in the hearing records, in this little segment with its parenthetical explanation:

> The Chairman: Who will be our first witness, Mr. Halley?
> Mr. Halley: Frank Costello.
> The Chairman: All right. Let us have Frank Costello here.
> (The testimony of Frank Costello, at this executive session, has been eliminated because it is virtually completely duplicated in the testimony given in the public hearings included in this publication, which were held in New York City on March 13, 14, 15, 16, 19, 20, 21, 1951.)[11]

So, the news consumer can try to see whether perspective is offered in complex stories which need it. If perspective is there, however, he must gauge it as carefully as anything else in the news. Unfortunately, it too can be inaccurate.

One of us remembers wincing in the editorial writers' sanctum after an extra edition was put out the day President Kennedy was killed, November 22, 1963. A reporter had been assigned to write a background article about presidential assassinations, and his long story said that Kennedy was the third U.S. President killed in office and provided historical detail about the Lincoln and

McKinley tragedies. A game try, but inept; the reporter entirely overlooked President James A. Garfield, victim of an assassin in 1881.

The authors of *An American Melodrama*, just mentioned for an example of clear perspective, can also be cited for an instance in which they muddled the scene.

Looking back on the Indiana primary of 1968, they somehow got the notion that Governor Roger Branigan was a monumental vote-getter who had won four one-year terms in a row in the Hoosier state, and that Robert Kennedy's 43 percent of the vote, against Branigan's 30 percent and Eugene McCarthy's 28 percent, was thus all the more significant of political drawing power.[12]

But no American state elects its governor to a one-year term (although 11 have two-year terms).[13] Branigan of course was rounding out a single four-year term, a standard record which made his mediocre showing behind Kennedy in his home state primary considerably less astonishing.

All of this suggests that erudite Englishmen need to check their data too, and that the news consumer has to be alert for error from any direction.

Another kind of perspective is often missing from news stories—the view from another country.

Plainly enough, different cultures have different ways of looking at matters. Here on our own continent, this has been strikingly evident ever since the Aztecs, who fought to take prisoners, encountered the Spaniards, who fought to kill. The blood runs a bit less frequently now when viewpoints clash, but the disagreement still may be intense.

Vancouver, British Columbia, and Seattle, Washington, are only a few hours apart by car. The language of the two cities is the same, and the cultures are closely similar. But the newspapers of these neighboring cities at the end of May, 1970, read as if the pair whirled through time on separate planets.

U.S. squeeze play on energy bared, read a front page headline in the *Vancouver Sun*.[14] The *Sun's* Washington, D.C. bureau reported that a White House staff member told a group of inquisitive legislators, "restrictions were slapped on Canadian oil imports in a move to put pressure on Canada to join a continental energy agreement."

The U.S. government's yearnings to have a pact with Canada on energy resources had been big and alarming news north of the border. J. J. Greene, the Canadian minister of energy, mines and resources, recently had told off a group of American oilmen in a speech. With Washington's confession of pressure tactics, Greene now vowed Canadians would "never negotiate anything with a gun at their head."[15]

Excited headlines and extensive coverage in Vancouver. In the *Seattle Times*, a page 12 column on the situation by Peter Thomson of the *Toronto*

Telegram Syndicate;[16] in the *Seattle Post-Intelligencer*, nothing. Add it all up, and you find that a major story in Vancouver for days received one slight mention in Seattle, 144 miles southward.

Many chapters of human events unfold as they do because one land's version of reality is not another land's. From August, 1964, until late in 1968, the U.S. air force systematically bombed targets in North Vietnam. The U.S. government described this as bombing of strategic military sites—anti-aircraft batteries, munitions depots, and the like. Not until a few U.S. newsmen visited North Vietnam in late 1966 did it become generally known in this country that what was described here as a precisely limited military response, the North Vietnamese regarded as full-dress war.[17] Our bombs were hitting civilian areas, and far from dispiriting the North Vietnamese into giving up, the bombing seemed to inspire the population to rally stubbornly against an outside threat, the way countless groups have defended themselves throughout history.

Later, when peace negotiations began in Paris, the difference between American and North Vietnamese concepts of time became evident. U.S. news reports described the talks as dragging on over the years, but in the Asian concept of time, a few years is insignificant.

As many national disparities of viewpoint exist as there are boundaries between countries. The news consumer can't hope to keep up with many of these conflicting perspectives, but he can turn to some sources for a sample of views from other lands.

The weekly television show *World Press*, on the Public Broadcasting Service, offers a review of newspaper coverage in several parts of the world. It is useful for the American consumer to realize that in a week when a congressional debate dominates the news here, the Japanese press may be focusing on elections for the Diet, the newspapers of India might headline the visit of a member of the Russian politburo, and many African newspapers feature the visit of Prime Minister Hastings K. Banda from the black nation of Malawi to the Republic of South Africa, the bastion of apartheid.

Saturday Review runs a sprightly feature called "As Others See Us," a roundup of editorial comment and letters to the editor, excerpted from newspapers throughout the world.

Atlas magazine is a monthly entirely devoted to reprint articles from other countries. The views there focus on a very different world than we are used to.

For instance, here are the main articles in a fairly typical issue of *Atlas*:

"The Private Lives of Russia's Leaders," from *Der Spiegel*, Hamburg.

"All Power to Baby Doc Duvalier," from *Siete Dias*, Buenos Aires.

"A Visit with a Liberated Lady from North Vietnam," from *The Vietnam Courier*, Hanoi.

"Chou En-Lai's Candid Talk with Arab Journalists," from *An-Nahar*, Beirut.
"Why is China Supporting West Pakistan?" from *Far Eastern Economic Review*,
  Hong Kong.
"Will Uruguay's Popular Front Win?" from *Panorama*, Buenos Aires.
"The Greening of a NATO General," from *L'Europeo*, Milan.[18]

Wherever a news consumer gets a sampling of foreign perspective, from
a reprint source or directly at a library or a newsstand with out-of-town publications, he is taking a step out of narrowness. His regular news media should
provide him some notion of the world beyond our borders, but the consumer
gains a better understanding if he makes an occasional foray himself.

Plugging the Holes

The U.S. Bureau of the Census counted 791,839 American Indians in
1970, a jump of more than 50 percent from the 1960 total of 523,591.[19]
An incredible explosion in the birth rate? No, said the census bureau.
The reasons for the precipitous increase, which compared to a rise of only
13.3 percent in the total population, were different classification procedures
and increased pride among Indians.

The simple but tricky explanation, then, was that in 1970 more people
were calling themselves Indians.

That story demanded an answer to the question "Why?" and the Associated Press reporter provided it. Sometimes, however, a vital question will go
unanswered, leaving what newsmen call a hole in a story.

Early in 1971, the Nixon administration struggled hard to save the U.S.
supersonic transport project, only to lose narrowly when Congress cut off federal money to build a prototype. Then, months after the epic congressional
battle that scuttled development of the SST, an eye-opening report came to
light.

NBC and CBS evening television news carried briefs, a few seconds of
narration mentioning the release of a hitherto secret report in which a scientific
review board commissioned by President Nixon himself had recommended
junking the SST a full two years before the administration's project was defeated in the Congress.

Had the report been made public during congressional debate, it's probable that the SST would have been grounded more quickly and easily. So the
story centered on the suppression of information unfavorable to the administration's dogged support of the project. The news briefs covered that point,
but left another question in viewer's minds. Why was the report released only
now?

United Press International cleared up the mystery.[20] The UPI story contained the information that the American Civil Liberties Union and two conservation groups, Friends of the Earth and the Sierra Club, had sued for release of the document under the Freedom of Information Act. As a result, the story added, the Justice Department had decided against trying to keep the Report secret any longer.

UPI also outlined the findings of the President's review board, which warned of the SST's potential impact on the economy, air traffic control, air fares, and noise.

To be put into fair perspective, the story demanded more than the headline treatment given it by the two networks.

Another of the holes into which newsmen may fall became apparent during civil disorders. The tension and confusion often lead to faulty eyewitness reports from those involved, and reporters face hard problems made even harder by an impending deadline, as Tim Reiterman's two versions of a Berkeley outburst, reprinted in chapter eight, testify.

Brandeis University's Lemberg Center for the Study of Violence looked at twenty-five such incidents from July and August of 1968, and pinpointed reports of sniping as frequently unreliable. Later news reports commonly had to revise downward the estimates of sniper activity, the Center said.[21]

Why? One of the key reasons was the damage done by isolated shotgun blasts. For example, the Center study team found that in Peoria, Ill., seven policemen were wounded in a single blast; in Harvey-Dixmoor, Ill., five out of seven police casualties came from one shotgun discharge, and in York, Pa., ten of eleven civilian casualties resulted from one blast.

In cases such as those, the Center admonished, the report of the number of people wounded is misleading. It makes the amount of sniping seem greater than it was. So, casualty figures should be coupled with information about the toll from the isolated shotgun shell.

The news business is pockmarked with informational craters. Another that the news consumer should look for is absence of local facets in a national story.

A wire service story tells about car repair frauds nationally. Do your news outlets add information about the situation in your area?

Congress has voted a tax increase. How did your congressman vote, and why? The news media should help consumers get a regular accounting from their elected officials by keeping track of their records on important legislation.

The four-day, 40-hour week is being experimented with. Is it being tried anywhere in your area? If so, with what results?

The state prison at Attica, New York, explodes in a prisoners' strike and wholesale shootings by the authorities attempting to put down the protest. What's the reporting on your state prison system? On your local jail? Are there investigative stories about both the prisoners and the guards, the offenders and the system?

Welfare costs have gone up and up nationally. Newsmen who have looked into the trend say the quick cliché explanation is wrong; the rises are not primarily because of welfare cheating. What's the news of welfare in your area, investigative or merely reflexive?

This country's news outlets generally support community fund drives with free advertising and favorable stories as publicity. Does any newspaper or broadcasting station, in the coverage it provides you, match major local problems against charitable expenditures, to see if the current uses are truly the best possible?

The pattern, then, is this: keep an eye on local coverage to see whether the implications of a national story are examined here in your own town—and if they are, whether the reasonable questions have been asked in the reporting.

A Quick Word From the Opposition

A few years ago James J. Vigilante, then president of the New Jersey State Patrolmen's Benevolent Association, gave a speech in which he said that when a potential criminal knows he faces the possibility of a death sentence, he will be much less eager to violate the law.[22]

"The PBA is in favor of capital punishment and believes that without it there would be a 100 percent increase in the crime rate," a news story quoted Vigilante as saying. "Criminals are not eager to die for their crimes but they would not hesitate to take part in more vicious acts if it were not for the threat of capital punishment."

The news story, a straight report of Vigilante's remarks, provided a good example of the old school of reporting which rates a story adequate as long as the words of the speaker are accurately reproduced. It's also an example of what's wrong with that kind of news.

Not until several days later did the information get straightened out, and then it came in a letter to the *Newark News*. "I challenge Mr. Vigilante to offer even one bit of evidence to support his claims," retorted the executive secretary of the Council to Abolish Capital Punishment. "Any serious student of the problem of capital punishment knows that all the evidence collected in this country for the last 50 years shows that long terms of imprisonment are as effective deterrents as the death penalty, and that nowhere in the world where capital punishment has been abolished has the crime rate risen because criminals were no longer executed."[23]

The reporter covering the speech should have had the wit to ask Vigilante what evidence prompted his statement. Failing that, the copy desk should have called Vigilante. And the Council to Abolish Capital Punishment should have been asked to provide balancing remarks.

As the story was printed, it reads as a serious comment on the value of capital punishment rather than what it is—a statement revealing only the frame of mind of the PBA president.

Through the centuries, criminals have been drawn and quartered, boiled in oil, broken on the wheel, thrown to wild beasts, stretched on the rack, strangled, crucified, disemboweled, and torn apart in ways that taxed man's ingenuity almost as much as his humanity.[24]

During the Middle Ages about 350 capital crimes were recognized in England, and as late as 1819 death penalties were decreed for more than 220 crimes, including picking pockets, shooting rabbits, and cutting down trees along an avenue or in a park.

Yet, Patrolman Vigilante's oratory to the contrary, no evidence exists that any form of capital punishment ever deterred anything.

Should a reporter be expected to be an historian? Yes, in fact, that's what his job is. He writes instant history every day and should be aware of major historical trends. In this case, however, the reporter or editor need have looked no further than an encyclopedia, which every serious newsroom contains. In its elongated English, the *Britannica* provides a comprehensive answer:

> Regarding deterrence, it is well established by statistical studies that (1) when comparisons are made between contiguous states with similar populations and similar social, economic, and political conditions—some of these states lacking and others retaining capital punishment—homicide rates are the same and follow the same trend over a long period of time, regardless of the use or nonuse of capital punishment; (2) the abolition, introduction or reintroduction of this penalty is not accompanied by the effect on homicide rates that is postulated by the advocates of capital punishment; (3) even in communities where the deterrent effect should be greatest because the offender and his victim lived there and trial and execution were well publicized, homicide rates are not affected by the execution; (4) the rate of policemen killed by criminals is no higher in abolition states than in comparable death-penalty states.[25]

The story of the PBA president's speech demanded not a slimly headlined letter to the editor several days later, but simultaneous rebuttal—balancing comment within the same story. The other side of an argument should not have to catch up later. In fact, it won't, because many readers may not see the follow-up.

Just as necessary for fair reporting is simultaneous rebuttal whenever charges are made by one person or group against another. And the newsman has to be alert, because normally careful sources can make mistakes, too.

The point was underlined when one of Ralph Nader's task forces released a 1200-page report, *Power and Land in California*, which charged that about one-quarter of the state's legislators were lawyers representing land interests, and another one-quarter were directly involved because "many operate their own real estate or construction firms or have their own large land holdings." The task force also contended that 70 percent of Governor Ronald Reagan's campaign funds came from land interests.

At a news conference, Nader summed up the report with the statement that corporate and government officials in California have "enormous power over the people . . . but no responsibility." He said salaries of government officials should be raised to high levels and that, in return, officials should be forbidden by law to be involved in business.

The task force estimated that 235 lobbyists for land interests spent more than $3.6 million in 1970, or more than $30,000 per legislator.

Nader added that the firms named as big political contributors "appear repeatedly in our study as recipients of massive public subsidies, as abusers of the environment, as beneficiaries of tax breaks, and as unprecedented violators of numerous laws."

Much more, of course, confronted newsmen in the massive report. Besides that, there is an almost irresistible glow about the paladins of consumer advocacy—students and young lawyers working diligently, at minimal or no pay, as investigators for the public.

Nevertheless, newsmen did what they had to do. Refusing to let motive substitute for method, they lobbed penetrating questions at the task force. A UPI reporter uncovered this example of a lack of simultaneous rebuttal:

One of Nader's Raiders, Robert Fellmeth, 26, a lawyer and head of the California team, conceded they had not talked to former governor Edmund G. Brown, former attorney general Thomas Lynch, and former deputy Charles A. O'Brien before making charges against those officials.[26]

Fellmeth defended the methods and credibility of the team, but admitted, "I guess we should probably have confronted them. It was probably a failing on our part."[27]

The Los Angeles Times, in a story that filled several news columns, uncovered other information for the reader, and sought specific rebuttals. On the financing of the task force:[28]

> Fellmeth disclosed in an interview that the conservationist Sierra Club Foundation financed $7,500 of the $18,500 cost of the study, the balance paid for by a small San Francisco foundation and Nader's Center for the Study of Responsive Law.

Then rebuttal to the implication that the study might have been stacked in favor of conservationist policies:

> While the California study takes many Sierra Club positions, it occasionally criticizes the club, and Fellmeth said it was "ridiculous" to think the twenty-five Nader investigators were subject to a conflict of interest.

The next logical question would be, Who compiled the report? The story promptly answers:

> The investigators included Fellmeth, author of "The Nader Report on the FTC" and "The Interstate Commerce Commission"; Lew Sargentich and Richard Parker, the top two men at Harvard law school in 1970 and now clerks for Supreme Court Justices Thurgood Marshall and Potter Stewart, respectively; and various other young lawyers, economists, biologists, and planners.

The report called for an immediate halt to the $900 million airport Los Angeles planned to build near Palmdale, and the *Times* covered that hometown angle with careful presentation of both sides, in this fashion:

> The Nader study sharply criticized not only the department's selection of the Palmdale site but also the parts played by the State Department of Aeronautics and the Federal Aviation Administration in approving it.
> "There was no consideration of the airport's effect on the deceptively fragile desert environment," the study complained.
> Once the site was approved, federal agencies "rubber stamped it," the report said. None of the involved agencies conducted the "bona fide" investigation required by the National Environmental Policy Act of 1969, the Nader group charged.
> The report also accused the Federal Aviation Administration of suppressing a file memorandum which recommended disapproval of the proposed site.
> In addition, Nader's task force said, the FAA "capitulated" to the Department of Airports and was "philosophically unable to rebuff" the city agency in approving the site.

Those were the charges. Next the *Los Angeles Times* story sought out simultaneous rebuttal to those charges.

> Responding to the Nader report, Clifton Moore, general manager of the Department of Airports, called it an "excellent example of environmental overkill."
> It is "contributing greatly to the rapidly widening credibility gap between the environmental movement and the general public," he told the *Times*.
> He said the report focuses on the Nader group's basic thinking which, according to Moore, is designed to stop all growth wherever possible, intimidate elected officials, and harass the normal processes of government without offering positive constructive solutions.
> Arvin O. Basnight, Western director of the FAA, said he had no knowledge of a suppressed memorandum but pointed out that the combined judgments of many individuals within the agency—not just one—went into the airport's approval.
> At the same time, he described references to the FAA's "capitulation" as "repugnant."

"We don't compromise our best judgment in matters of air space and air safety," he said.

Throughout its story, then, the *Los Angeles Times* included comments from some of the people criticized by the Nader task force. Here's one more example.

Some of the officials singled out said that the statements made about them were untrue. State Controller Houston Flournoy said: "If the mere fact of a campaign contribution is to be construed as conflict of interest, then no controller will ever be elected who can serve free of conflict of interest as Nader uses that term." He said Nader's "real quarrel seems to be with our system of campaign financing. In this regard I share his concern."

Readers may draw different conclusions from the information supplied by the newspaper, but at least they have a fair perspective on a complex story.

The *Los Angeles Times*, to its credit, is not afraid to run articles that spread over several columns, or even several pages, if that amount of space is necessary to make sense of the news.

And in this case it provides an excellent example of a story which plugged holes by including simultaneous rebuttal.

The Editor's Shears and The Shorn

Magazine and newspaper writers have bylines to mark their work. Radio and television reporters identify themselves in their sign-offs. But editors in any medium rarely catch public attention and, for all the news consumer is usually aware of their craftsmanship, they could be mute and invisible as well as anonymous.

Editing a news story is a matter of riding herd on someone else's work.[29] An editor can cut or lengthen a story, change phrasing, doublecheck information, anything he thinks should be done to make the story as strong as possible. Because the editor's task requires some skill in writing, some in reporting, some in researching, and plenty of intuition both about his newsmen and the subjects they tackle, the job advertises itself as the abode of the newsroom's more complex souls.

Media legend and lore abound with tales of editors who read the encyclopedia in their spare moments and who can do a telephone impersonation of any official in town when the story needs hard-to-come-by information.[30] The editor as a rather odd virtuoso—sort of like the fellow who excels at putting jigsaw puzzles together—happens naturally enough in the newsroom. He must contend with all the mistakes made by the rest of the staff. Through the generations, editors try in self-defense to spoonfeed wisdom and wile into reporters. A lot of their effort is in the spirit of old-time deskmen such as Austin P. Cristy, who laid down these guidelines at the *Worcester Telegram* in 1909:

> The body of a person drowned should not be called a floater. No dead body should be called a stiff.
> Cut out "colored," "American," "Irish," "English," "Swede," "French," "Jew," or any term indicating race or religion when used to describe an individual. Omit booze, cop, swipe, swat, tough mug, bat in the eye, jab in the jaw, punch in the slats, got wise, and similar expressions, other than in quotations.[31]

Generally, an editor's aura doesn't catch attention beyond the circle of his working colleagues. As far as the consumer is concerned, the work an editor does is usually indistinguishable from the reporter's. Corrections and changes are made before the story gets into print or on the air, and only the result, with the snags out and the holes chinked, is the consumer's concern. So it is that the personalities who man the most vital checkpoints in the news process go unknown. *Fortune* magazine writer Carol J. Loomis provides this example from the prestigious *Wall Street Journal*:

> Most of the copy turned in by the reporters hits the desk of William C. Kreger, a block-like figure who sits near the middle of the newsroom, looking like a very large paperweight, and who functions as "inside" editor, riding herd over all of the news-hole except the front page, the editorial page, and any back-page features. Since the *Journal* does not run on its masthead either the name of its managing editor or his chief assistants ("it just never has been done," says *Journal* president Bill Kerby), Kreger is largely unknown in the business world. Yet he probably exercises more control over what business news the country reads than any other person alive. It is Kreger who decides that a story is a "must" and he who determines the prominence of the headline. If he does not see a story as important, it does not make the *Journal*.[32]

A recent exception to editing's customary anonymity flared in television news, in which film and videotape footage has to be cut down to usable length on the TV screen. Early in 1971 the editing process attracted unusual attention because of the CBS documentary, "The Selling of the Pentagon." In examining the public relations projects of the U.S. military, the news program featured filmed segments of the public relations officers at work and portions of interviews with Pentagon officials. Before long, Congressman William E. Minshall of Ohio bundled together the complaints by the show's critics when he introduced legislation which would:

> Require a continuous identifying label on any television film or videotape showing staged or edited events or interviews where quotes had been shifted

from their original sequence. Similar editing on radio would require an announcement of what had been done before and after the broadcast.

Make complete unedited transcripts available on request immediately after all edited interviews.

Require a "reasonable opportunity" for presentation of opposing viewpoints when a station presents only one side of a controversial issue.[33]

Unfortunately, the battle about "The Selling of the Pentagon" didn't deal squarely with the editing ethics involved—the question of whether the network distorted the news by the way edited segments of interviews were arranged in the final version.

CBS, in making its defense, fended off a House subcommittee's demand for its unused film footage as an intrusion on freedom of the press. When the subcommittee chairman tried to cite CBS President Frank Stanton for contempt of Congress, the House refused to back the action and instead voted the issue back into committee.[34] Spiked there on a side issue, the legal dispute died away.

The critics of the network, for their part, seemed motivated by outrage that the Pentagon had been criticized and by the desire to kick an obstreperous news operation into line. It is hard to imagine that the same ruckus would have occurred if the CBS documentary team had used identical techniques on the Soviet Union's ministry of defense, or even Great Britain's.

But all sides concerned, and especially the consumer, are better off when television news does try for the visual equivalent of quote marks and ellipses which are used in printed material. Fred W. Friendly, who pioneered in documentary work and is now one of the most perceptive critics of television news, points out that a mention of the editing is simple enough:

> . . . Every effort should be made to let the viewer know that the quotations are the result of editing. For example: "Former President Johnson presents his account of great events, issues, and decisions . . . edited from several lengthy conversations with Walter Cronkite, filmed in the autumn of 1969 at the LBJ ranch in Texas." Or: "The participants in this controversy were filmed at different places and different times, and their opinions have been edited here in juxtaposition to reflect the debate."[35]

Chapter 10

Putting One Word
After Another

Item: A seminary student approached his superior and asked, "Father, may I smoke while I pray?"

"No, my son, you may not," the priest told him.

A second student watched, thought for a moment, and approached the superior.

"Father, may I pray while I smoke?" he asked.

"Of course, my son," the priest replied.

Item: Describing the settlers' push into native lands in Australia, an early governor wrote approvingly of "the natural progress of the aboriginal race towards extinction."[1]

Item: Headline from an idle moment at the *New York Times* copy desk . . .[2]

Moses, On Sinai,
Gets 10-Pt. Plan

Item: Once upon a time in a parking lot at the University of California at San Diego, a sign instructed: No Parking Prohibited Without a Permit.

Item: Despairing of the American vocabulary of the 1970s, writer Melvin Maddocks concluded: "There is an adequate language for fanaticism, but none for ordinary, quiet conviction."[3]

We know ourselves by our language. By careful attention to the lines of language which course through his head every day, the news consumer quickly discovers we don't know ourselves with much clarity. Patterns of word and thought, euphemism, unclear context, confusion, passion: these and other items waylay us. Throughout the news process, that endless cycle of putting one word after another, the tangles and traps can be found . . . *if* the consumer stays alert.

War and Peace That Passeth All Understanding

Now for the latest world news from your local dictionary:

> **peace** (pēs) *n.* 1. The absence of war or other hostilities. 2. An agreement or treaty to end hostilities: *the Peace of Westphalia.* 3. Freedom from quarrels and disagreement; harmonious relations. *They made peace with each other.* 4. Public security; law and order: *disturbing the peace.* 5. Inner contentment; calm; serenity: *peace of mind.* . . .[4]

> **war** (wôr) *n.* 1. a. A state of open, armed, often prolonged conflict carried on between nations, states, or parties. b. The period of such conflict. 2. Any condition of active antagonism or contention: *"O, what a war of looks there was between them!"* (Shakespeare). 3. The techniques or procedures of war; military science; strategy. . . .[5]

A dictionary entry is a printed report about how a word generally has been used in our language—a roundup of information about the word. But instead of the who, what, when, where, why, and how, the elements that pulse in the work of a newspaperman or a broadcaster, the dictionary entry provides a series of definiens. Definiens are those words that define another word or expression.

A dictionary entry, then, handily clusters the most common meanings a word has had. Not so the latest news from a newspaper or broadcast. What the news consumer hears or reads may have had one definition at its source, another as the newsman handled the information, and still another in the consumer's mind.

In a single newscast or newspaper, the consumer may encounter peace and war several times, each one different.

There was peace along the Suez Canal today . . . But isn't that peace also war, in the sense of definien number two: any condition of active antagonism or contention (*"O, what a war of looks"*)?

The world has not been at war since 1945, the Secretary of State pointed out. . . . Yet some forty-five wars below the World War II level of fighting have flared since then.[6] The United States has been in two wars—Korea and Vietnam—one of them the longest in this country's history, and both of them without declaration of war.

Hopes for peace in Vietnam . . . The American peace plan aimed for a transfer of warfare, from U.S. versus Vietcong to the South Vietnamese government versus Vietcong, and "pacification" has been a term to describe the U.S. strategy of warfare there.

"The peace of God, which passeth all understanding," runs a lovely line from the King James version of the Bible.[7] That's not the only kind of peace which, in the mechanical chant we get from our modern news apparatus, is far beyond understanding, nor are war and peace the only words garbled by a confusion of tongues. The news is thick with words and phrases which may have sundry definiens.

Negotiation, policy, law and order, free enterprise, American way of life, communist menace, protest, balance of trade, discipline, restraint: by now, an entire vocabulary is available to a person in public life for the manufacture of statements without ever risking a precise explanation of his belief. But if the news comes without definiens, how does the consumer know what it means?

The odds are that he doesn't. When you think about it, not knowing how someone else is using a word is nothing new or out of the ordinary. Our talk is full of generalities without definiens—so much so that the American tribal rite is to gather to discuss a problem, then chorus something such as "First, we have to have a working definition of discrimination."

The consumer can remind himself that any of a number of definiens may be behind the words relayed to him in a news story. Sometimes, this will be due to the sloppiness within the news media. A more difficult source of confusion is imbedded within our everyday language itself, and the way we use it.

Why is it possible for a word to mean more than one thing? A word is like a section of telephone cable, a sheath with several conduits inside it. Each of the conduits can carry a different meaning, but all within the same unit.

This is possible because words are sound combinations, certain noises we assign to features of our world. For ancient reasons, laziness and lack of imagination probably high among them, man the vocalist casually uses the same sound combinations to convey different meanings. That's why we have definiens. This human habit of attaching more than one meaning to a word has brought about an entire field of study—semantics, the study of meaning in language.[8]

In the summer of 1971, the Tasaday tribe was discovered in a jungle in the Philippines.[9] The culture of the Tasadays still was back in the Stone Age; they had lived through the centuries unaffected by the outside world's changes. Anthropologists found that the Tasadays' greatest fear was thunder or, as they called it, "the big word." The Tasaday recognition of the link between noise and language was clearer than ours usually is.

Many of us confuse the descriptive noise—the word—with the thing itself. But the first semantic point is that the word is not the same as the thing, and the news consumer needs to firmly grasp the idea that no number of words ever can duplicate a news event. A reporter can *tell about* an airplane crash, but he can never tell everything about it, and he can never exactly duplicate it.

A second major semantic principle is that no two things are alike. A chippendale chair is not a rocking chair, and neither one is a straight-back chair. Furthermore, no two chairs are identical, even duplicates stamped from the same mold. Minute differences will exist, even if we cannot easily see them.

Nor does any single chair remain exactly the same. The continual whirl of the electrons in its molecular structure, a speck of dust that is not on the chair one moment but is the next, the amount of light in which we perceive the chair at any instant: the chair is always changing imperceptibly, one way or another. Only because the change is imperceptible are we able to talk about things in the manner we do. The chair *seems* the same, so each time we refer to it we can call it "chair," and that is an essential convenience for making ourselves understood.

This illusion of constancy can also cause problems. For instance, the words *the United States* have been used an infinite number of times in our history. But which United States does each set of words mean? The entity is constantly changing, in countless ways. It's undergone basic changes in boundary alone more than three dozen times since the days of the thirteen original states, and each newly admitted state up to our present total of fifty meant an altered version of the United States.[10] Political administration changes, social moods fluctuate, the look of the landscape changes, the population total is different every instant. In short, despite the single phrase, *the United States* has meant—and means—countless entities. The name may remain the same, but the reality behind it changes.

Context: In, Out, and Around

Sometimes words can distort, even when their individual meanings are clear. Writer Leo Rosten explained:

> Recently I addressed a large group of educators and I pointed out to them that if I were to say, "Our chairman was sober last night," it would not be an untruth, because he was, in fact, sober. But it certainly would suggest, through that way of patterning, that this was unusual behavior on his part.[11]

Rosten was making the point that individual words mean nothing until they are arranged and patterned with other words.

We call the larger pattern of words the context of a statement, and context is essential to understanding. Even when what is said is literally accurate, and the meaning plain and unmistakable, the news consumer may be fooled if the context is askew. Take this example.

In the summer of 1963, a resident of the Mississippi delta area was arrested in the sniper killing of Black civil rights leader Medgar Evers. The *Jackson Clarion-Ledger* carried the front-page headline: **Californian is Charged With Murder of Evers.**[12]

The suspect had been born in California, all right, and had spent the first five years of his life there. The other 37 years he had lived in Mississippi.

Another form of lifting out of context is the art of snippetry, which flourishes in advertisements for movies and books. One of the movies with a booklength title—*Who is Harry Kellerman and Why is He Saying Those Terrible Things About Me?*—was advertised with the blurb from *New York Times* critic Vincent Canby: "Fancily and stylishly put together."

That excerpt, Canby noted, was "the feeble-minded remains of a sentence that once read: 'The movie, which opened last night at the Sutton, has been rather fancily and stylishly put together by Mr. Grosbard, although I suspect much of this look comes from the look of the fancy sets and from the dozens of stylishly abrupt flashbacks that are never as revealing as they promise to be."[13]

One segment of news the consumer gets with slim context: headlines. Newspapers use headlines to sum up stories, and at this writing, two of the three evening network news shows on television begin with headlines of some sort.

Headlines stand out as a definite world which doesn't actually exist. Writing headlines is a difficult chore, and to expect every newscast and newspaper to have nothing but precisely crafted headlines is like expecting the news to be rewritten into Shakespearean sonnets.

Furthermore, even the best of headlines are too brief to contain the necessary qualifiers.

Sometimes the misleading is piquant. Headlines about federal funds often resurrect a Civil War hero: **Rutgers Gets U.S. Grant For Course,**[14] or **U.S. Grant To Study Retarded Children.**[15]

Nudity sometimes appears as a headline writer strains for a revealing verb: **Bare Writer's Marriage to Sculptor.**[16]

Some newspapers show their personalities within the context of their headlines. Readers of the *New York Daily News* easily savvy the terse slangy heads with which the tabloid punches across the news: **3 Baddies in Black Pull a 40G Beaut.**[17]

But the stately competitor of the *News* in the morning field, the *New York Times*, is so grave and history minded that deskmen there once made a game of writing heads for the world's great stories as the Times might have told the news in one solemn column:

Jehovah Resting
After 6-Day Task[18]

French Are Urged
To Consume Cake[19]

Sometimes headline writers can entertain as well as inform their readers by combining unlikely contexts. When race driver Stirling Moss was hit by a stone thrown up from a tire as he tried out a car at Milan, the headline read: **Rolling Moss Gathers Stone.**[20]

Headlines are both art and craft, and the play of language within them can be entertaining. But the headline writer's knack carries a serious responsibility as well, because the words atop a story can skew the reader's perception of the news item.

The *St. Louis Post-Dispatch* demonstrated, through three editions of the same story, the problems that even a first-rate newspaper can have with headlines.

City edition: *Rights Militants Take Over Meeting*
Second edition: *Militants Take Over Meeting on Rights*
Three-star final: *Activists Are Heard at Rights Meeting*

As the *St. Louis Journalism Review* explained it, the city edition headline "conjures up visions of Black Panthers or H. Rap Brown storming into a meeting and grabbing microphones.[21] But those who were at this particular meeting— and those who read the *Post* story carefully—know that it didn't happen that way. The 'militants' were, in fact, given time to speak by prearrangement . . .

"The head was changed in the second edition—but its meaning wasn't. Apparently it just fit better that way.

"In the three-star final—after the reporter who wrote the story complained—the headline was changed to reflect more accurately what happened. Gone is the false impression of force. Moreover, the accurate headline fits just as well—proving that the old bugaboo, lack of headline space, wasn't really the problem."

But the best example of how to rearrange a context comes out of medieval history.

In 1478 Laurent Guernier was hanged in Paris. As it turned out, the hanging had been one of those unfortunate mistakes; a reprieve had been granted, but arrived too late. A year later his brother got permission to have the body honorably re-buried, and Jean de Roye tells the tale in his chronicle:

Before this bier went four town criers of the aforesaid town sounding their rattles, and on their breasts were the arms of the aforesaid Guernier, and around that bier were four tapers and eight torches, carried by men dressed in mourning and bearing the aforesaid crest. And in this way it was carried, passing through the aforesaid city of Paris . . . as far as the gate of Saint Anthony, where the aforesaid corpse was placed on a cart draped in black to take it to Provins to be buried. And one of the aforesaid criers who walked before the aforesaid corpse cried:

"Good people, say your pater nosters for the soul of the late Laurent Guernier, in his life an inhabitant of Provins, who was lately *found dead under an oak-tree!*"[22]

Galloping Gobbledygook

President Franklin D. Roosevelt could wield a sharp chisel on verbal rococo, as his subordinates were reminded time and again. One day during World War II, when the Washington press corps still was small enough that newsmen could gather in the oval office of the White House for impromptu sessions, the President picked up a civil defense announcement. He hadn't seen it before, and his astonishment mounted as he read the lingo aloud:

> Such preparations shall be made as will completely obscure all federal buildings occupied by the federal government during an air raid for any period of time from visibility by reason of internal or external illumination. Such obscuration may be obtained either by blackout construction or by terminating the illumination. This will of course require that in building areas in which production must continue during a blackout, construction must be provided that internal illumination may continue. Other areas, whether or not occupied by personnel, may be obscured by terminating the illumination.[23]

When the laughter finally dwindled, Roosevelt directed that the order be reworded. Tell them, he said, that in buildings where work will have to keep going, put something across the windows. In buildings where work can be stopped for a while, turn out the lights.[24]

With those strokes, FDR showed how to cut through the congealed bureaucratic language called gobbledygook.[25]

Gobble, from the noises made by turkeys, and *gook*, a sludgy, slimy substance. *Gook*, in turn, may come from the Scottish *gowk*, meaning simpleton.

Gobbledygook often enough sounds like meaningless noises from a simpleton.

Gobbledygook seems to increase with the size of the organization, so we characteristically look to government for prime examples.

A few years ago, the city of Berkeley, California, sent out an explanation of why garbage rates were increased:

> This change in procedure is occasioned by our efforts to effect more economic and efficient city operation by consolidating certain functions.[26]

Translation? We're becoming more efficient, so you'll have to fork over more money.

Gobbledygook shows up in the news for a number of reasons.

1. The writer or speaker himself isn't clear about what he wants to say.
2. He doesn't know how to say it.
3. He believes that a reader or listener will be impressed by a barrage of polysyllables thudding against the brain.
4. He has something unpleasant to say, and he tries to hide it among slushy, slippery words, or to find inoffensive ways of delivering offensive messages —the art of euphemism.

Some gobbledygook experts have had long training. They started in school, where their instructors seemed to be saying that they should never use one word when they could cram in two or more.

Say the assignment is to write 800 words about the dangers of speeding. The student, who has never heard of research or who is too lazy to do any, puzzles over how to spin that many words out of his head. He may begin with a straightforward

Fast driving is dangerous.
But after a little thought it becomes
In my opinion, fast driving is dangerous.
With more tender, loving care that stretches to
In my opinion, fast driving would seem to be rather dangerous.
And if he's unusually agile he may make it
*In my humble opinion, though I do not claim to be an expert on this compli-
cated subject, fast driving, in most circumstances, would seem to be rather
dangerous in many respects, or at least so it would seem to me.*

"Thus," says linguist Paul Roberts, who provided the example, "four words have turned into 40, and not an iota of content has been added."[27]

A scintillating start for a gobbledygooker. That student will grow up to be at least an undersecretary in the Department of Health, Education and Welfare.

When we get into the habit of smudging our words like that, sentences begin to turn back upon themselves.

Take the words of a national commander of the American Legion, quoted by columnist Herb Caen in the *San Francisco Chronicle*. Of the need to protect the American dollar, the commander declared: "I believe the government should enforce some voluntary limit on the money spent by tourists."[28]

Exactly what we need, quipped Caen. More voluntary enforcement.

That such verbal meanders are not rare was forcibly impressed on the authors while this chapter was being written. During a supper break we were watching the NBC *Nightly News* when it switched to a clip of President Nixon answering questions about his wage-price freeze. At a meeting in Detroit he was asked about the charge that the freeze was unfair to some workers.

"One of the inevitable results of a freeze is that there will be inequities," the President began, reasonably enough. Then he lost his bearings and added, "And those inequities must be equally shared during the period of the freeze."[29]

Equal inequities? Voluntary enforcement? Maybe such sputter is becoming the mother tongue here in the home of the luxury economy car, but if it is, what's ahead? Some dark illumination of the national spirit? Or merely an abrupt easing of any concern at all about what we're really saying?

Sometimes what we're really saying is that honest language is uncomfortably harsh. Whatever the nation that happens to be a combatant, for instance, its war will spawn euphemisms, as if new terms could soften the actions.

Many of them come perilously close to what George Orwell projected in his novel of tyranny, *1984*, where Newspeak was contrived to change not only the language, but people's thought patterns as well. The Ministry of Truth had charge of propaganda, the Ministry of Peace waged war, the Ministry of Love maintained law and order, and the Ministry of Plenty was responsible for strict rationing.

In another example of what he called doublethink, Orwell gave the ruling party three slogans: War is Peace, Freedom is Slavery, and Ignorance Is Strength.[30]

How far have we come since Orwell's fantastic novel was published in 1949?

Back in reality in Southeast Asia, the Department of Defense solemnly announced in 1971 that U.S. troops had entered Laos in an incursion, leaving the news consumer to wonder whether an invasion by any other name is less of an invasion.[31] And if the entry into Laos was an incursion, was the departure of the U.S. task force from South Vietnam an excursion?

Similarly, the U.S. didn't bomb North Vietnam. It conducted preventive reactions. The deadly weapons tried out in the Vietnam jungles were sophisticated hardware. Combat patrols became missions to search and clear or, on truly euphemistic days, reconnaissances in force.[32]

It may be more than mere coincidence that in 1947, not long before Orwell's novel appeared, the U.S. Cabinet office which for 158 years had been called the Department of War was dubbed the Department of Defense.

Nor is the ultimate in Orwellian Newspeak, the doubleflip of a phrase to confound the brain, merely a remote fantasy. In 1936, at the outbreak of the Spanish Civil War, General Millan Astray rallied forces for Franco with the mad slogan, "Long live death!"[33]

Back on the U.S. home front and in a lesser state of belligerence, the Secretary of Health, Education and Welfare in 1970 was telling senators he wished they'd refer to the poor as being on family assistance instead of welfare. Welfare itself, he might have noted, once was a euphemism for relief, which was a euphemism for the earlier charity, which was a euphemism for the dole.[34]

All this circumlocution, plus whatever problems he has with his own use of language, hinders the newsman in his attempt to report. Perhaps it's remarkable anything comes through the verbal fog. As the news consumer fights his way through the garble, he can appreciate just how remarkably plainspoken was the proclamation issued by Haile Selassie, emperor of Ethiopia, when his country was invaded by Italy in 1936. The emperor had few weapons, but if clarity could have won the day, he would have been the clear victor:

> Everyone will now be mobilized and all boys old enough to carry a spear will be sent to Addis Ababa.
> Married men will take their wives to carry food and cook.
> Those without wives will take any woman without a husband.
> Women with small babies need not go.
> The blind, those who cannot walk, or for any reason cannot carry a spear are exempted.
> Anyone found at home after receipt of this order will be hanged.

Loaded

One U.S. Representative voted against U.S. entry into both world wars, the only member of Congress to cast such a pair of votes. To some editorial writers, Congresswoman Jeannette Rankin, a pacifist, had courageously stood by her principles. To others she had been defiant, stubborn, and unpatriotic.

At work here are loaded words—those that plant either favorable or unfavorable ideas in the minds of readers.

First, a simple, straightforward report:

> Congresswoman Jeannette Rankin voted against U.S. participation in World War I and World War II.

But then, emotionally charged judgment:

> (Positive) She had *courageously* stood by her *principles*.
> (Negative) She had been *defiant, stubborn*, and *unpatriotic*.

Consciously and subconsciously, we all deal in words that slant in one direction or another. In fact, most terms except such structure words as *a, the, and, of* do have some positive or negative associations. In many cases, however, the reactions differ with the individual. If you have pleasant memories of a faithful pet you once romped with, you may react favorably to the word *dog*. But if you were once bitten by a dog, you may react negatively to the word.

Other words can be either positive or negative to broad groups of people. Libel laws recognize that reality. If a term is so loaded that merely pairing it with a person's name will injure that person in his business and social relations, then it will be considered the most clear kind of libel.

Included in a long list of terms found libelous in U.S. courts in the last quarter century have been *communist, homosexual*, and *abortionist*.

Interestingly, as a society's values change, so will the list of libelous words. Now that abortion has been legalized in some states, the stigma is disappearing from that word. Communist does not sound as reprehensible to as many American ears now as it did in the 1950s. While it still is not safe to print or broadcast that a person is a communist unless he is provably or admittedly so, the time may come when being called a communist will no longer ruin any person's reputation in his community. And, as lifestyles in our society become more diverse, the same may be true of homosexual.

With knowledge that some words are loaded so that they will affect his reaction to the news, the consumer needs to keep a wary eye on the media to determine how often he is fed judgments rather than—or along with—reports. Loaded judgments can come from both the reporter and from the newsmaker who is being interviewed.

Report: In 1970 the U.S. space program was faced with a budget cutback that meant the loss of 50,000 jobs.

Reporter: Would you describe this as a *slash*?

Space agency director: No. It's *austere but forward-looking*.[35]

Some editorial writers and newsmagazine editors showed their prejudices during the Truman and Eisenhower years by their choice of terms for the men who accompanied those Presidents during vacations. Eisenhower was described as having *friends*, but Truman was surrounded by *cronies*.

Inside this double standard, businessman George E. Allen, who was a frequent companion of both Presidents, underwent one of the most prompt editorial transformations ever. In a *Saturday Evening Post* article in May, 1956, Allen is pictured on one page with Truman, above a caption which says "he became one of Harry Truman's closest cronies . . ." On the facing page, Allen is pictured with "his fishing pal and Gettysburg neighbor, Ike Eisenhower."[36]

Time magazine, which never made a secret of its distaste for *HST* and its enthusiasm for Ike, described Truman as *barking, preaching*, and *grinning slyly*, while the good President Eisenhower *chatted amiably, cautiously pointed out*, and spoke *with a happy grin*.[37]

Loaded statements are not much problem where no attempt is made to hide the slant. Writer Jack London, who nurtured undiluted venom for strike-breakers, is credited with this classic piece of vituperation against the "scabs" during the early days of this century:

> After God had finished the rattlesnake, the toad and the vampire, he had some awful substance left with which he made a scab. A scab is a two-legged animal with a corkscrew soul, a water-logged brain, and a combination back-bone made of jelly and glue. Where others have hearts he carries a tumor of rotten principles.
>
> When a scab comes down the street men turn their backs and angels weep in heaven, and the devil shuts the gates of hell to keep him out. No man has a right to scab as long as there is a pool of water deep enough to drown his body in, or a rope long enough to hang his carcass with. Judas Iscariot was a gentleman compared with a scab. For betraying his master, he had character enough to hang himself. A scab hasn't.[38]

There's more, but that's a fair sample of a piece that's loaded, outraged, and doesn't try to pretend otherwise.

What the news consumer must guard against, however, are statements which may at first appear to be even-handed, but which aren't.

David Brinkley of NBC News at times has been charged with bias for the way he raises an eyebrow or intones a phrase.[39] After videotaping some of his reports and replaying them for friends and students, we're convinced that Brinkley could sit mute and immoveable before an audience and still be accused of prejudicing the news. The mischief is the message, in the case of many a viewer watching the Brinkley visage. Nevertheless, as one of the most deft stylists among television news writers, on occasion Brinkley might legitimately be charged with loading a report.

When President Nixon announced that he would ask Congress for money to build supersonic transport prototypes, Brinkley used it as the lead story on the evening news, with opening lines that included this summary statement:

> Its virtue is that it'll save a few hours on trips across the Atlantic or Pacific. Its shortcoming is that wherever it goes it will leave a shattering sonic boom, rattling dishes and cracking windows, so it will not be allowed to fly over land and it won't be used inside the U.S. unless somebody finds a way to stop the noise.[40]

Aside from being a vast oversimplification of an exceedingly complex problem, this obviously is not as even-handed as the virtue/shortcoming format ordinarily suggests.

Brinkley throws away the plane's virtue with an offhand comment that it'll save a few hours on overseas flights.

But its shortcoming includes shattering, rattling, and cracking noise. The implication in the words strung together this way: who wants all that, just to save international travelers a few hours?

A mayoralty campaign produced another prime example of how a writer can work his words to tilt the report. The day after the primary election, an evening newspaper printed an editorial, which legitimately could be expected to contain the newspaper's opinion. But in this case, the editorial writer announced his impartiality in the race between a 63-year-old Republican businessman who owned a printing company and a 34-year-old Democratic state senator who had served on several important legislative committees. The editorialist concluded:

> From the 10 candidates who sought mayoralty nominations in Tuesday's primary, we think the voters chose the best of the lot and thereby set the stage for what should be an absorbing and constructive final campaign.[41]

But how had he characterized the two candidates?

> The basic issue, in fact, resolves itself into a matter of choosing between a quietly solid progressive wise in the fundamentals of public policies and an energetic and photogenic liberal willing to experiment in untried areas.[42]

That neatly pits quiet, solid wisdom against a glamor boy's untried experimenting. Try loading the summary in the other direction:

> The basic issue, in fact, resolves itself into a matter of choosing between an inarticulate capitalist with a slavish devotion to past policies, and an energetic and experienced state senator who is willing to try imaginative solutions to stubborn problems.

Sometimes, because of the values of a society, words are loaded in ways we hardly notice until they're forcefully brought to our attention.

Women's rights activists lately have been quarreling with the way that many terms are ordinarily expressed in the masculine. This book, for example, uses newsmen when it means both men and women. That isn't unthinking usage, either.

The authors needed a familiar term which would include print and electronic news, and which would also cover reporters, editors and others directly involved in the news process. To accomplish all that we settled, uneasily, for the standard grammar book rule that the masculine can be used to cover both sexes.

Journalist is a less sexually biased word, but it refers only to print media. Reporter and editor are too narrow to cover the wider range of newsroom jobs.

Other terms may develop. The Associated Press now officially calls its female employees newswomen, and some women's right organizations have opted for person: chairperson, congressperson, newsperson.[43]

Mr., Miss, and Mrs. are also under siege. A man's designation doesn't indicate whether he's married, so why should a woman's? Some women now use Ms., while others prefer no title at all.

Others point to the standard marriage ceremony, which concludes with the words, "I now pronounce you man and wife." Not man and woman; not husband and wife; but man and wife, which seems to turn the woman into a piece of man's property.

That's what a lot of the complaint is about, the historically subservient role of women which has been reinforced through many centuries of loaded language: women as second-class workers, as housewives without identities separate from their families, as sex objects.

"Betty Garrett is 35, looks about 25 and sits like 16, her high-breasted figure poured into a turquoise knit dress, one well-shaped leg tucked under her," the story began.[44]

Take a guess at why Betty Garrett was interviewed. Model? Go-go dancer? Hardly. She's a top-flight reporter, a feature writer for the Columbus, Ohio, Citizen-Journal. The story appeared in Editor & Publisher magazine, which frequently prints articles about writers and editors. Normally, such stories begin with a comment on the significance of the writer's work. Eventually, after the physical inventory, this one got around to that subject, too.

The story was not written "before people knew better." It appeared in July, 1971, right in the midst of a barrage of information about women's roles in society.

Furthermore, the story was written by a woman.

In another case, Dianne Witkowski, a consumer's news specialist for Chicago Today, testified before a committee of the Illinois Senate on the perfectly serious subject of sales taxes. Her own paper topped the story with a photo and a cutline which described her as "Shapely Miss Witkowski, in a lavender minidress."[45]

Lois Wille, Pulitzer prize-winning reporter for the Chicago Daily News, calls this the our-girl-as-a-sex-symbol treatment.

"For years," she says, "the Daily News had a policy of having one female as general assignment reporter. She was 'our girl.' When she left, a new one was drafted from the woman's department.

"For decades, as far back as the Hecht–MacArthur era, most Chicago papers had a woman around to do foolish things: Sky-dive, collect garbage, ride a race horse. 'Our Girl in a Mental Hospital,' said the headlines. Or, 'Our Girl Meets Cary Grant."[46]

"Our girl" is a put-down, much the same as the tokenism of hiring one display-window Negro.[47] And many women today believe that such actions and use of language reinforce prejudices—a complaint far from new in the history of protest movements.

Studies of textbooks illuminate the charge. Author and professor Florence Howe reports:

> Late or early, in catalogues or on shelves, the boys of children's books are active and capable, the girls passive and in trouble . . . Ask yourself whether you would be surprised to find the following social contexts in a fifth-grade arithmetic textbook:
>
> 1. girls playing marbles; boys sewing;
> 2. girls earning money, building things, and going places; boys buying ribbons for a sewing project;
> 3. girls working at physical activities; boys babysitting and, you guessed it, sewing.
>
> Of course you would be surprised—so would I. What I have done here is to reverse the sexes as found in a fifth-grade arithmetic text.[48].

Despite the limitations built into the society and into the language, a few women succeed in "men's" jobs. Then what happens?

Israeli Prime Minister Golda Meir may be "Her Excellency," but in an article reporting on rumors of her romance with a wealthy Californian, a mid-east correspondent referred to her four times as just plain "Golda."[49] Nowhere in the story was she identified as the Prime Minister of Israel.

The writer defended himself by pointing out that the ninth paragraph included the comment, "Maybe when she resigns as premier she will be willing to remarry."[50]

But how often has anyone seen a similar first-name-only usage in a news story about Britain's Prime Minister Edward Heath, who also happens to be unmarried, or about any other prime minister?

Pow! Zonk! Bam!

Rock music, aircraft engines, and ordinary highway traffic, at the scale we now endure, threaten to harm our hearing, fog our brains, and unsettle our nervous systems.

As the decibels have heated up, we have also suffered a rise in the temperature level of language. It's rather like trying to sort through the messages of ever-larger neon signs, each one trying so hard to outscream the others that none stands forth in the garish blur.

While intemperate language is nothing new, today we have the means to hurl it faster and farther than ever before, and more people to do the hurling.

Fascist . . . racist . . . pig . . . hippie . . . honky . . . sexist.

Is every movement that dubs itself revolutionary truly that momentous? Is every cause that claims the title really the key to survival?

Can every advertised product which makes the boast actually be the biggest, best, whitest, brightest, least polluting, most money saving?

Columnist Russell Baker of the *New York Times* has remarked that if every minor irritation now is called agony, what then is left for the truly agonizing?[51]

Television newsman Harry Reasoner has observed that when every crisis is described as grave, a plain old crisis doesn't seem to carry any urgency.[52]

And in the political season which always seems to be upon us, can all those politicians who orate the answers to our problems actually produce any?

The extravagance of language truly can be perplexing. Consider the mailman interviewed by CBS television newsman Roger Mudd after hearing a campaign speech by Senator Fred Harris of Oklahoma. The fellow wasn't much impressed.

"All he's doing is talking about humanity," the voter told Mudd, "and the problem's much deeper than that."[53]

That dubious listener may have been trying to apply what Russell Baker calls the lie-discount mechanism.[54] Baker figures that the man-in-the-street, just to maintain his cool, is forced to discount 80 percent or more of advertising claims, and much of political oratory as well.

But if we have reached the point of having to discount so much before even examining the message capsuled in the words, haven't we hyped our everyday language beyond effectiveness? The question is a severe one for the newsman and the news consumer who, except for news pictures, deal entirely in language.

On the one hand the newsman knows that he must not overstate. On the other, he knows that he cannot adequately report on a war or a prison riot or a campus demonstration without also reporting the language of those events.

The perplexities can be judged from the number of times commentators and columnists and editorial writers talk and write about language problems.

If our words hung in air like the talk balloons spoken from the mouths of cartoon characters, we could legislate against the garish clutter, the way screaming neon has been purged in such communities as Carmel, California; Williamsburg, Virginia; and Princeton, New Jersey. Small, precise signboards have not impeded communication or commerce in such places.

But while berserk signs can be halted by ordinance, language is not so easily controlled. First Amendment guarantees of free speech and free press may stop short of allowing a man to yell "fire" in a crowded theater, but they rightly do not permit close restrictions on language, even in a good cause.

The newman's difficult task is to use the language with as much precision and as little hysteria as possible. The consumer's job is to be wary of imprecision and extravagance in the language of the news, and to complain when it's foisted on him.

Chapter 11

Miss Peach by Mell Lazarus. Courtesy Publishers-Hall Syndicate.

When Rights Collide:
Information Versus Privacy

The two rights showed up in the scripture of American law a century apart, but they appeared at all only because each must contend at close quarters with the other.

Freedom of the press, a constitutional guarantee, is not possible if an absolute right of privacy can turn aside inquiry.

The right of privacy, a complex legal weave, has little meaning if the news media wield an absolute right to intrude publicity on anyone, any time.

Never separated very far, these rights sometimes jostle together unnecessarily, as when the news media come into someone's life for a story lacking in genuine news value, or when a government declares the privilege of privacy in what should be public knowledge.

Other times—when the news media cover the courtroom, and when government gathers information for the intricacies of modern rule by bureaucracy —the rights inevitably have to collide, like locomotives on the same track. The question then is how great the impact of collision has to be.

Privacy Comes—and Goes

It's 1890, and Benjamin Harrison presides over a nation which will welcome Idaho and Wyoming as states this year. No radios, no television, no electric guitars punctuate the air. No jet planes embroider the sky; no cars belch noise and fumes across the landscape. The machine age has arrived at the factories, but nevertheless a relatively calm country sprawls the width of the continent. Americans, almost sixty-three million of them, count space and time on their side.

An exception in the still portrait is a shrieking metropolitan press led by publisher Joseph Pulitzer and his *New York World's* peephole reporting of sex, scandal, and gossip. Pulitzer arrived in New York journalism on May 11, 1883, with front page features about a wronged servant girl, a hanging in

Pittsburgh, a riot in Haiti, a Wall Street speculator, and an interview with a condemned slayer.[1] By 1890, he is polishing human interest techniques, while William Randolph Hearst hones them even more adroitly in San Francisco.[2]

Some readers, however, are disgusted, and revulsion brings a potent appeal for a new right—the right of privacy—which at once sets a collision course with the constitutionally guaranteed freedom of the press.

The call for legal recognition of privacy comes from two Boston lawyers, Louis D. Brandeis, who later is named to the Supreme Court of the U.S., and Samuel D. Warren.[3] They grump in the pages of the *Harvard Law Review* that the excesses of the press, "overstepping in every direction the obvious bounds of propriety and decency," make it essential for the law to recognize a right of privacy which will go beyond libel law and protect the citizen's right to be let alone.[4]

Strangely, from the viewpoint of the crowded twentieth century, English common law doesn't mention privacy, the Declaration of Independence doesn't list it as one of the inalienables, and the U.S. Constitution fails to recite its virtues.

Brandeis and Warren set the doctrine under way, however, and it ran an erratic course of victories and setbacks in courtrooms until June, 1971, when a Supreme Court decision struck stunningly at legal theory on both libel and privacy.[5] The justices did it to enhance press freedom.

The Court ruled that no one involved in an event of public interest can collect damages for libel—printed or broadcast material that robs him of his good reputation—even if what is said about him is untrue, unless he can prove the statements were calculated lies or made with reckless disregard for whether or not they were.

The case began when police raided the home of George A. Rosenbloom, a Philadelphia distributor of nudist magazines, confiscated about a thousand publications, and charged him with possessing obscene literature. Radio station WIP covered the story and reported a crackdown on "the smut literature racket."

Rosenbloom was acquitted of the charge in a state court after the judge instructed the jury that, as a matter of law, the nudist magazines weren't obscene. Then Rosenbloom sued WIP for libel, claiming his reputation had been damaged and he had been forced out of business by WIP's references to him in several broadcasts as a "smut distributor" and "girlie book peddler."

He won. The jury said the radio station had to pay him $25,000 in actual losses and $725,000 as punishment for sloppy reporting and failing to check the facts. The trial judge reduced the punitive damages to $250,000, after which a court of appeals wiped out the whole judgment. The Supreme Court agreed with the court of appeals, on the basis of a radical shift in libel law which had begun in 1964.

At that 1964 turning point, in the *New York Times* v. Sullivan decision the Supreme Court had ruled that since free discussion of government is so important, public officials are not automatically entitled to good reputations as everyone else.[6] In subsequent cases, the category has been expanded to include public figures,[7] then political candidates,[8] and finally, in the Rosenbloom case, anyone involved in an event of public interest.

Justice William J. Brennan Jr. said in the majority opinion on the Rosenbloom case that:

> In libel cases we view an erroneous verdict for the plaintiff as most serious. Not only does it mulct the defendant for an innocent misstatement—the three-quarter-million dollar jury verdict in this case could rest on such an error—but the possibility of such error . . . would create a strong impetus towards self-censorship which the First Amendment cannot tolerate.
>
> We are aware that the press has, on occasion, grossly abused the freedom it is given by the Constitution. All must deplore such excesses. In an ideal world the responsibility of the press would match the freedom and public trust given it. But from the earliest days of our history, this free society, dependent as it is for its survival upon a vigorous free press, has tolerated some abuse.[9]

And what of privacy, which, in this case, was closely involved? Justices Thurgood Marshall and Potter Stewart, dissenting, called the decision inadequate to protect the reputations of millions of Americans who live their lives in obscurity "from unjustified invasion and wrongful hurt."[10]

Ramsey Clark, the former U.S. attorney general who argued the case for Rosenbloom, warned that the ruling would apply to every future libel suit, "for experience demonstrates that the media, not the courts, determine who and what is newsworthy. Since public curiosity is boundless, particularly when skillfully stimulated, so is the concept of newsworthiness. Virtually any event in a man's life may surface, after the fact, as newsworthy."[11]

The majority opinion of the Court contained a similar significant comment: "Voluntarily or not, we are all public men to some degree."[12]

The Court majority indicated clearly that freedom of the press will be weighted more heavily than an individual's right to privacy or to a good reputation. Courts can shift their opinions, but at the moment freedom of the press is riding the high side of the seesaw.

It comes down to this. The individual's right to privacy from media intrusion depends today, much as it did before 1890, largely on the ethics and decency of newsmen.

Stories That Shouldn't Be Told

Blind Judge Gets License to Remarry, the headline reads.[13]
Well, asks the wary reader, aren't judges supposed to remarry? Or is it

only blind judges whose remarriage seems so remarkable to the headline writer?

The illogic amplifies in the first sentence: "Luis Miranda, the state's only blind judge, has filed for a new marriage license only 10 days after divorcing his wife."

The next paragraph reveals that the ex-wife is also blind, while in the eighth and, mercifully, final paragraph we learn that none of their five children is.

In between are trickled the tidbits of information that Miranda worked as a court stenographer during the day while attending law school at night, and that hard work and a political appointment propelled him to a $32,000-a-year judgeship. Close by is an inspirational statement, borrowed from an earlier story, in which Miranda tells how to succeed despite handicaps.

How? Think positive and work hard.

This meandering account contains a grab bag of hoary clichés about human interest: handicapped / minority / married to a handicapped / minority / had normal children / but didn't live happily ever after / now plans to try again only ten—*ten*—days after divorce.

It's remarkable that the family dog—there must have been one—was omitted.

Why was this printed? Gossipy stories loaded with innuendo about people's private lives get read, that's why, even if they are badly written.

To their credit, many news outlets strive to weed out such schlock, and compassionate newsmen cultivate a sense of fair play by continually asking whether the public's right to know is involved, or merely public curiosity.

A newsroom rule of thumb says that every story should be absolutely accurate and that the newsman should have a good motive for using it. Defining "good motive" is the tough part.

Unfortunately, no one has yet programmed a computer astute enough to gulp the raw materials of a story and flash *TILT* if they invade privacy. And human computers considering a story may calculate differing conclusions.

The aftermath of Chappaquiddick, 1969: Is Senator Edward Kennedy entitled to any privacy? He goes to a party on Chappaquiddick Island in Massachusetts, then drives his car off a bridge and a young secretary drowns.[14] Is that information vital to the public interest, as opposed to being interesting to the public?

Newsmen disagree. Some say the senator's private life should be just that—private. Others contend that private actions are tied to public performance. The bare structure of that Kennedy story could be told in a dozen paragraphs. The hundreds of thousands of words actually published and broadcast mount up into a case study of varied news policies. The Chappaquiddick coverage also shows news values, discussed in chapter two, interacting and conflicting with ethical standards.

Not all invasion of privacy questions are so compelling or weighty. Consider an event as pleasant as the marriage of New York Mayor John Lindsay's daughter in June, 1970. No press and no pictures, said the mayor in fatherly style; this is private.[15]

Much press and many pictures, responded the *New York Daily News.* The newspaper first masterminded a helicopter assault that was ultimately scrapped because of bad weather. Next, a photographer was assigned to take advance photos of the mayor's official residence, Gracie Mansion. The results confirmed the photo editor's hunch that a three-man commando operation was needed. And so it was done, with one photographer perched on a nearby rooftop and two others hoisting tripods over the mansion's 8-foot stone walls. All used Nikon-F motorized cameras, and the trio kept in communication by walkie talkie.

"My camera was fastened upside down by a C-clamp on a Unipod which telescoped up to five feet," one of the cameramen explained. "With the penta-prism viewer removed from the camera, I had as good a periscope as any U-boat commander."[16] His shot of the bridal couple made page one.

"This carefully planned, coordinated communication setup paid off," deadpanned newspaperdom's trade journal, *Editor & Publisher.*[17] The photographers were congratulated by *Daily News* executives for a job well done.

Editor & Publisher's letters column bristled with outrage from fellow newsmen. "It seems to me," wrote Professor Ralph Holsinger of Indiana University, the former managing editor of the *Cincinnati Enquirer,* "the *Daily News* team's assault on the privacy of Mayor Lindsay's daughter illustrates one of the reasons the press is in trouble today. It merely confirms the opinion of those who think newsmen spend their time snooping into things that are none of their business."[18]

Whether or not the statistic is related, the *New York Daily News,* a tabloid that does run heavily to human interest stories, sells more copies each day than any other U.S. newspaper—more than two million.

A judge, a senator, a mayor: public people. How much private life can they and their families expect? Libel and privacy decisions in the courts say they can demand little, but news organizations vary significantly in what they will allow.

How about an anonymous citizen's private life? Here's a story about one who asked for publicity, and got it in a national wire service feature:

WASHINGTON—This is to inform former mailman Ronald Zilch, wherever he is, that Sadie loves him and wants him to come back.

It wasn't you, Ronnie, that she was upset with that last morning at the post office. It was just that her head ached from sorting mail. That's why she wouldn't talk to you.

"He never gave me a chance to explain," Sadie related to her congressman, in the first of several letters he has received about the ill-starred post office romance.

"He stopped coming to work," she wrote, "and they dismissed him for excessive absence. He became despondent and left his parents' home."

That was more than two years ago and Sadie Bronwin has been directing letters to congressmen and newspapers ever since, seeking help in tracking him down. "He is a human being and wherever he is he still reads newspapers."

The Sadie Bronwin file in the congressman's office is getting fat now, despite his insistence he cannot ask newspapers and press associations to publish her appeal.

"I am sorry you are so unsympathetic to the humane act of having the press inform former letter carrier Ronald Zilch that his fiancee, Sadie Bronwin, loves him and he should return to me and his family," she said in her latest letter.

But Sadie wasn't giving up. "I again beseech you," she closed the letter, "to aid us with our great and desperate personal problem. Please ask the English language news media to help us communicate with Mr. Ronald Zilch."[19]

Along with the story came a wirephoto of the woman, which defies kindly description.

But she asked—begged—for publicity. Isn't providing it a public service? No. The whole tone of the story is wrong. It snickers; it pokes fun at heartache, and if Ronnie is on the lam, it certainly invades *his* privacy.

Alas. On a busy news day, with too little time to consider, one of the authors rescued this story from the wire and reflexively slapped it onto page one, under the headline **Come Back, Ronnie, Wherever You Are**, to brighten an otherwise gray front page. Not with the photo, she says defensively, but the decision to use the story at all was the wrong one. To avoid repeating the error, the names in the story above (and in the case of the remarrying blind judge) have been changed, and references to the hometown deleted. The rest of the story stands as written and, lamentably, published.

Many cliched words and pictures of tragedy should be forgotten, too: mothers crying over lost children, widows weeping at mine shafts, dead gunmen's relatives and neighbors observing what good and quiet boys they were.

On the other hand, few newsmen want to rob the news of three-dimensional people, and broadcasters and writers have been working particularly hard during the last decade or so to make complicated events come to life in terms of their impact on individuals. So you may read about the welfare system, not in statistics alone, but in a story that starts with a welfare family's dilemma.

The boundary between humanizing the news and invading privacy is fuzzy and slick, much like driving through fog on an icy road, where any small mistake in judgment may lead to disaster. Newsmen, as noted, sometimes make mistakes. It's true, too, that the public's right to know is defined a little differently in each person's head.

What a news consumer can do is to judge the day-to-day tone of his news sources. Although he will disagree with some of their judgments, he should expect, overall, as much respect for each person's privacy as is consistent with the public's need to know. When the two collide, as they sometimes will, most newsmen will respond as did the majority of the Supreme Court in the Rosenbloom case—for the public's right.

All Hush-hush Along the Potomac

A law exists, the most careful and earnest law of its kind this country has ever had, to deal with the governmental tendency to keep matters from public scrutiny.

Called the Freedom of Information Act, it went into effect in 1967. The law goes step by step into methods of procuring information from government agencies, and provides that a person who can't get information to which he is entitled can go into court to enjoin a federal employee from withholding that information.[20]

In the summer of 1971, a 47-volume study of the Vietnam war began bulking into the news like the peaks of an iceberg. The New York Times published three installments of its analysis of the "Pentagon Papers," then was restrained by court order from publishing any more until legal arguments could be heard.[21] The Washington Post also came out with stories drawn from the same study, and was just as promptly stopped by court order.

The U.S. Department of Justice was seeking an injunction against any further publication of material from the "Pentagon Papers," which were classified "top secret—sensitive." The government brief cited the Freedom of Information Act as justification for keeping the "Papers" out of the papers. This argument read:

> Congress has recognized the authority of the President to protect the secrecy of information relating to foreign relations and national defense. The first exemption to the Freedom of Information Act, which generally provides for making public information in the hands of the government, specifically exempts from the statute's provisions matters that are—(1) specifically required by Executive order to be kept secret in the interest of national defense or foreign policy.[22]

The argument of information versus privacy takes many intricate paths, but none more sinuous than this question of the government's right to private conduct of affairs. Parading an anti-secrecy law before the bench to justify top secret classification for an historical study of foreign policy is merely one of the supple ironies which can be found.

Two other instances are close at hand:

The Supreme Court decision on the "Pentagon Papers" both resolved and didn't resolve the case. Yes, the *Times* and the *Post* were allowed to publish their material drawn from the classified volumes, *but* five of the nine justices suggested that after publication, there might be grounds for prosecution on grounds of violating national security rules.[23]

As for the Freedom of Information Act itself, *yes*, this bill is a long-awaited key to closed files, *but* it hasn't been much used by newsmen.[24]

On the banks of the Potomac, or wherever else government and media dwell together, law alone can't contain the issue of information versus privacy. Newsman or official may bring legislation in on his side at one time or another, but the continuing story is a contest of attitudes.

In the best of all possible bureaucratic worlds, government secrecy might not matter so much. So long as human communities are at odds with each other, there is an argument for some secrecy as a measure of self-defense. But keeping matters confidential soon turns into a habit of regarding a public office as a haven of privacy.

Even a government of the highest intentions and most upright public servants can persuade itself that secret maneuvering is necessary and proper. Tasks go smoother on the quiet, the element of surprise can be used, failure is less costly that way, the decisions are too complex to be debated out on the cobblestones. The self-persuasion adds up impressively, and most of it comes in cozy reasoning that tells a person he is only doing his job the best way he can.

The newsman's constant rankle, and the news consumer in this instance should share it just as irritably, is that officials get carried away with themselves.

Most of the dubious rites of privacy go on in government in the name of national security. Others are there—well, because they've always been there. For example: by custom, a President leaving office takes with him his "presidential papers." In our modern era of a powerful presidency, these records amount to a gigantic historical treasure.

Lyndon Johnson's archives in the presidential library in Austin, Texas, total more than 30 million sheets of paper, invaluable data which it took a caravan of trucks to carry away when Johnson left the White House.[25] Every modern President who has lived into retirement—Truman, Eisenhower and Johnson—has written from such files his own version of history, meanwhile classifying portions of his presidential records to keep anyone else from research in them for as long as 25 years.

Presidential libraries have become an extreme case, but secretiveness lives on and on throughout government offices. This habit of secrecy would be silly if its captives were in a less vital line of work. But they are in the business of running the country for us, and a few days after the "Pentagon Papers" hit the news, a former Pentagon censor told something of how his colleagues view that task. William G. Florence, who had been a security classification policy officer in the Department of Defense, said "hundreds of thousands" of federal employees over the years have classified an estimated 20 million documents. Florence added that in his opinion, 99.5 percent of that total could safely be made public.[26]

Into the endless contest between official and newsman came the Freedom of Information law in 1967.

As you might guess, a measure which the government can wave smugly as justification for keeping the "Pentagon Papers" hush-hush is not the perfect antidote for official secrecy. The FoI law ends with a list of exceptions—some vague and limber, such as the proviso about national defense secrets and one about paperwork "related solely to the internal personnel rules and practices of an agency";[27] others legally tight and humane, such as the protection of "personnel and medical files and similar files the disclosure of which would constitute a clearly unwarranted invasion of personal privacy."[28]

The effects of the act haven't been spectacular. One of Ralph Nader's task forces charged in 1969 that "the Freedom of Information act which came in on a wave of liberating rhetoric is being undermined by a riptide of bureaucratic ingenuity." Nader's Raiders said in many cases government officials were finding ways to slip around the law, while the news media were not pressing the bureaucrats hard enough.[29] Sigma Delta Chi, the professional journalistic society, in its 1970 report admitted that "newsmen do not appear to have been the principal users" of the law. SDX added, perhaps a bit defensively:

". . . the mere existence of the law—and the ability to remind uncommunicative officials that it exists and contains court remedies—often is sufficient to enable the reporter to pry loose the desired records or information without having to resort to the courts."[30]

Earlier, we said the issue of how much privacy the government is entitled to is a contest of attitudes. That contest can go on endlessly, through laws and court cases and past censors' stamps and newsmen's pilfered photocopies, but it boils down to a pair of quotes produced by the case of the "Pentagon Papers."

1. Robert Mardian, head of the Internal Security Division of the U.S. Department of Justice:

   "I couldn't believe that a responsible newspaper would print top-secret sensitive documents."[31]
2. Neil Sheehan of the *New York Times:*

   "This history is public property, not the property of Lyndon Johnson or Robert McNamara or the Bundy brothers or any other public figure involved in the Vietnam war. The story belongs to the people. They paid for it with their lives and treasure. As far as I'm concerned, they own it and have the right to know of its contents."[32]

The Snoops from Sam City

When a newsman invades someone's privacy the result is on the record, in print or on a broadcast script which can be read or heard, evaluated and protested. By their nature, then, news outlets provide a forthright accounting of their own activities.

Other intruders don't.

Forthrightness, in fact, is an enemy to their task. Their forays are the type of undercover threat to individual rights that can be understood only through widespread coverage in the news. Also, the tactics used frequently weaken forthrightness by a form of sabotage against consumer's trust in newsmen themselves. Despite such mauling of both the citizen's rights and freedom of the press, the news media generally have not covered themselves with glory in sleuthing the snoops.

Prying into private lives goes on daily as part of the big-business big-government syndrome now holding sway in this society. An American with any alertness at all knows now that many businesses collect information about citizens; that some is illegal and some is inaccurate. But from the confines of his own concerns, he can probably see just the top of the mound. Only when he is refused credit will he learn that his credit records are wrong, that a fumble some office functionary made—in secret, naturally—counts for more than does paying bills conscientiously on time. Only accidentally does he discover that an insurance company evaluates him by asking the folks next door about his moral character. Only occasionally will a classic of corporate spying break into the open, such as the unusual spectacle of the president of General Motors apologizing before a congressional committee for GM's snooping into the private life of consumer advocate Ralph Nader.[33]

Though a few cases are documented each year in the news media, whatever else lurks in the business files has been exceedingly difficult to determine. And if private business threatens the citizen who values his privacy, far more unsettling is the complex of government agencies bent on charting the course of his life.

The point is as lofty or as clipped as you want to make it. In terms Thomas Jefferson might parse approvingly: The official quest for information marauds out from the national capital over all considerations of privacy and tramples the Bill of Rights.

In a phrase Elliot Horne used in *The Hiptionary:* "Sam City is the main vein. What shakes Sam rattles the whole bit."[34]

Beginning in the fall of 1970, Senator Ervin of North Carolina, a political conservative with strict constitutional views, convened the Senate Subcommittee on Constitutional Rights to investigate the investigators—federal agencies that collect and disseminate intelligence.[35]

The proceedings should be read and evaluated in their entirety, but start with just one case: the documentation in December, 1970 that the Army, which is *never* supposed to engage in domestic spying, was keeping under surveillance hundreds of law-abiding political figures, including Senator Adlai Stevenson of Illinois.

Back in January, Christopher Pyle, a former Army Intelligence officer, had spelled out details of the Army's domestic espionage system. "Today," he wrote, "the Army maintains files on the membership, ideology, programs and practices of virtually every activist political group in the country." These, he carefully pointed out, included groups and individuals absolutely nonviolent and law abiding who merely were exercising their constitutional rights.[36]

According to Pyle and others, military undercover agents sometimes posed as news cameramen and reporters. The same subterfuge has been standard practice for countless police departments keeping tab on demonstrations of all sorts. News veterans who have encountered such pseudo-newsmen vehemently protest the deception because it can utterly destroy any reporter's credibility and access to news sources. Who will talk to a reporter who may instead be a secret investigator? Staffers of the *Washington Star* pledged to expose, on the spot, any secret agent they found pretending to be a newsman.[37] Other protests from the media have been loud in their outrage, but probably not as efficient as the *Star* brand of direct action.

Newsmen cannot safely assume the fakes have eyes only for other targets. The spying can easily enough focus on them, too, especially in filing away information about which newsmen may have material worth subpoenaing in any eventual court action. Critic Nat Hentoff has chastised the news media for not filing suit to find out how many newsmen are themselves being monitored by government agents.[38]

After Pyle's disclosures of the espionage system the military uses on its own country, Army officials promised to destroy the files and tapes of domestic political activities. But the Ervin committee's hearings indicated that hadn't been done.[39] In fact, the spying continued. This revelation and others demonstrated several points:

1. Most citizens have failed to make the connection between other people's civil rights and their own. Unless the snooping has roiled their own lives, citizens haven't responded with the sense of outrage which would pressure the snooping to a richly-deserved end.
2. Few news organizations have bestirred themselves for investigative reporting on the subject, and not many have handled cleanly and extensively the

stories readymade for them by legislative hearings and citizens' rights groups.

3. Few public officials, including legislators, have taken a serious interest. New York Congressman Ogden Reid, one in the handful of legislators actively critical of the intelligence gathering, points out both the dangerous ineptness of the surveillance and the dangerous inattention of elected leaders. "It looked like amateur night at its worst" Reid said of Army surveillance.[40]

"Sometimes the computer got mixed up between the object and subject," he said. "There's a report of a general who stopped to take a look at an incident and sent in a report, and the computer made a mistake and decided he was the suspect."

The most disturbing fact of all, Reid stresses, has been civilian acceptance of the spying: "The Army plan was sent to 319 civilians, including all 50 governors, and none of them blew the whistle."[41]

The Ervin hearings during 1970 and 1971 did spark additional interest, although the best coverage still came from news organizations which previously had been most alert. From what sampling of the news media we have been able to do, it seems plain the much-criticized "elitist" metropolitan press has done the sturdiest job of handling the snoopery story. Smaller papers which ordinarily trumpet loud noises about the American heritage haven't had much to say against the secret raids on the citizen's private affairs. The unvigilant could take their cues from a few of the outspoken critics. From such editorializing as the *Saturday Review's*, for instance:

> What is most disturbing about the recent disclosures, however, is what they suggest about the pervasiveness of domestic political surveillance. Even if the Army were to get out of the domestic intelligence business entirely—and there is little likelihood that it will—we would still be subject to the activities of hundreds of other agencies, governmental and private, would still have to bear the suspicion that the files, the tapes, and the computer banks keep growing, and would still live in a country where privacy from official intrusion is increasingly jeopardized by a network of interlocking data storage systems that collect everything from credit and tax records and Social Security numbers through data on criminal arrests, political affiliations and personal associations.[42]

After Senator Edmund Muskie of Maine released a document showing that the FBI spied on environmentalists' Earth Day activities in 1970, a *New York Times* editorial reflected:

> When a Senator of the United States makes public one of these documents and rightly complains about such practices, the Attorney General blandly says that there might have been dangerous radicals at these meetings. The fact that

many people passively accept this excuse shows how corrupted American standards of liberty have become.

No one should forget that when the most radical dissenter speaks at a public meeting, he is only exercising a constitutional right. But the Attorney General says violence might have broken out. This rationalization is itself an affront to truth since FBI agents leave peacekeeping in such situations to the local police.[43]

The *St. Louis Post-Dispatch* published an overview of the state of liberty in the U.S. In that *Post-Dispatch* series, the chilling phrase "post-Constitutional America" emerged.[44] The chief counsel for the Senate Subcommittee on Constitutional Rights commented on the meaning of post-Constitutional:

"When it becomes known that the government is taking notice of people who engage in certain kinds of activity, people will stop doing these things regardless of whether or not they're perfectly legal. The First Amendment goes out the window if people don't do things they think the government doesn't approve of. And at this point, you're well on the way to thought control."[45]

Political philosophers and historians have documented across centuries and around the world that rights do not stand in isolation—that yours are threatened unless the same rules apply to "that radical hippie," "that racist bigot," and "everyone-else-I-don't-like." Most of the quotations used in this section are snippets from the case against government snooping; whatever the directions of his political leanings, the news consumer should be riled enough that he'll do some digging of his own, and will also check his news outlets to see if they are reporting—adequately or at all—the issue of intrusion into private matters.

Chapter 12

"Generally comprehensive and incisive, but with an excessively negative tone over-all, wouldn't you say?"

How Do You Know If It's Right?

Dear Sir:

    You cur! . . .

This forthright start of a letter to the editor comes from back in the legends of newspapering, along with horsewhippings of newsmen by even angrier readers. Any follow-through on the news today is likely to be more subdued—we don't lay tongue much any more to such stylish denunciations as "cur," and horsewhips are scarce—but the consumer can still cue in with a little effort.

He can start by reminding himself of the basic problem in knowing whether a story is accurate or not: the news doesn't hold still. Often a story is open-ended—open to amplification or correction or rebuttal after it appears in print or on the air.

So, the consumer stays alert for further developments, for what happens next at that far end of a story. He keeps track of how individual newsmen and news outlets handle stories, to see whether their record of performance is reliable. He watches for added chapters from news figures, competing media, the original reporter himself. He turns to critics who watch how the media are doing. All this he watches and listens to, and fits in any later items which set a story right.

Sherlocking the Day's News

A consumer who has not yet learned to get the most mileage out of news is apt to read or listen to a report uncritically, accepting whatever his laziest brainwaves tell him, and believing he has the news straight.

Not likely. First of all, the consumer extracts from what he hears or sees the things he wants to believe—those that match his biases. Beyond that, he may unconsciously distort the message to fit his expectations, or he may block out whole sections of it.

On a crisp October evening in 1938, thousands of Americans panicked as their radios crackled with reports that Martian invaders, landing near Grovers Mill, New Jersey, had incinerated defenders with strange weapons and were heading toward New York City.[1]

The "invasion" was science fiction in a news format, an updated production of the H. G. Wells classic, *The War of the Worlds*. Before the show went on the air, the script editor had worried that listeners wouldn't react well to the tale and would flip the dial. On top of that, CBS had demanded thirty-eight script changes to make the plot less realistic.

Nevertheless, before the program was over, people were digging World War I gas masks out of closets and calling their priests for confession. Sailors on leave in New York were recalled to their ships. The Associated Press was sending explanatory bulletins to its members. Cars raced along roads between New York and Philadelphia as the fear-stricken sought escape. Around the country, people reported *seeing* Martians.

Incredibly, the terror erupted despite the obvious contrivances of the plot and this clear introduction:

> The Columbia Broadcasting System and its affiliated stations present Orson Welles and the Mercury Theater on the Air in *The War of the Worlds* by H. G. Wells. Ladies and gentlemen: the director of the Mercury Theater and star of these broadcasts, Orson Welles.

The fictional nature of the program was announced three more times: before and after the station break, and at the end.[2]

Sociologists, professional and amateur, had a field day offering explanations. Some said that Americans were so worried about the Depression at home and war abroad that they were ripe for panic. Whatever the reason, thousands of people did block out the explicit statements and many clues that they were listening to fiction.

The consumer must also worry about more than his own slanting or blocking as he tries for accuracy, for the reporter too has viewpoints that will affect the way he constructs a story. Two honest, well trained reporters, covering the same event, may relay entirely correct information, but from significantly different angles.

During the city's 1970 boat show, *Chicago Today* told its readers, **Boat industry finds clear, rich sailing,** while on the same afternoon the *Chicago Daily News* headlined, **It's rough sale(ing) in boating industry.**[3]

The reporters had interviewed and quoted different industry analysts whose estimates were, indeed, as far apart as the headlines indicate.

In St. Louis, the *Post-Dispatch* informed its readers, **Environment Magazine in Financial Trouble,** but the *Globe-Democrat* galloped to the rescue the next day with **Environment Magazine Solves Financial Crisis.**[4] In this case, the solution was illusory. The magazine promptly folded.

Whether the subject is a rock music festival, the Democratic national convention, or the international monetary system, the consumer who hears and reads the greatest diversity of reports about an event should have the best chance of understanding its many sides and drawing his own conclusions.

So a cardinal rule of news is that the consumer needs more than a single version of any story which is important to him. That's one reason why each community needs a variety of news outlets.

It's vital, too, to understand that television and radio newscasts function primarily as headline services, from which the consumer must grab information in mid-air. He cannot go back and re-read electronic reports, and so he distorts them more easily than printed stories. Nevertheless, repeated surveys indicate that most Americans point to television as their primary source of news, and far too many as their *only* source.

The consumer also needs to watch out for what's said tomorrow, and next week, about subjects making news today. He should develop a habit of suspending judgment, or at least of holding his conclusions loosely, knowing that additional reports may change the picture.

In 1969 a drilling platform blowout spawned a four million gallon oil slick that contaminated forty miles of prime recreational and residential coastline near Santa Barbara, California.[5] As indignation mounted, the Senate subcommittee on air and water pollution summoned Union Oil president Fred Hartley to defend his company's offshore drilling practices.

The next day the *New York Times* story quoted Hartley as saying, "I'm amazed at the publicity for the loss of a few birds."

That evening David Brinkley repeated the quote on NBC. The next day the *Wall Street Journal* printed it. It appeared in an outraged editorial in the *Washington Post*, and the *New York Times* used it again the following Sunday in its "Week in Review." *Time* magazine quoted it in its February 14 issue.

"Lord, I wish he hadn't said that," mourned another Union Oil official.

Well, he hadn't.

What happened was that the *New York Times* reporter, Warren Weaver, Jr., had been called out of the subcommittee hearing and, when he returned, the *Christian Science Monitor's* Robert Cahn filled him in on what had happened.[6] Cahn later figured out that, in the noise of the hearing room, Weaver mistook his quick paraphrase for a direct quote.

Hartley's statement, as later released in the official transcript of the hearing, read: "I think we have to look at these problems relatively. I am always tremendously impressed at the publicity that death of birds receives versus the loss of people in our country."

He made the comment while explaining the oil company's efforts to clean up what he himself called the desecration of the California coastline.

"Sixteen of our top research people were sent to Santa Barbara to establish a bird cleaning and care center and have been very successful," he said, and the company's task forces were working diligently to restore the beaches.

"We picked the quote from the *Times*," admitted Edward Cony, managing editor of the *Wall Street Journal*. "It's embarrassing and it violated our rule that we never take anything from a secondary source."[7]

Hartley wrote letters to the news organizations which had used the erroneous quote, and the newspapers printed the correction. All the erring news outlets apologized, including NBC.

Then Union Oil, afraid that the corrections would not draw the attention of the original reports, bought full-page newspaper advertisements throughout the regions where the company does business. **Please**, headlined the ads in thirty-five states and Canada, **let's set the record straight.**

Although most stories don't get that garbled, important additional information often does follow initial reports. Readers and viewers should watch especially for:

1. follow-up news reports;
2. explanatory or conflicting stories by columnists;
3. letters to the editor;
4. corrections and apologies.

Follow-up stories are common. Yesterday your governor protested the federal government's plans to close a major military base. Our economy is already shaky, the governor said, and the loss of the base will cost 5,000 more civilian jobs.

But today the mayor of the city nearest the base hurries to the media with another estimate. "It'll be more like 500 than 5,000," he predicts.

Who's right? Check down into the stories to see what the estimates are based on. The reporter should have included that information. A clue in this case turns out to be that the governor was aiming his remarks at the White House—trying to have the order reversed—while the mayor was trying to calm his constituents.

Perhaps the truth lies somewhere between. It's like estimating the value of your house for a prospective buyer, then for the tax collector.

Statistics often demand skeptical inquiry. Otto Friedrich, writing in *Time*, gives these examples:

The federal government's Center for Disease Control announced that a drug company may have infected 5,000 hospital patients with contaminated intravenous solutions, contributing to the deaths of 500 people. Asked how this figure had been determined, a government spokesman said that one estimate of 2,000 was "unrealistic," and another estimate of 8,000 was "unfair." So the authorities split the difference.[8]

In another case, estimates of the amount stolen by New York's heroin addicts usually range from $2 billion to $5 billion a year. Max Singer, president of the Hudson Institute, decided to find out how the figure came to be computed. Why, by multiplying an estimated 100,000 addicts by an estimated average habit of $30 a day, which would mean the addicts need $1.1 billion a year. Since a thief generally sells stolen property for about a quarter of its value, that produces a total of $4.4 billion.

The hitch in the calculation, as author Friedrich points out: the value of all the goods stolen in New York each year does not amount to nearly that much.[9]

No one, it seems, had checked the figure until Singer came along. Yet, any good reporter should routinely and automatically do so.

A second category of stories for the consumer to watch are comments by columnists, who sometimes will add background to straight news reports. Yesterday your state legislature refused to pass a bill limiting the height of buildings along lakefronts. Today a political columnist may tell you why, detailing the lobbying pressure from real estate groups which contribute to the campaigns of key legislators.

Such commentary, as suggested in the preceding chapter, should be carefully scanned for sources—the names, facts, and figures which can be checked and which lift a story beyond unsubstantiated speculation.

National affairs columnists such as James J. Kilpatrick, Marianne Means, Tom Wicker, William F. Buckley Jr., James Reston, and Mary McGrory often provide a circus of political punditry. During campaigns, it's instructive to keep score of which columnists say which candidates will win, and why, then to check back after the election.

Letters to the editor are another effective means of following up news stories. They rank as one of the most popular parts of the publications and provide a check on the accuracy of reporters. Letters cascade onto editors' desks, with the *Seattle Times*, for example, receiving an estimated 7,000 a year[10] and the *New York Times*, 40,000.[11] While some are just peevish, others contain a well-documented correction of the record.

In our file of letters-to-the-editor clipped from newspapers and magazines during the past dozen years, the most frequent outpourings of exasperation are aimed at Jack Newfield, a frequent contributor to national magazines and assistant editor of *The Village Voice*, a New York weekly whose readers thrive on pithy, pointed retorts.[12]

One of them reads:

> Dear Sir. The scurrilous attack by Jack Newfield on the *Times* in your issue of May 21 contains among its many vicious distortions the statement that the *Times* has failed until this month to publish a single editorial protesting the

murder of Fred Hampton . . . I am enclosing an editorial entitled Police and Panthers, dealing entirely with the Chicago raid and its aftermath . . . John B. Oakes, editor of the editorial page, *New York Times*.[13]

"Mr. Oakes is obviously correct about the editorial," Newfield admitted, "and I apologize. But the main thrust of my piece—all the news articles assigned, and then not printed by the managing editor and the city desk—still stands."[14]

Does it? Not in the minds of careful readers. Another letter, protesting another Newfield article, sets forth why:

"It is my impression that Jack Newfield reports more than his share of small pieces of misinformation," says the writer. "These errors accumulate in the mind of the reader and undermine Newfield's effectiveness as a reporter. Why is Newfield so careless? He has put himself in the position of investigating other news organizations and yet he has left himself vulnerable to the charge of misrepresentation."[15]

Newfield is capable of first-rate investigative reporting. In 1971 he won special recognition from Columbia University for a series on conditions in New York City's jails and a report about the city's attempt to evict sixty-nine homeowners in Queens.[16] By now, however, some readers are loathe to believe any article that carries a Newfield byline.

They were not reassured when he wrote for *Harper's* magazine, then under the editorship of Willie Morris, an article about the *New York Post*.[17] *Ten months later*, those readers who scan every scrap of type noticed on the contents page in tiny print of the size generally found in classified ads, "Erratum: We are advised that there were a number of factual inaccuracies in an article about the *New York Post* by Jack Newfield in our September issue. We regret any harm that may have been done as a result of its publication.— The editors."[18]

This brings us to a final point—corrections. When a news organization distributes an article which contains a serious error, it should be corrected promptly.

If a publication is to retain readers' confidence, it cannot do what editor Morris did: run a minuscule apology ten months later, which does not, even then, confess what was wrong with the original report.

Both editor and consumer need the impulses of a detective.

Voices Within and Some Choruses Without

The consumer's sherlocking in the living room can also draw on new vigilance at the newsroom and its environs. Many newsmen themselves are regularly criticizing the media, on the basis of ethics and standards of performance. Such critics within the profession and an always willing crowd nearby both provide help for the consumer.

As with much of our history in the 1960s, the trend of systematic criticism of the news media by media workers was born on the pavement. Throughout the four days of the Democratic National Convention in Chicago in late August, 1968, police and protesters contended by the thousands in the streets. Newsmen trying to report the clashes often found themselves the targets of the police; at least forty-three reporters and cameramen were injured during the uproar.[19] The Chicago media lodged complaints with the city administration of Mayor Richard J. Daley. But a few months later, a small group of journalists were still dissatisfied with their local media's coverage of the Daley regime. They began publishing the monthly *Chicago Journalism Review*.

The *Review* outlasted expectations of its early death, and its tough commentary impressed groups of newsmen elsewhere. In the autumn of 1970, two other bright and ambitious reviews appeared—the *St. Louis Journalism Review* and *The Unsatisfied Man* in Denver. Through the rest of 1970 and 1971, local journalism reviews were started by newsmen in at least eight other cities.[20]

Such reviews aren't a miracle cure for the news media. Only a minority group of newsmen, after all, contributes the time, effort, and bankroll—and risks the jeopardy to their jobs—to put criticism into print. The upper echelons of editors and management are still the powers-that-be in the major media. The reviews themselves are not flawless either; occasionally they fumble in their task of watching the watchdogs. Finally, it's anybody's guess what their survival rate is going to be. Writing in the magazine *Saturday Review*, author Norman Hill skeptically concluded:

". . . There are many signs that the local journalism review is just a passing fad, a safety valve for one college generation afflicted with extraordinary irritability and impatience, and an ideological vogue."[21]

If Hill proves to be right, media and consumer will both be the poorer. Reviews of the sort which showed up with the opening of the 1970s at least provide some corrections or explanations of shoddy work by the newspapers and broadcasting stations, and at best can put pressure on those news enterprises to do a more diligent and more honorable job. Beyond that, they provide the conscientious newsman some reassurance that he is not alone in his desire to get the news told accurately.

And for the consumer directly, *The Unsatisfied Man* in the spring of 1971 showed how a journalism review can provide inside information on local coverage. The topic: the 1976 Winter Olympics, to be held in the Rockies near Denver.

The Olympics—skill and sportsmanship, grandeur and glory, a festival of nations and a pot of visitors' money for the host city. What could ever be wrong with the fabled Winter Games? Well, look back to California's Squaw

Valley, site of the 1960 Winter Olympics. That Olympic wonderland became a financial white elephant for the state of California, which within a decade had lost $3.3 million and was trying to sell its half of the valley's ski slopes.[22] Also, the notion of carving any vast new winter sports complex out of mountain scenery is now guaranteed to rile conservation groups.

New moods and old journalistic habits are rarely in tune. *The Unsatisfied Man* took a critical look at the *Denver Post's* coverage of the making of the '76 winter olympiad:

> . . . There are strong indications that the chief *Post* excess of the 1970s will be its coverage of the 1976 Winter Olympics, which it favors strongly. A few cases in point:
>
> . . . Although environmentalists have raised serious objections to the Olympics, *The Post* prefers the Chamber-of-Commerce, Olympics-is-profitable view. For example, in one of its few strong editorials since its editorial page recently was milquetoasted . . . the paper protested that "the sniping at the Denver Olympic Committee . . . is getting out of hand."
>
> When *Post* staffer Joanne Ditmer . . . used her "Raising the Roof" column to criticize the editorial writers for their stand, she was called into the front office for a chat.
>
> On March 8, (Executive Editor William H.) Hornby, Managing Editor John Rogers, and even the top *Post* Editor and Publisher Charles Buxton, agreed to serve on a DOC-organized "press advisory committee" to help with the Olympics press coverage. (Michael Balfe Howard, new managing editor of the *Rocky Mountain News*, declined to become a party to this obvious attempt at systematic news management.)
>
> The next day, word came down from Hornby that "*All* materials (his emphasis) relating to the 1976 Winter Olympics for Denver must henceforth be cleared at the copy stage either with myself or the Managing Editor." The directive, Hornby made clear, "includes columns, sports stories, editorials, letters, news stories, features, etc."
>
> Why the tender, loving care for all Olympic stories—and even for letters to the editor? Said Hornby in a masterful example of managementese: "The purpose is coordination of effort and centralization of our understanding as to what is going on." . . .[23]

The Unsatisfied Man didn't stop with nay-saying. In a subsequent issue, the review recommended to its readers a trenchant six-part series in Denver's other major daily, the *Rocky Mountain News*, on preparations for the Olympics and citizen opposition to the plans.[24]

In this case, the local journalism review helped the consumer get a more accurate version of the news by showing the shortcomings at one news operation, then pointing out another source of information on the topic. These gadfly publications can put up alerts about sundry media sins:

Official sourceitis: The *Chicago Journalism Review* showed that the police version of the fatal shootings of Black Panther party members Fred Hampton and Mark Clark on December 4, 1969, at first had been uncritically accepted by some of the Chicago media.[25] Since then, discrepancies in the official story line have brought on grand jury indictments of fourteen law enforcement officials involved in the raid on the Panthers.[26]

The ethic of the mega-dollar: In the pilot issue of (*MORE*), a New York City review of the media, J. Anthony Lukas pointed out that a *Reader's Digest* special section on the environment was actually an advertising supplement, in the same format as the *Digest's* usual articles. Major industrial firms paid up to $59,000 a page in that September, 1971, issue to tell about their efforts against pollution.[27]

Diligence on the half shell: Staffers of the *St. Louis Journalism Review* timed the late evening news shows on the three major St. Louis television stations for three nights in a row, then reported that, weather and sports aside, the half hour news consistently amounted to about thirteen minutes.[28]

As noted, local journalism reviews began appearing in quantity during 1970 and 1971. The elders of journalism's critical periodicals come not from the after-hours efforts of working newsmen, but from the schools of journalism at Columbia University and the University of Missouri.

The bimonthly *Columbia Journalism Review* began publication in 1961, and its back issues can provide the news consumer solid information on many media topics. Its contents are broad-ranging, as this lineup in a typical issue indicates: articles on the ill health of mass magazines, journalism on black campuses, the Baltimore Sunpapers, applying social science research techniques to reporting, and outmoded habit patterns of editors; a review of Atlanta journalism; a roundup of articles about the media in other publications; opinion pieces about women's pages and the underground press; and regular sections which comment on recent boners or triumphs in news coverage.[29]

Missouri's Freedom of Information Center was established in 1959 as a clearing-house for data about "the people's right to know."[30] The FoI Center Report is devoted each time entirely to a single current topic within the media. In a typical span of several months, for instance, the Reports were titled:

Newsmen's Sources and the Law	*An Answer to Television Critics*
Student Press Revisited	*The Metamorphosis of the FTC*
The Free Market Place Dilemma	*Why Network TV News is Criticized*[31]
Press Passes: Patent or Privilege	

Time and again, newsmen hear it suggested that a public committee evaluate their work. Such echoes have been recurring ever since the Commission on the Freedom of the Press, an ambitious inquiry into media responsibilities, put the idea this way in 1947:

"We recommend the establishment of a new and independent agency to appraise and report annually upon the performance of the press."[32]

Great Britain has such a Press Council, and so does the province of Quebec. In the U.S., a statewide press council has been set up in Minnesota, and local versions are being tried in several communities ranging in size from Sparta, Illinois, to Honolulu, Hawaii. If a person who has a complaint against a newspaper can't resolve the matter with the paper's management, he can take his complaint to the council, which usually has a membership drawn both from the public and from the media.

"If the council finds the newspaper is not in error, it will attempt to resolve the misunderstanding by the complainant," explains C. Donald Peterson, the State Supreme Court Justice who heads the Minnesota Press Council. "If the newspaper is found to be in error, the findings will be transmitted to the newspaper, the complainant, and to the media for publication. This is as far as the council can go in imposing penalties for confirmed violations of good journalistic practice, but we believe such adverse publicity can effectively correct any abuses."[33]

From the news consumer's viewpoint, a press council seems a mixed bag. The theory sounds good; a device to handle complaints ought to be a public boon, just as the journalism reviews attempt to be. But in Great Britain, when a complaint is lodged with the Press Council "the chances are only one in ten that a newspaper will eventually be reprimanded in a formal adjudication issued by the Council," according to a study by Donald E. Brown, an American journalism professor.[34] Such odds suggest to the average reader that the Press Council is less than a stern headmaster of British newspaperdom.

Opposite the problem of a press council being too tame is the worse prospect that it could become too ferocious. How would a national media council have reacted under such pressure as Vice President Agnew's hammering at the news media, for instance? Or if the government itself was the complainant in cases brought to the council?

At the moment, the pros and cons of criticism by committee seem to add up this way for the news consumer. You should be aware that a local or state press council *might* provide a way to pressure a news enterprise into correcting itself, but don't count on the coming of a national press council as a panacea for woes you find in the news media. At any rate, such a national body does not appear likely any time soon. A 1971 report by the American Society of Newspaper Editors, whose support a council would need, waxed notably unenthusiastic. "To set up an American Press Council or comparable procedures is fraught with such grave difficulties that we cannot recommend it," the ASNE committee said.[35]

Besides the journalism reviews and fledgling press councils, the consumer can turn at times to individual critics for scrutiny of the media. American journalism has had some dutiful critics within its own ranks, but never enough of them.

Criticism of newsmen by fellow newsmen is not new. Reporter Will Irwin wrote an analysis of the U.S. press which ran through 15 issues of *Collier's* in 1911.[36] Robert Benchley began a column called "The Wayward Press" in *The New Yorker* in 1927.[37] Benchley's successor, A. J. Liebling, wrote periodic press criticism in the same column until his death in 1963.

Liebling, a freewheeling soul who loved gourmet food, boxing, and journalism, was the bane of some newspapermen but a hypnotic beacon for many serious news consumers. His book, *The Press*, still is worth reading as a rousing lover's quarrel with American newspaperdom. Liebling was particularly caustic about owners who kept buying more and more newspaper companies, and this excerpt is fairly typical of his goading style:

> Mr. Samuel I. Newhouse, the archetype, specializes in disgruntling heritors, or profiting by their disgruntlement. A family feud is grist to his mill, but if he can't get a paper that way he will talk beautifully of the satisfactions of cash, rapidly quoting sections of the capital-gains law as he accepts his hat. If the owner shows him the door, he exhibits no resentment.
>
> "I regret that you do not feel you can sell me the overcoat now, Madame," he says as he backs down the porch steps, "but if your husband dies and you should reconsider, I do hope you'll give me the first chance to make you an offer." (Mr. Roy Thomson, the Canadian who has taken to buying newspapers in Britain, is the same sort.) Newhouse and Thomson, quizzed about their politics, are evasive. They have no political ideas; just economic convictions.[38]

No critic since has been the virtuoso with acid which Liebling was, but some have done vital work for the news consumer. Here are perhaps the best-known, in a rundown too brief to do them real justice:

Ben Bagdikian was an excellent reporter on the news business before leaving that task in 1970 to become an editor at the *Washington Post*, where his job includes in-house criticism.

Robert Lewis Shayon, a contributing editor of *Saturday Review*, is a long-time critic of broadcasting. In his column on radio-television, Shayon frequently examines the business and ethical sides of the media as well as current programming.

Nat Hentoff's column in the *Village Voice* bangs into stories done and undone by the New York media.

William L. Rivers, a former Washington correspondent and now professor of communication at Stanford University, writes a "Monitoring Media" column in *The Progressive* magazine.

Chris Welles, general editor of *Institutional Investor*, doubles as a freelance critic and writes for magazines about the financial side of major journalism enterprises.

James Aronson, author of a book charging the U.S. press with a Cold War mentality, now writes a column of media criticism for the quarterly *Antioch Review*.[39]

Edwin Diamond, a veteran magazine editor, began in 1970 as media critic for WTOP-TV in Washington, D.C., and has written articles for *New York* magazine about specific news enterprises.

Harry Ashmore, formerly editor of the *Arkansas Gazette* in Little Rock, has done thoughtful criticism for the publications of the Center for the Study of Democratic Institutions, and often discusses current media problems in his syndicated newspaper column.

Most such critics work for big city news enterprises, while the great need for skillful criticism is in smaller communities where monopoly newspapers and a skinflint budget of television news may hold forth. A small but promising trend may help this situation; a few dailies outside the metropolitan media circuit are using in-house critics to stick up for the readers. So far, the innovation still is in sizeable cities such as Louisville and St. Petersburg, but new ideas usually seep at least into some enterprising small dailies around the nation.

The *Louisville Courier-Journal* has had an ombudsman since 1969.[40] His job: act on readers' complaints against the newspaper. The *St. Petersburg Times*[41] and *Evening Independent* began a similar system, called "The People's Voice," in November, 1970.

The Louisville and St. Petersburg ownerships have long been known as exceptionally enlightened. Run-of-the-mill managements perhaps are reluctant to undertake the sort of tough self-examination which drew attention to the *Washington Post's* Richard Harwood during his period as "resident critic" at the outset of the 1970s. Harwood watched the *Post's* news stories and pointed out to top editors any errors or shortcomings he saw. And periodically, he wrote a column in which he singled out what his newspaper recently had done wrong and discussed the reasons why. A sample:

> The problem begins with the information we receive—several hundred thousand words a day. It represents, Walter Lippmann once said, "an incredible medley of fact, propaganda, rumor, suspicion, clues, hopes and fears . . ." Our daily task is to select from this mass of information—and misinformation—those things that seem to us to be "important" and "true" and to get them into print within a period of a few hours. The process is fallible every step of the way.
>
> Who, for example, are the people who gather and supply us with this torrent of words? In many cases we don't know. They may be employees of other companies that are in the business of selling information to newspapers—the Associated Press, United Press International, Reuter, and so on. They may be

"stringers"—correspondents scattered around the country or around the world who sell us (on someone's recommendation) stories from time to time. In some cases our only dealings with them are through long-distance communication. Are they all competent and reliable? Are they free of conflict of interest? Sometimes we don't know.[42]

Two other sources within the news business which the consumer can make use of are the major trade periodicals, *Broadcasting* magazine and *Editor & Publisher*. Both lean heavily to the management side of the industry, and they should be read with an eye to their special quirks. *Broadcasting*, for example, is likely to treat stories about challenges to station licenses in this fevered fashion:

"A disgruntled Mexican-American job seeker has initiated the latest phase of what is rapidly becoming a reign of terror for Texas broadcast stations—their license renewals on the line amid an outpouring of challenges from chicano communities."[43]

Editor & Publisher sometimes lapses into easy stereotyping. When one of us wrote an article for E & P which mentioned a crew-cut middle aged newsman doing a reporting job "amid ten thousand young people at a rock music festival," an editor sharpened and slanted the point to read "amid ten thousand young people dressed in the accouterments of hippiedom."[44]

Amid the countinghouse flourishes, however, both magazines produce useful information week in and week out. *Broadcasting* is strong in the quantity of topics it covers regularly, and in lengthy special reports; typically, an issue in August, 1971, had a depth story by chief correspondent Rufus Crater about the Boston melodrama in which WHDH-TV and its license challenger, WCVB-TV, were both investing heavily in the future although it was uncertain which station would win the right to broadcast on the one available channel.[45] *Editor & Publisher* runs to shorter articles, but keeps abreast of newsroom innovations. It's a copious source for news about government-press conflicts, and it reports consistently on what newspaperdom's professional organizations are doing.

Neither publication has a regular critic of the industry-at-large whose columns could spark off ideas about how well the newsgatherers are performing. *TV Guide*, the immensely prosperous little weekly, does somewhat better, both in its regular columns and in articles. Profiles of newsmen and serious discussions of TV coverage show up in its pages. One of the best sources the consumer can find about what's involved in local news coverage is Richard Townley's four-part series in May and early June of 1971: "Television Journalism—An Inside Story."[46]

The consumer also can step outside the media to a throng of eager critics. And that's fine, as long as he treads warily there, too.

Groups with causes can unreel long lists of what they think the media are doing wrong. Many of their complaints about stereotyping in news stories and emblazoning the sensational over the solid are justified. But be careful. Organizations have their own biases and loose habits of stereotyping.

This brings up a reminder which applies to all critics of the news media, within and without: they must be read and heard as skeptically as the media themselves.

Take this example. Susan Davis, editor of the monthly roundup of women's news called *The Spokeswoman*, told a *Chicago Daily News* reporter that the women's rights movement was "doing great things but the media doesn't report it."[47] But *The Spokeswoman*, which summarizes news from newsletters and other sources within the movement, also frequently refers to articles which a clipping service gathers from—where else?—the news media. And newsgatherers have been sufficiently interested in stories about the women's rights movement that in late 1971, about 250 of *The Spokeswoman's* 2,600 subscribers were media outlets. Finally, Editor Davis's statement lambasts the media as a singular entity, a single current of information when in fact the streams are numerous and diverse. Coverage of news about women has deserved many gripes (we discuss a few of them on pages 154–56) but her criticism must be more precise to have real bite.

Organizations usually have their own publications, which can be useful to the news consumer for their specialized information. Some environmental groups, which run heavily to membership from universities and the professions, put out skillful periodicals which concentrate on information usually given short shrift by the national media.

For example, the *Sierra Club Bulletin* in February, 1971, listed the oil spills since the day the tanker *Torrey Canyon* broke apart off the southwest coast of England—straight-forward data on the kind of petroleum, source of each spill, and the amount. Decide for yourself whether you need such information collected for you; make a guess about the total number of oil spills between the *Torrey Canyon* disaster of March, 1967, and the *Bulletin's* last listed spill, the collision of two tankers in San Francisco Bay in January, 1971. The answer is in the end-notes for this page.[48]

At the local level, anti-establishment newspapers can provide alternative views on some news stories. Countless communities have such publications— which have been dubbed underground papers even though most operate as openly as the giant dailies—of some sort or another. A paper such as the bimonthly *Bay Guardian* in San Francisco takes the job of critic seriously. Besides watchdogging the city's two big dailies, the *Guardian* filed a legal challenge against their use of a joint publishing company, a major test case of the Newspaper Preservation Act which benefited the country's major newspapers.[49]

You don't have to confine your reading of alternative sources to the liberal side. Publications tending towards the conservative are plentiful; two leading examples are *Human Events*, a weekly newspaper featuring such writers as John Chamberlin, Victor Reisel, and Edgar Ansel Mowrer, and the monthly publication of the *Young Americans for Freedom, New Guard.*[50]

The final note of this chapter is the same chime we've been hitting throughout: whatever your political persuasion, read all critics as meticulously and warily as the offerings from the news media.

Think back, for instance, to the malady of highfaluting statistics, and try this case. David Brower of Friends of the Earth is the patron saint of ecology in the U.S., and a seasoned debater who brings facts as well as eloquence to bear in his fights against the SST, river damming, mining the wilderness, and other conservation issues. Yet, John McPhee of *The New Yorker* found that one Brower remark which has become oft-quoted within the environmental movement can charitably be described as nebulous:

> . . . After he gave a lecture at Yale once, I asked him where he got the interesting skein of statistics that six per cent of the world's population uses sixty per cent of the world's resources and one per cent of the six per cent uses sixty per cent of the sixty per cent. What resources? Kleenex? The Mesabi Range?
>
> Brower said the figures had been worked out in the head of a friend of his from data assembled "to the best of his recollection."
>
> "To the best of his *recollection*?"
>
> "Yes," Brower said, and assured me that figures in themselves are merely indices. . . .[51]

Chapter 13

Thou Shalt Not
Commit Mockery

The news consumer is continually aware of the great world coursing into his own sphere, we said early in this book. That's the major reason why news is so often discomfiting, and why the media are resented for the information they transmit to us. For in truth or in fantasy, you are liable to perceive in the news all the bogies that have ever haunted you. . . .

Before, They might have been decently out of sight and hearing, somewhere beyond the next ridge with their treacherous notions and shabby customs. Their mockery might drift near on rumor, but at least our tempers could be spared the daily prance of Their ways of life.

Centuries back, in the heyday of religious crusades, the most distressing heretics might be so far away that a serious citizen had to travel months to lay lance upon Them.

Later, with the colonizing of the Americas, the dissenters in the new lands were weeks by sea from the ruling powers, so far that the administrative lines on Them could not hold across the oceans.

As this country was settled, the spread of people still scattered much of Their impudence safely beyond the horizon—rowdy miners and cowboys and other adventurers on the frontier fringes, grumbling farmers remote on the prairies, socialists and bizarre religionists and other eccentric thinkers in their communes.

When the distance of miles dwindled, social distance provided some last security from Them. The immigrants could seethe in their ghettoes down in the lower class, the factory worker shut from mind in his dark sullen mill.

Distance stood as the buffer from Them, all of those down through history who would make mockery of the right order of the world. But no more. Today's reader and viewer lacks the old spans of safety between himself and those who veer from his mode of life. Today, the edginess is jittering toward discombobulation of the sort in this line from the typewriter of an editorial writer:

"It may be news to beardies, weirdies, pot heads and freaks, but one of the things America is all about is fair play for the other fellow."[1]

The beardies and weirdies, and the fascists and backlashists—and all the other epithets that can be hurled from one viewpoint toward another. Along with the news, the modern media transmit the emotional currents of society, and this flow from mankind's nerve ends isn't often soothing.

If each of us had emotions under control in our own wiring, there would be no complaint about what comes into the living room from the lines of the media. Of course, there would be no news either, except for weather forecasts and accident reports, because our criteria of what is worth attention is based on mankind's quibbles, not its milliseconds of calm.

But matters are hardly ever under control, either within us or out in society. It's no easy life with mockery, the denial of certainties our soul can be comfortable with, always so close at hand. Especially, it's no calm life. This country fairly zings with the intensities of mockery here.

To some older Americans, the clothing and hair and music and life style of the young have been mocking the standards of decency.

To some of the young, the social ills and the heft of our military power are a mockery of national ideals.

Street disorders by racial minorities loom to many in the white majority as a dangerous mockery of law and order.

The wealth and privileges within the white majority antagonize many in the minorities as an infuriating mockery of equal chance.

And all the angry illusions now are graven on videotape and newsprint; the news media carry a cargo they are blamed for.

Well, don't carry it, some news consumers say through gritted teeth. Stop delivering the disturbers of the peace into the living room all the time.

A tantalizing notion, but it doesn't work.

One major nation in the family of Western civilization tried it—France. The DeGaulle government in the late 1960s tightly controlled broadcast news. Discontent among French students and workers was not reported. While American viewers saw and heard campus protests, such stresses did not exist on France's state-run broadcasting channels.

The trouble didn't drain away when kept from sight. In May, 1968, accumulated protest began erupting in France in the worst upheaval any Western nation has undergone in recent times.

The tottering of the surprised Fifth Republic proved, in the words of an American television correspondent in Paris, "that when people want to demonstrate and riot, they will do so whether or not TV cameras are there to film them."[2]

With little notice, some similar blinkering closed around the campus mood in the United States as the 1970s began. After the flareups of the 1969–70 school year, with the intense protests against the U.S. role in the invasion of Cambodia and the fatal shooting of four students at Kent State, the general assumption was that American universities and colleges lapsed into quiet.

Scenes of mass meetings and campus-wide turmoil faded from the newspapers and television screens, not because of any government edict but because the prevailing standards of reporting did not discern such events.

But researchers for the American Council on Education found that campus protest had continued in the 1970–71 school year, with about one out of every five institutions of higher learning hit by at least one protest in which a building was taken over, classes were disrupted, someone was injured, or property was destroyed.[3]

These flashpoints, however, were not the Berkeleys and Harvards and Cornells of past news sagas, but lesser-known colleges and two-year schools. "Unrest has permeated into the Podunks," one of the researchers said of the "quiet" year's results. It did so in spite of the inattention of the national news media.

The mockery, then, goes on with or without the media, and will do so as long as there are stresses within society. It simply crowds in upon the mocked more promptly and more insolently when it comes in the news each day.

Like it or not, each of us is a news consumer—which in today's social turbulence means each of us is going to feel the mockery of disagreeable events all too often. But if the consumer lets the distaste and distress which come along with more agreeable information turn him from the news, he forfeits any chance to influence what's happening to the world. It's a costly forfeit.

Afterword

Regular sources of criticism and useful works about the news media are available to the consumer. Here is a selective list.

Books

Ben H. Bagdikian, *The Information Machines* (New York: Harper & Row, 1971).

Alfred Balk and James Boylan, eds., *Our Troubled Press*, (Boston: Little, Brown and Co., 1971).

Erik Barnouw, *A History of Broadcasting in the United States* (New York: Oxford University Press)
>   Vol. I: *A Tower in Babel*, to 1933 (1966);
>   Vol. II: *The Golden Web*, 1933–1953 (1968);
>   Vol. III: *The Image Empire*, 1953–1970 (1970).

Marvin Barrett, ed., *Survey of Broadcast Journalism*, published annually by the Alfred I. duPont–Columbia University Survey and Awards (New York: Grosset & Dunlap, Inc.)

Les Brown, *Televi$ion: The Business Behind the Box* (New York: Harcourt Brace Jovanovich, Inc., 1971).

Otto Friedrich, *Decline and Fall* (New York: Ballantine Books, Inc., 1970).

Donald M. Gillmor and Jerome A. Barron, *Mass Communication Law* and *1971 Supplement to Mass Communication Law* (St. Paul: West Publishing Co., 1969 and 1971).

Morton Mintz and Jerry S. Cohen, *America, Inc.*, Ch. 2, "Hear No Evil, See No Evil, Speak No Evil" (New York: The Dial Press, 1971).

W. A. Swanberg, *Citizen Hearst* (New York: Bantam Books, Inc., 1963).

Gay Talese, *The Kingdom and the Power* (New York: Bantam Books, Inc., 1970).

Magazines

Atlas (Best From the World Press), monthly, The World Press Co., 1180 Avenue of the Americas, New York, N.Y., 10036.

Broadcasting, weekly, 1735 DeSales St. NW, Washington, D.C., 20036.

Columbia Journalism Review, bimonthly, 700 Journalism Building, Columbia University, New York, N.Y., 10027.

Editor & Publisher, weekly, 850 Third Ave., New York, N.Y. 10022.
Freedom of Information Center Reports and *FoI Digest,* Freedom of Information Center, School of Journalism, Box 858, Columbia, Missouri, 65201.
Newsweek, weekly, 444 Madison Ave., New York, N.Y. 10022. See regular section, The Media.
Time, weekly, Rockefeller Center, New York, N.Y. 10020. See regular section, The Press.

Television

(Regularly scheduled "magazine" programs, 1971–72 season)
CBS: *60 Minutes*
NBC: *Chronolog*
  Quarterly Report
Public Broadcasting Service: *Black Journal*
        This Week
        Washington Week in Review and *30 Minutes With . . .*
         (At this writing, the National Public Affairs Center for Television has been created to produce this pair and other news shows for PBS.)
        World Press
WNET–TV, New York: *Behind the Lines*

Local Journalism Reviews

Atlanta Journalism Review, published as experimental supplement to *Columbia Journalism Review,* 700 Journalism Building, Columbia University, New York, N.Y., 10027.
Buncombe: A Review of Baltimore Journalism, 2317 Maryland Ave., Baltimore, Md. 21218.
Chicago Journalism Review, 11 E. Hubbard St., Chicago, Ill., 60611.
Hawaii Journalism Review, 603 Koko Isle Circle, Honolulu, Hawaii, 96821.
(MORE), A Journalism Review, Box 2971, Grand Central Station, New York, N.Y., 10017.
Philadelphia Journalism Review, Room 918, 1001 Chestnut St., Philadelphia, Pa., 19107.
St. Louis Journalism Review, P.O. Box 3086, St. Louis, Missouri, 63130.
TCJR: Twin Cities Journalism Review, P.O. Box 17113, St. Paul, Minn. 55117.
The Unsatisfied Man, P.O. Box 18470, Denver, Colorado, 80218.

Critics and Ombudsmen

Antioch Review, James Aronson, critic.
Louisville Courier-Journal and *Louisville Times,* John Herchenroeder, ombudsman.
Minneapolis Star, The Reader's Referee (editorial committee).

Minneapolis Tribune, Bureau of Accuracy and Fair Play (editorial committee).
St. Petersburg Times and Evening Independent, Del Marth ("The People's Voice").
Saturday Review, Robert Lewis Shayon (weekly TV-radio columnist).
The Progressive, William L. Rivers, critic.
Village Voice, Nat Hentoff, critic.
Wall Street Journal, Robert L. Bartley (periodic editorial page articles on the media).
WTOP-TV, Washington, D.C., Edwin Diamond, critic.

Articles

Harry S. Ashmore, "Uncertain Oracles," *The Center Magazine*, November/December
1970, pp. 10–21.
Stephen Grover, "Many in Broadcasting Fear the Rising Attack from the Government,"
Wall Street Journal, April 28, 1971, p. 1.
Nicholas Johnson, "What Do We Do About Television?" *Saturday Review*, July 11,
1970, pp. 14–16.
Carol J. Loomis, "One Story *The Wall Street Journal* Won't Print," *Fortune*, August
1971, pp. 140–43.
Martin Mayer, "How Television News Covers the World (In 4000 Words or Less),"
Esquire, January 1972, pp. 86–91.
Richard Townley, "Television Journalism—An Inside Story," *TV Guide*, May 15–June
5, 1971.
Sander Vanocur, "How the Media Massaged Me," *Esquire*, January 1972, pp. 82–85.
Max Ways, "What's Wrong with News? It Isn't New Enough," *Fortune*, October 1969,
pp. 110–13.

Source Notes

1. Anchor Man, Digger, Prime Timer, Arouet, and You

[1]Dan Rather is slugged: *Broadcasting*, September 2, 1968, p. 24.

[2]"I think we've got": *New York Times*, August 28, 1968, p. 30.

[3]President Eisenhower said: *Time*, February 15, 1960, p. 74.

[4]"At that precise moment": *New York Times*, July 26, 1971, p. 6.

[5]His speech was worked out: Neil Hickey, "The President Goes to The People," *TV Guide*, August 22, 1970, p. 10.

[6]His predecessor, Lyndon B. Johnson: Hugh Sidey, *A Very Personal Presidency* (New York: Atheneum, 1966), p. 97.

[7]Typed out the way: Hickey, "The President Goes," *TV Guide*, August 22, 1970, p. 10.

[8]The thinker lived: Leo Rosten, "Voltaire," *The Many Worlds of Leo Rosten* (Evanston: Harper & Row, 1964), pp. 99–102.

[9]"I disapprove of what you say": *The Oxford Dictionary of Quotations* (New York: Oxford University Press, 1955), p. 557. The sentence was attributed to Voltaire by author E. Beatrice Hall in her 1907 book, *The Friends of Voltaire*. She later explained she used the phrase "as a description of Voltaire's attitude to Helvetius—and more widely, to the freedom of expression in general. I do not think and did not intend to imply that Voltaire used these words *verbatim*, and should be surprised if they are found in any of his works. They are rather a *paraphrase* of Voltaire's words in the Essay on Tolerance—*Think for yourselves and let others enjoy the privilege to do so too.*" *Saturday Review of Literature*, August 17, 1935, p. 13.

2. If It's Good, Is It News?

[1]"Placidity is not news"; Interview on Public Broadcast Laboratory, December 22, 1968.

[2]"It's a little bit": Speech excerpt televised on *60 minutes*, November 25, 1969.

[3]"News is the unusual": Interview on Public Broadcast Laboratory, December 22, 1968.

[4]"Warts on society's skin": Interview on KCTS-TV, Seattle, June 23, 1971.

[5]Under the headline: Richard O'Connor, *The Scandalous Mr. Bennett* (Garden City, N.Y.: Doubleday, 1962), p. 301.

[6]Manila: UPI story in *Seattle Post-Intelligencer*, September 27, 1967, reprinted by permission of United Press International.

[7]Tricia Nixon's wedding: *Chicago Tribune*, May 2, 1971, p. 1.

[8]Dead Sea scrolls: "Dead Sea Scrolls," *Encyclopaedia Britannica* (1971), VII, pp. 117–20.

[9]Love Letters from President Harding: *New York Times*, July 10, 1964, p. 1; Francis Russell, *The Shadow of Blooming Grove* (New York: McGraw-Hill, 1968), pp. 657–59.

[10]My Lai massacre: *Editor & Publisher*, December 13, 1969, pp. 9–11; *Newsweek*, December 8, 1969.

[11]Won Hersh a Pulitzer Prize: Pulitzer Prizes are awarded each spring in several fields of journalistic endeavor (there also are prizes in Letters and Music) by trustees of Columbia University. Prizes are awarded upon recommendation of the Advisory Board on the Pulitzer Prizes, from a bequest of two million dollars by the late Joseph Pulitzer, publisher of the *New York World* and *St. Louis Post-Dispatch*. For a history of the Prizes, see John Hohenberg, ed., *The Pulitzer Prize Story* (New York: Columbia University Press, 1959), pp. 329–31.

[12]Pentagon Papers: *Newsweek*, June 28, 1971.

[13]Hearst was first: The next three paragraphs are based on material in W. A. Swanberg, *Citizen Hearst* (New York: Bantam Books, Inc., 1963).

[14]"Scoop is a dying art": David Halberstam, "Reflections on a Professional," (*MORE*), June 1971, p. 9.

[15]NY Times did not rush: *Newsweek*, June 28, 1971, p. 26.

[16]"The widely prevalent concept": *Editor & Publisher*, September 28, 1968, p. 108.

[17]Pinpoints of "good news": See James Bylin, "Papers and TV Outlets Stress 'Good' News; Response is Positive," *Wall Street Journal*, September 24, 1970, p. 1; *Time*, February 8, 1971, p. 65; John Leonard, "There's Bad News Tonight," *Life*, February 5, 1971, pp. 12–13.

[18]"KIRO has gone as far": *Seattle Post-Intelligencer*, September 28, 1970, p. 21.

[19]Wall Street Journal reported: Bylin, " 'Good' News," *Wall Street Journal*, September 24, 1970, p. 14.

[20]KIRO's audience was lowest: *Seattle Post-Intelligencer*, January 15, 1970, p. 12.

[21]Dead last: *Seattle Post-Intelligencer*, November 11, 1971, p. E5.

[22]The lead of WLS: *Time*, February 8, 1971, p. 65.

[23]J. Edward Murray: Quoted in *Wall Street Journal*, September 24, 1970, p. 14.

[24]Clif Kirk disagrees: Excerpt from panel discussion televised on KCTS-TV, Seattle, June 1, 1971.

[25]Charles Kuralt reporting: See *Time*, January 19, 1968, p. 44; *Newsweek*, January 1, 1968, p. 54.

[26]"The 'good news' concept": *Seattle Post-Intelligencer*, September 28, 1970, p. 21.

[27]Kirk seems to agree: KCTS-TV panel discussion, June 1, 1971.

[28]John Keasler tells it: John Keasler, "A non-violent paper? try it—it's murder!" *Editor & Publisher*, May 31, 1969, p. 16.

[29]Dan Wakefield: *Newsweek*, February 26, 1968, p. 62.

[30]Ward Just: *The Atlantic*, October 1970, p. 4.

[31]Meyer Berger: For samples of Berger's reporting, see *Meyer Berger's New York* (New York: Random House, 1960).

[32]"The writing is done": Ruth Adler, ed., *The Working Press* (New York: Bantam Books, Inc., 1970), p. 17.

[33]Historian Carl Becker: Carl Becker, *Progress and Power* (New York: Alfred A. Knopf, Inc., 1949), p. 16.

[34]"They may not be": Walter Lippmann, *Public Opinion* (New York: The Macmillan Company, 1960), p. 95.

[35]"To all appearance": Quoted in Alan Moorehead, *The Fatal Impact* (New York: Harper & Row, 1966), p. 104.

[36]"The facts that put together": Rebecca West, *The Meaning of Treason* (New York: The Viking Press, Inc., 1947), p. 56. Copyright 1947 by Rebecca West.

3. The News Apparatus

[1]The Luddite Disturbances: "Luddites," *Encyclopaedia Britannica* (1971), XIV, p. 402; E. J. Hobsbawm, "The Machine Breakers," *Labouring Men* (Garden City, N.Y.: Anchor Books, 1967), pp. 7–26.

[2]Johann Gutenberg: "Gutenberg, Johann," *Encyclopaedia Britannica* (1971) X, pp. 1051–52; Arthur T. Turnbull and Russell N. Baird, *The Graphics of Communication* (New York: Holt, Rinehart and Winston, Inc., 1968), pp. 12–15.

[3]" 'Prithee, friend' ": Louis L. Snyder and Richard B. Morris, *A Treasury of Great Reporting* (New York: Simon and Schuster, 1962), p. 8.

[4]News-Times-Herald: According to a 1970 study by Marge Grogan, these eight names —in the order listed—are the most common for U.S. and Canadian daily newspapers. The totals for dailies with these mastheads:

News—355	Press—87
Times—196	Tribune—75
Herald—155	Star—70
Journal—137	Sun—52

"What's in a name?", *Editor & Publisher*, March 13, 1971, p. 52.

[5]Refinements in cylinder press: John Tebbel, *The Compact History of the American Newspaper* (New York: Hawthorn Books, Inc., 1969), p. 93; Edwin Emery, *The Press and America* (Englewood Cliffs, N.J.: Prentice-Hall, Inc., 1962), p. 258.

[6]Mark Twain lost fortune: Justin Kaplan, *Mr. Clemens and Mark Twain* (New York: Simon and Schuster, 1966), pp. 282–332.

[7]With several thousand employees: "The Associated Press has 3,301 employees world-wide. It also has many hundreds of string correspondents." Letter to the authors from Ted Boyle, promotion manager for Associated Press, September 7, 1971. UPI, in a different and apparently more general system of counting, says it "operates 238 bureaus in 62 nations and employs more than 10,000 full and part-time reporters, photographers, editors, telegraphers and technicians." Enclosure in letter to the authors from Kenneth Smith, UPI promotion manager, September 16, 1971.

[8]As late as Sunday morning: Newsweek—"In general, the magazine closes its news columns sometime early Sunday morning and, providing there are no 'stop press' orders —very rare, indeed—is on-press on or near 7 A.M. Sunday. The first "makeready' copies are airlifted in to New York a few hours later. It is not, however, at all unusual for changes to be made throughout Sunday while the magazine is being printed. . . ." Letter to authors from Edward H. Le Zotte, publicity director of Newsweek, August 31, 1971. *Time* magazine—"Late-breaking news of an unusual nature can get into *TIME* magazine as late as Saturday night/Sunday morning. The magazine is usually 'put to bed' shortly after midnight Sunday morning, goes to press during Sunday in 17 printing plants around the world, and is distributed in 185 countries beginning on Sunday night and Monday." Letter to authors from Alex Burnham, publicity director for *Time*, September 20, 1971.

[9]Leslie's Weekly: Frank Luther Mott, *A History of American Magazines, 1850–1865* (Cambridge: Harvard University Press, 1938), pp. 456–57.

[10]KDKA: Erik Barnouw, *A Tower in Babel* (New York: Oxford University Press, 1966), pp. 69–70.

[11]Wire service reports granted: Erik Barnouw, *The Golden Web* (New York: Oxford University Press, 1968), p. 21.

[12]"There were two rows": quoted in Barnouw, *Golden Web*, p. 205.

[13]KAIM: The station's roundups "are features of B.F.A.—Broadcasting Foundation of America. . . . These reviews are 15 minute tapes. They are first-quality and professionally done. They are aired Monday-Friday at 12:30 P.M. and 10 P.M. on KAIM-AM. . . ." Letter to the authors from Cliff R. Scott, general manager of KAIM, October 7, 1971.

[14]WCCO: Letter from Jim Bormann, director of community affairs, to authors, August 31, 1971.

[15]John Cameron Swayze reads: *Cleveland Plain Dealer*, March 17, 1951; confirmed by letter from John Cameron Swayze to authors.

[16]Swayze showed up nationwide: Erik Barnouw, *The Image Empire* (New York: Oxford University Press, 1970), pp. 41–42.

[17]Staffs of hundreds: For instance, "it takes about 12 control room technicians and an equal number of studio technicians—in New York alone—to get the 'ABC Evening News with Howard K. Smith and Harry Reasoner' on the air each night. In addition, we have about six control room technicians and six studio technicians nightly in our Washington studios. . . . If we originate reports from elsewhere in the country—or from other parts of the world via satellite—it takes between four and six technicians at each sending point. We have nine foreign bureaus and six domestic offices, staffed by about 50 correspondents and 125 camera crewmen. . . . We have about 20 producers around country and the world, 15 writers, a dozen graphic artists and 21 film editors. . . . There are also between 25 and 35 researchers, production assistants, desk assistants and secretaries directly concerned with our Evening News." Letter to authors from George Merlis, director of public relations, ABC News, September 21, 1971.

[18]"He's been shot": Barnouw, *Image Empire*, p. 233.

[19]KYW-TV: Robert Lewis Shayon, "Philadelphia Wedding," *Saturday Review*, July 24, 1971, p. 50. Shayon's version is verified in a letter to the authors from John M. Rohrbach Jr., general manager of KYW-TV, September 28, 1971.

[20]KCRA-TV: Telephone conversation between Robert E. Kelly, KCRA station manager, and Ivan Doig, August 30, 1971.

[21]"With as many as twenty": Marvin Barrett, ed., *Survey of Broadcast Journalism, 1968–1969* (New York: Grosset & Dunlap, Inc., 1969), p. 51.

[22]The planes whine down: Hamilton D. Perry, *The Panay Incident* (New York: The Macmillan Company, 1969), pp. vii, p. 230. For more about newsreels, see John Tebbel, "The Eyes and Ears of the World," *Saturday Review*, June 12, 1971, pp. 60–62, and "The Last Reel," *Newsweek*, January 1, 1968, p. 53.

[23]Mount Vernon, N.Y.: Nick Egleson, "An unblinking vigil on Main Street, USA," *Village Voice*, May 20, 1971, pp. 11–12; "Big Brother Is Watching," *TV Guide*, August 7, 1971, pp. 12–13.

[24]At the Providence Journal: excerpt from a letter from Charles H. Spilman, executive editor of the *Providence Journal* and *Evening Bulletin*, to the authors, August 11, 1971: ". . . The *Journal-Bulletin* has high standards of editing which were not always met by the tape. Additionally, we have four wire services available to us . . . and we found that we were using a very small amount of the tape in any event." Spilman concludes:

"The *Journal-Bulletin* has no policy on the use or non-use of tape. We simply suspended its use for the time being because we considered that we could do a better job without it."

[25]St. Louis Post-Dispatch: Excerpt from a letter from Evarts A. Graham, Jr., *Post-Dispatch* managing editor, to the authors, August 10, 1971: ". . . Our slot man, George Cooper, participated in an American Press Institute seminar a couple of years ago. There he stated orally his apprehension about tape and its inhibiting effect on changes at individual newspapers. In effect, it guarantees mediocrity throughout the press." Graham concludes: "On the other side of the coin, there appears to be no doubt that increased use of technology in newspapers, which clearly is inevitable, will tend to have a similar result. . . ."

[26]"So I tried various ways": Letter from Robert G. Abernethy, NBC News, Los Angeles, to the authors, March 11, 1971.

[27]William F. Schanen, Jr.: Material about the Schanen episode is drawn from Bernice Buresh, "Boycott turns on Wisconsin Publisher," *Chicago Journalism Review*, September 1969, pp. 7–8; Bernice Buresh, "Wisconsin publisher folds papers in boycott," *Chicago Journalism Review*, April, 1970, p. 15; and John Pekkanen, "The Obstinacy of Bill Schanen," *Life*, September 26, 1969, p. 59. Mr. Schanen died on February 9, 1971; our version of the 1969 boycott is verified by his son, William Schanen III, in a letter to us.

[28]An estimated $20 million: F. C. Shapiro, "The life and death of a great newspaper," *American Heritage*, October 1967, p. 97.

[29]Newspapers average 42 percent: Ben H. Bagdikian, *The Information Machines* (New York: Harper & Row, 1971), p. 84.

[30]"The quality of journalism": *Philadelphia Journalism Review*, June 1971, p. 9.

[31]1,000 jobs vanished: Story from New York Times News Service, *Seattle Post-Intelligencer*, March 17, 1971, p. 11.

[32]Ten of fifteen newspapers: *ibid.*

[33]More than $200 million loss: *Broadcasting*, January 11, 1971, p. 40.

[34]Andrew Heiskell assured: Material about cigarette advertising in the next few paragraphs is drawn from Thomas Whiteside, "Selling Death," *The New Republic*, March 27, 1971, pp. 15–17. Reprinted by permission of *The New Republic*, copyright 1971, Harrison-Blaine of New Jersey, Inc.

[35]Inquisitive U.S. senator: Frank E. Moss of Utah.

[36]Journalism Quarterly reported: Barry M. Feinberg, "Content Analysis Shows Cigarette Advertising Up Twofold in 14 Magazines," *Journalism Quarterly*, Autumn 1971, pp. 539–42.

[37]Jack Kauffman forecast: *Broadcasting*, January 11, 1971, p. 39.

[38]RCA owns: Morton Mintz and Jerry S. Cohen, *America, Inc.* (New York: The Dial Press, 1971), p. 92.

[39]Study of twenty-nine conglomerates: *Broadcasting*, August 2, 1971, p. 14.

[40]1,748 dailies: Raymond B. Nixon, "Half of nation's dailies now in group ownerships," *Editor & Publisher*, July 17, 1971, p. 7.

[41]Chicago had four big dailies: Emery, *Press and America*, pp. 729, 754.

[42]Lost an estimated $7 million: *Time*, August 9, 1971, pp. 52–53.

[43]New York boasted fourteen dailies: Tebbel, *Compact History*, p. 220.

[44]Two of thirty-seven cities: *Editor & Publisher*, July 17, 1971, p. 32.

[45]7,100 radio and 901 television: Totals from Federal Communications Commission

as of October 1, 1971. The breakdown of broadcasting stations: AM radio, 4,350; commercial FM radio, 2,279; educational FM radio, 471; commercial UHF TV, 186; educational UHF TV, 117; commercial VHF TV, 511; educational VHF TV, 87.

[46]FCC announced: *New York Times* story in *Seattle Post-Intelligencer*, March 27, 1970, p. 1. However, at this writing the FCC has just authorized total purchase of KOIN-AM-FM-TV in Portland by Newhouse Broadcasting Corporation, despite Newhouse ownership of both major daily newspapers in the same city. See *Broadcasting*, October 4, 1971, p. 7.

[47]Publishing executives began objecting: "Publishers attack FCC rule requiring sale of stations," *Editor & Publisher*, June 12, 1971, p. 42.

[48]FCC voted: *Broadcasting*, August 23, 1971, p. 27.

[49]142 percent increase: *New York Times* story in *Seattle Post-Intelligencer*, March 17, 1971, p. 11.

[50]Newspaper Preservation Act: "Text of Newspaper Preservation Act signed by President," *Editor & Publisher*, August 1, 1970, p. 10.

[51]Author James Lipton: James Lipton, *An Exaltation of Larks* (New York: Grossman Publishers, 1968).

[52]Joseph Goulden described: Joseph Goulden, "The *Washington Post*," *The Washingtonian*, October 1970, p. 56.

[53]Stories appeared: The list of newsmen "who accompanied members of the UC Board of Regents on their visit to the Cerro Prieto geothermal site, October 29, 1970" was provided to the authors by E. A. Lopez, information officer of the U. of California, Riverside. Correspondence with individual newsmen confirms the total number of stories resulting from the trip.

[54]*Life* and *Newsweek*: see *Life*, August 13, 1971, and *Newsweek*, August 16, 1971.

[55]*Time* and *Newsweek*: see issues of February 8, 1971.

4. Stories Untold

[1]Conference of governors: For a journalist's criticism of news coverage of the governors, see John Fischer, "A Shipload of Doomed Men," *Harper's*, January 1968, pp. 9–12.

[2]Hired by National Geographic: See Em Hall, "In the Global Village, Life's Not 'Geographic,' " *Village Voice*, August 27, 1970, p. 19.

[3]Great stadium binge: Since 1960, stadiums have been built or are planned in Anaheim, Atlanta, the Boston area, Buffalo, Cincinnati, Honolulu, Houston, Kansas City (two stadiums), Los Angeles, New Orleans, the New Jersey Meadows, New York, Oakland, Philadelphia, Pittsburgh, St. Louis, San Diego, San Francisco, Seattle, and Washington, D.C. For details of individual stadium projects, check the index of *Engineering News-Record*, 1960–1971.

[4]Dean Rusk told reporters: AP story in *Seattle Post-Intelligencer*, February 24, 1968.

[5]Newsmen relied on NASA handouts: See James A. Skardon, "The Apollo story: what the watchdogs missed," *Columbia Journalism Review*, fall 1967, pp. 11–15.

[6]Arrested more than 12,000: See *New York Times*, May 4–8, 1971.

[7]Another question pressed: See Weekly Compilation of Presidential Documents, June 7, 1971, pp. 848–49; "The Art of Follow-Up," *The Nation*, June 14, 1971, p. 739.

[8]Totem of "national security": The extent of one major news enterprise's dedication

was indicated in this excerpt from a letter *Life* publisher C. D. Jackson wrote to a critical reader in November 1961: "We have dedicated *LIFE* to every effort that journalism can bring to bear to guarantee victory in the Cold War against Communism. We intend to pursue this policy with vigor and determination until such a time as it is no longer necessary." Copy of letter in the authors' possession.

[9]Frank Barnako covers: See Frank Barnako Jr., "How the Mayor uses the media," *Chicago Journalism Review*, October 1971, pp. 10–12.

[10]"We're trying to do": *ibid.*, p. 12.

[11]Howard K. Smith anchored: *Time*, November 23, 1962, p. 69.

[12]Max Ways cites: Max Ways, "What's Wrong with News? It Isn't New Enough," *Fortune*, October 1969, p. 111.

[13]About 15,000 to 10,000: 15,000 persons a century old or more—Newspaper Enterprise Association story in *Seattle Post-Intelligencer*, May 14, 1971; 10,000 industrial designers—*Occupational Outlook Handbook*, U.S. Dept. of Labor Bureau of Labor Statistics, 1970–1, p. 176.

[14]Golden weddings: Richard Scammon and Ben Wattenberg, *This U.S.A.: An Unexpected Family Portrait of 194,067,296 Americans* (Garden City, N.Y.: Doubleday & Co., Inc., 1965), p. 200.

[15]Now cover environmental topics: See Everett Skehan, "New England seminar spawns environment story exchange," *Editor & Publisher*, July 3, 1971, p. 24.

[16]Editor Thomas Pew: See Francis Pollock, "Consumer Reporting: Underdeveloped Region," *Columbia Journalism Review*, May/June 1971, p. 43. Pollock's version is verified in a letter from Editor Pew to the authors, July 13, 1971. For a depth report about policies on specifying brand names, see Stanford N. Sesser, "Some Papers Hesitate To Specify Brands in Critical Stories," *Wall Street Journal*, July 6, 1971, p. 1.

[17]One of the largest sellers: Letter to the authors from *New York Magazine* publisher George A. Hirsch, July 23, 1971.

[18]News divisions in the red: See "TV can't cover losses in covering the news," *Business Week*, November 2, 1968, pp. 64–66; "3 nets spent $118 million for tv news," *Editor & Publisher*, August 22, 1970, p. 41.

[19]Fred Friendly quit: Kendrick, *Prime Time*, p. 32.

[20]Friendly quoted Murrow: Fred W. Friendly, "The Responsibility of TV Journalism," in *The Responsibility of the Press*, ed. Gerald Gross (New York: Simon and Schuster, 1969), p. 312.

[21]Struggle at Harper's: See Stuart W. Little, "What Happened at Harper's," *Saturday Review*, April 10, 1971, pp. 43–47; Charlotte Curtis, "An Adventure in 'the Big Cave,' " *(MORE)*, June, 1971, pp. 11–13.

[22]Lem Tucker remarked: Lenora Williamson, "It's Lem Tucker time—listening to a tv station's news director," *Editor & Publisher*, August 29, 1970, p. 46.

[23]Walter Cronkite estimates: Edward Rapetti, "A Look at Tv News With Walter Cronkite," *Editor & Publisher*, October 14, 1967, p. 72.

[24]Murray Kempton: "The Trouble With Newspapers," an interview with Murray Kempton by David Gelman and Beverly Kempton, *The Washington Monthly*, April, 1969, p. 24.

[25]"Feeling acute guilt": *Seattle Post-Intelligencer*, December 17, 1970, p. 12.

[26]The Journal's profitability: See Carol J. Loomis, "One Story The Wall Street Journal Won't Print," *Fortune*, August 1971, p. 140. An inquiry from the authors to the *Journal* verified that "the statistics are accurate" in the *Fortune* article.

[27]Jayne Mansfield died: See *Columbia Journalism Review*, Summer 1967, p. 21.

[28]Dick Hutchings works: Material about Hutchings and his crew is from Jeanie Kasindorf, "He Just Prays It Will Be an Easy Day," *TV Guide*, July 10, 1971, by permission from *TV Guide Magazine.* Copyright 1971 by Triangle Publications, Inc., Radnor, Pa.

[29]"A still camera": Williamson, "Lem Tucker time," *Editor & Publisher*, August 29, 1970, p. 46.

[30]NBC photo essay: *NBC Nightly News*, July 12, 1971.

[31]Roswell Garst: See *Time*, October 5, 1959, p. 44.

[32]Mob scenes: For discussion of crowded coverage of stories, see Gerald B. Healey, "Wolf pack journalism is assailed," *Editor & Publisher*, August 31, 1968, p. 15.

[33]"The spectacle of a half dozen": UPI story in *Seattle Post-Intelligencer*, March 11, 1971.

5. Lies, Half Truths, and Evasions

[1]"The trouble with Adlai Stevenson": Robert Alan Aurthur, "The Wit and Sass of Harry S Truman," *Esquire*, August, 1971, p. 118.

[2]"On May 5, 1960": excerpt from William McGaffin and Irwin Knoll, *Anything But the Truth* (New York: G. P. Putnam's Sons, 1968), p. 67.

[3]"*From beginning to end:*" Victor Bernstein and Jesse Gordon, "The Press and the Bay of Pigs," *The Columbia University Forum*, Fall 1967, p. 11.

[4]"Mr. Johnson next strained": *Newsweek*, December 19, 1966, p. 25.

[5]"As evidence that Americans": *New York Times*, March 7, 1970, p. 10.

[6]"The White House said": *New York Times*, March 10, 1970, p. 4.

[7]Samuel Pepys spent hours: J. H. Plumb, "The Public and Private Pepys," *Saturday Review*, October 24, 1970, p. 31.

[8]It's called atropine: See Robin Clarke, *The Silent Weapons* (New York: David McKay Co., 1968), pp. 190–91; Steven Rose, ed., *Chemical and Biological Warfare* (Boston: Beacon Press, 1968), p. 31.

[9]"I wanted FDR": *Newsweek*, April 22, 1957, p. 76.

[10]Page one of La Hora: material in this paragraph and the next is based on Bernstein and Gordon, "Press and Bay of Pigs," *Columbia U. Forum*, Fall 1967, pp 5, 10–13.

[11]"If you had printed": Clifton Daniel, *The Press and National Security*, pamphlet by *New York Times*, 1966, p. 9.

[12]Even in ancient China: See Lin Yutang, *A History of the Press and Public Opinion in China* (Chicago: University of Chicago Press, 1936), pp. 2, 6.

[13]"In my country": Walter Lippmann, "On the Profession of Journalism," *Editor & Publisher*, May 29, 1965, p. 64.

[14]"The press is a mirror": Quoted in *Time*, April 1, 1957, p. 62.

[15]When delegates met: Catherine Drinker Bowen, *Miracle at Philadelphia* (New York: Bantam Books, 1968), p. 22.

[16]"So great is unanimity": *ibid.*, p. 178; Max Farrand, *The Framing of the Constitution* (New Haven: Yale University Press, 1913), pp. 114–15.

[17]Mayors across the political spectrum: Tension between some newsmen and such mayors as Lindsay of New York, Daley of Chicago, Fasi of Honolulu, and Yorty of Los

Angeles broke into headlines many times in the late 1960s and early 1970s. But less well-known feuds went on in other cities as well; see "Paper's long feud with mayor heats up," *Editor & Publisher*, December 26, 1970, p. 22, about Mayor Henry Maier of Milwaukee; and Ralph Z. Hallow, "The Mayor is 'Nobody's Boy,'" *The Nation*, April 19, 1971, pp. 492–96, about Mayor Peter F. Flaherty of Pittsburgh.

[18]Some protest groups have refused: In Denver, for example, newsmen were banned in 1970 from some meetings on the basis of race or knowledge of Spanish; for the list of incidents and the protest by the local journalism review, see *The Unsatisfied Man*, September 1970, p. 6.

[19]Eighteen states have "shield" laws: Richard P. Kleeman, "Subpoenas, Shields and SDX," *Report of the 1970 Sigma Delta Chi Advancement of Freedom of Information Committee*, p. 10; since the SDX compilation, Illinois has passed a shield law. See *Broadcasting*, September 27, 1971, p. 7.

[20]Ramsey Clark: *Chicago Tribune* counsel Don Reuben quoted about Clark, *Editor & Publisher*, May 2, 1970, p. 52. For discussion of subpoenas, see Brian Boyer, "Reporters threatened by subpoena actions," *Chicago Journalism Review*, March 1970, pp. 13–15.

[21]*Fortune* magazine was subpoenaed: See Paul Cowan and Jack Newfield, "Media Response: Medium Fool," *Village Voice*, February 12, 1970, p. 67; confirmed by letter to authors from Donald M. Wilson, vice president for corporate & public affairs, Time, Inc., September 28, 1971.

[22]Don H. Reuben: Quoted in *Editor & Publisher*, May 2, 1970; verified by letter to authors from Mr. Reuben's associate, Lawrence Gunnels, August 26, 1971.

[23]*Broadcasting* magazine reported: *Broadcasting*, September 27, 1971, p. 37.

[24]Upheld reporter Caldwell's refusal: *New York Times* story in *Seattle Post-Intelligencer*, November 18, 1970; *New York Times* analysis by Fred P. Graham in *Seattle Post-Intelligencer*, November 25, 1970.

[25]Mitchell said he would modify: See *Editor & Publisher*, August 15, 1970, pp. 9–10.

[26]"Compelling need": *New York Times* analysis by Fred P. Graham in *Seattle Post-Intelligencer*, November 25, 1970.

[27]"To reach agreement": *New York Times*, February 6, 1970, p. 40. As this book goes to press, the question of newsmen's privilege to withhold information is headed for the Supreme Court. See "Is 'newsman's privilege' nonexistent?" *Broadcasting*, September 20, 1971, pp. 46–47, and "Reporters should testify on crime U.S. brief argues," *Editor & Publisher*, September 18, 1971, p. 13.

[28]"Carries a heavy burden": For the text of the Supreme Court opinions in the "Pentagon Papers" case, see *Editor & Publisher*, July 10, 1971, pp. 11–19.

[29]For publishing inaccuracies: Curtis D. MacDougall, *The Press and Its Problems* (Dubuque: Wm. C. Brown Company, 1964), p. 69.

[30]Ban them from polling places: *Editor & Publisher*, June 26, 1971, p. 37.

[31]For broadcasting faulty information: *Report of the 1969 Sigma Delta Chi Advancement of Freedom of Information Committee*, p. 24.

[32]To keep them from scenes: *Report of the 1967 Sigma Delta Chi Advancement of Freedom of Information Committee*, p. 19.

[33]To license newsmen: *Report of the 1970 Sigma Delta Chi Advancement of Freedom of Information Committee*, p. 11; MacDougall, *Press and Its Problems*, pp. 69–70.

[34]Comer introduced a bill: *Editor & Publisher*, July 3, 1971, p. 40; August 14, 1971, p. 12. The vote on Comer's amended bill was 101 to 92; 102 votes were needed to pass the measure.

[35]Law inspired by Sen. Huey Long: Donald M. Gillmor and Jerome A. Barron, *Mass Communication Law* (St. Paul: West Publishing Co., 1969), pp. 105–110.

[36]President Kennedy suggested: "The Vietnam Case History," *Current*, August 1965, p. 36.

[37]Another technique is to hide: This paragraph is based on Tom Littlewood, "Nixon's 'Smoothies' Manage Some News," *Chicago Sun-Times*, October 5, 1969; Nixon news conference stories and Medicare story, *Washington Post*, September 27, 1969, p. 1; Nixon news conference stories, *New York Times*, September 27, 1969, p. 1; UPI story about Medicare in *New York Times*, September 27, 1969, p. 67.

[38]A more acrobatic example: This paragraph is based on McGaffin and Knoll, *Anything But the Truth*, pp. 131–32; stories on President Johnson and Senator Kennedy in *Washington Post*, March 3, 1967.

[39]Franklin D. Roosevelt: For brief discussion of Roosevelt's "fireside chats," see William E. Leuchtenburg, *Franklin D. Roosevelt and the New Deal, 1932–1940* (New York: Harper & Row, Publishers, 1963), pp. 330–31.

[40]Thomas E. Dewey: John Crosby, "Television's Future Effect on Politicians," *Reader's Digest*, January 1951, p. 4.

[41]Dwight Eisenhower's campaign: Louis G. Cowan in *Village Voice*, December 11, 1969, p. 8.

[42]Richard M. Nixon was accused: *New York Times*, September 24, 1952, p. 23.

[43]"Respectable Republican cloth coat": *ibid.*, p. 22.

[44]The Checkers speech: In August 1971, the Inner Circle Theatre in Washington, D.C., featured a 30-minute film of the "Checkers" speech. Young audiences reportedly found it uproariously funny; see Robert J. Donovan's column in the *Los Angeles Times*, August 27, 1971.

[45]"I can only say": *Newsweek*, November 19, 1962, p. 32.

[46]Boxed out the working newsmen: See Joe McGinniss, "Packaging the President: The New Political Values," New York, September 8, 1969, pp. 39–48. For a longer version of the Nixon media strategy in 1968, as reporter McGinniss recorded it in his travels with the Nixon staff, see McGinniss's book, *The Selling of the President* (New York: Trident Press, 1969). Nixon's relations with the news media after he became President are discussed in William Rivers, *The Adversaries: Politics and the Press* (Boston: Beacon Press, 1970), pp. 34–48.

[47]Permitting news conferences more infrequently: His first two years plus in office, President Nixon held news conferences about once every two months; see *Christian Science Monitor*, August 24, 1971, p. 3. "Nixon's three immediate predecessors held an average of 22 to 27 press conferences a year," noted *Editor & Publisher*, December 19, 1970, p. 44.

[48]Spiro T. Agnew: Quote from AP text of Agnew's November 13, 1969, speech in *Seattle Post-Intelligencer*, November 16, 1969, p. 22.

[49]President visited editors: *New York Times* story in *Seattle Post Intelligencer*, August 24, 1970, p. 11; Luther A. Huston, "Nixon's press visits are kept under wraps," *Editor & Publisher*, August 29, 1970, p. 53.

[50]Herbert G. Klein: See Bob Wilson, "Klein and Ziegler: Nixon's PR Men," *Freedom of Information Center Report #244*, June 1970, and John Pierson, "President Maps Drive To Sell His Program by Going to the People," *Wall Street Journal*, February 9, 1971, p. 1.

[51]In 1798: Totals of newsmen indicted and jailed under the Sedition Act—and in a few cases under common law for seditious libel shortly before the Sedition Act was

passed—were compiled from James Morton Smith, *Freedom's Fetters* (Ithaca: Cornell University Press, 1956), and Frank Maloy Anderson, "The Enforcement of the Alien and Sedition Laws," American History Association Annual Report for 1912 (Washington: Gov't Printing Office, 1914), pp. 115–26.

[52]"Must I shoot": Harold R. Nelson, ed., *Freedom of the Press from Hamilton to the Warren Court* (Indianapolis: Bobbs-Merrill, 1967), pp. 229–30.

[53]At least twenty-eight Northern newspapers: Total of newspapers suppressed was compiled from Wood Gray, *The Hidden Civil War* (New York: The Viking Press, 1942); James E. Pollard, *The Presidents and The Press* (New York: The Macmillan Company, 1947); Sidney T. Matthews, "Control of the Baltimore Press during the Civil War," *Maryland Historical Magazine*, June 1941, pp. 150–70; Thomas F. Carroll, "Freedom of Speech and of the Press during the Civil War," *Virginia Law Review*, May 1923, pp. 516–51.

[54]Committee on Public Information: Emery, *Press and America*, p. 587.

[55]Espionage Act of 1917: Gillmor and Barron, *Mass Communication Law*, pp. 89–90.

[56]Seventy-five papers restricted: Emery, *Press and America*, p. 594.

[57]Milwaukee Leader case: Gillmor and Barron, *Mass Communication Law*, pp. 89–99; Elmer A. Beck, *Autopsy of a Labor Daily: The Milwaukee Leader, Journalism Monograph #16*, published by Association for Education in Journalism, August 1970. (The incident involving the Leader was decided in the case of Milwaukee Social Democratic Publishing Company v. Burleson.)

[58]Decision still stands: However, in the 1964 case of Lamont v. Postmaster General, the Supreme Court ruled that "if the Government wishes to withdraw a subsidy or a privilege, it must do so by means and on terms which do not endanger First Amendment rights." *Supreme Court Reporter*, 1964, p. 1498.

[59]Smith Act: Don R. Pember, *The Smith Act as a Restraint on the Press, Journalism Monograph #10*, published by Association for Education in Journalism, May 1969, pp. 6–7.

[60]Voluntary censorship again: Emery, *Press and America*, p. 604.

[61]Hawaii military censorship: Jim A. Richstad, *The Press Under Martial Law: The Hawaiian Experience, Journalism Monograph #17*, published by Association for Education in Journalism, November 1970, pp. 8, 13, 15.

[62]Khe Sanh: *Washington Post*, July 29, 1968.

[63]"Embargo" on Laos coverage: *Editor & Publisher*, February 6, 1971, p. 15; *New York Times* story in *Seattle Post-Intelligencer*, February 15, 1971, p. 1; *Los Angeles Times* story in *Seattle Times*, March 22, 1971.

[64]Morley Safer: "CBS News' Friendly Takes Lid Off In Tabulating Pentagon Pressures," *Variety*, December 22, 1965, p. 30.

[65]Don Webster: *New York Times*, May 22, 1970, p. 25; Edwin Diamond, "The atrocity papers," *Chicago Journalism Review*, August 1970, pp. 3–4.

[66]Stevenson was trapped: For accounts of Stevenson's use of phony photos at the UN, see Kenneth S. Davis, *The Politics of Honor* (New York: G. P. Putnam's Sons, 1967), pp. 455–59; Herbert J. Muller, *Adlai Stevenson: A Study in Values* (New York: Harper & Row, 1967), pp. 282–83; Richard J. Walton, *The Remnants of Power* (New York: Coward-McCann, Inc., 1968), pp. 30–33.

[67]Murray Kempton made: "The Trouble With Newspapers," an interview with Murray Kempton by David Gelman and Beverly Kempton, *The Washington Monthly*, April 1969, pp. 32–33.

[68]Sen. Hugh Scott blasted: AP story in *Seattle Post-Intelligencer*, September 18, 1970, p. 45.

[69]President Nixon's reception: *New York Times*, September 17, 1970, p. 1.

6. Who Says So?

[1]A "slight cold": Pierre Salinger, *With Kennedy* (Garden City, N.Y.: Doubleday, 1966), pp. 251–52.

[2]"It didn't seem logical": James Reston interviewed by Richard E. Steele, April 17, 1963. Richard E. Steele, "The Anticipation of History: A Study of Speculative Reporting," (Master's thesis, Northwestern University, 1963), p. 84.

[3]When one reporter asked: Steele, "Anticipation of History," p. 82.

[4]"I started calling": Murray Marder interviewed by Richard E. Steele. Steele, "Anticipation of History," p. 87.

[5]Marine Moves: *Washington Post*, October 21, 1962, p. 1.

[6]President Kennedy told country: *New York Times*, October 23, 1962, p. 18.

[7]In a staff memo: Alfred Friendly, "Attribution of News: Memo to All Hands," *Nieman Reports*, July 1958, p. 11.

[8]Off-the-record: For discussion of off-the-record ground rules, see Samuel J. Archibald, "Rules for the game of ghost," *Columbia Journalism Review*, Winter 1967–8, pp. 17–23.

[9]Use of a single word: Philip Geyelin, *Lyndon B. Johnson and the World* (New York: Frederick A. Praeger, 1968), p. 105; Jacob Ornstein, "Let's Mend Our Speech a Little," *Chicago Daily News*, Panorama section, January 16, 1965, p. 3.

[10]A noteworthy case: For an example of press coverage of the possibility that President-elect Kennedy would name his brother to the Cabinet, see *New York Times*, November 19, 1960, p. 1. Note that reporter William H. Lawrence's story is unattributed, and says "no final decision has been made."

[11]McGeorge Bundy: Quoted in Delbert McGuire, "Editors permissive on non-attribution," *Editor & Publisher*, August 24, 1968, p. 15.

[12]Alan Otten: Alan Otten, "Background Briefings In the Capital Are Used For Both Good and Ill," *Wall Street Journal*, April 10, 1968, p. 1.

[13]"Dregs of society": *New York Times*, December 18, 1970, p. 1.

[14]"A woman giving the name": Laurence R. Campbell and Roland E. Wolseley, *Newsmen at Work* (Boston: Houghton Mifflin Co., 1949), pp. 168–69.

[15]Stan Opotowsky: Quoted in McGuire, "Editors permissive," *Editor & Publisher*, August 24, 1968, p. 51.

[16]Since live telecasting: Some of President Eisenhower's news conferences were videotaped for later televising. President Kennedy first held a news conference televised live on January 25, 1961. See *New York Times*, January 26, 1961, p. 1; January 27, 1961, p. 22.

[17]Rehearsed with their aides: See the introduction by Pierre Salinger in Harold W. Chase and Allen H. Lerman, eds., *Kennedy and the Press* (New York: Crowell, 1965).

[18]President Johnson was asked: McGaffin and Knoll, *Anything But the Truth*, p. 26.

[19]"Here is a man": *U.S. News & World Report*, August 17, 1970, p. 70.

[20]"His obvious intention": *ibid.*

[21]"My remarks were:" *ibid.*

[22]James Reston once suggested: Quoted in *Newsweek*, April 8, 1963, p. 59.

[23]The Royal Society: For discussion of this intriguing group, see Margery Purver, *The Royal Society: Concept and Creation* (Cambridge: The M.I.T. Press, 1967).

[24]Alvin Toffler estimates: Alvin Toffler, *Future Shock* (New York: Random House, 1970), p. 27.

[25]Evaluations of political scene: Emery, *Press and America*, p. 567.

[26]Isolation of a gene: *New York Times*, November 23, 1969, p. 1.

[27]William McGaffin provided: *Chicago Journalism Review*, January 1969, p. 9.

[28]When heart transplants: For discussion of the heart transplant record in the first few years of the surgical experiments, see Thomas Thompson, "The year they changed hearts," *Life*, September 17, 1971, pp. 56–70.

[29]Burlington Free Press: *Columbia Journalism Review*, Spring 1962, p. 64.

[30]*Wall Street Journal* story: "Nominee Fails to Win Some of the Executives Who Bolted GOP in '64," *Wall Street Journal*, October 16, 1968, p. 1.

[31]112,000 interned: John D. Hicks, George E. Mowry, and Robert E. Burke, *A History of American Democracy* (Boston: Houghton Mifflin Co., 1966), p. 729. For discussion of the internment of the Nisei, see Bill Hosokawa, *Nisei: The Quiet Americans* (New York: Wm. Morrow & Co., Inc., 1969), pp. 223–432.

[32]Daniel Boorstin made: Daniel J. Boorstin, *The Image* (New York: Atheneum, 1962), p. 61. Copyright 1961 by Daniel J. Boorstin.

[33]"Of the subjects": *ibid.*, p. 59.

[34]Famous supporters: *Time*, May 31, 1968, pp. 11–12.

[35]John Glenn announced: "Glenn in Orbit," *The Nation*, February 3, 1964, p. 111.

[36]Colonel Glenn explained: Richard L. Maher, "Countdown in Ohio," *The Nation*, February 10, 1964, p. 131.

[37]If a white man wrote: *Race and Violence in Washington State*, Report of the Commission on the Causes and Prevention of Civil Disorder, 1969, p. 48.

[38]*Wall Street Journal* quoted: *Wall Street Journal*, March 1, 1968, p. 12.

[39]"The media are in midst": *Race and Violence in Washington State*, p. 48.

[40]"The Commission's major concern": *Report of the National Advisory Commission on Civil Disorders* (New York: Bantam Books, Inc., 1968), pp. 382–83.

[41]*New York* magazine's exposé: Craig Karpel, "Ghetto Fraud on the Installment Plan," *New York*, May 26, 1969, pp. 24–32, and June 2, 1969, pp. 41–44.

7. Hoaxing and Hornblowing

[1]U.S. force of destroyers: UPI story, August 3, 1964.

[2]Lincoln's Love Letters: The Lincoln letters hoax and its aftermath runs through five issues of *The Atlantic Monthly*: December 1928, pp. 834–56; January 1929, pp. 1–14; February 1929, pp. 215–25, 283–84; March 1929, pp. 288a–88d; April 1929, pp. 516–25.

[3]The rectangular survey: See Ray A. Billington, *Westward Expansion* (New York: The Macmillan Company, 1960), pp. 207–9; Roy M. Robbins, *Our Landed Heritage* (Lincoln, Neb.: University of Nebraska Press, 1962), p. 8.

[4]Hoaxes infiltrate: For studies of hoaxes, see Curtis D. MacDougall, *Hoaxes* (New York: The Macmillan Company, 1940); Daniel Cohen, *Myths of the Space Age* (New York: Dodd, Mead and Company, 1967).

[5]The ups and downs: *Columbia Journalism Review*, Fall 1966, p. 64.

[6]Edward M. Miller wired: *Time*, February 9, 1959.

[7]Who cut big footprints: AP story in *Seattle Times*, April 1, 1971.

[8]Might be called elephantsitis: The Seattle version appeared in *Seattle Post-Intelligencer*, April 28, 1969, p. 7. Portland and Tacoma versions are cited in *Seattle Post-Intelligencer*, April 29, 1969.

[9]Editor William Bronson spoofed: See "Home Is A Freeway," *Cry California*, summer 1966, pp. 8–13. In a letter to the authors, October 14, 1971, Bronson remarks that two other articles he thought were obvious satire fooled some readers and newsmen. See "Paradise in a Nutshell?" *Cry California*, summer 1967, pp. 27–31, and William Bronson, "Beer Can Crackdown," *Cry California*, fall 1968, pp. 28–29.

[10]"I named her Marilee": Quoted by Curt Gentry, *The Last Days of the Late, Great State of California* (New York: Ballantine Books, 1968), p. 172.

[11]Editor John Meyer spread: MacDougall, *Hoaxes*, pp. 283–84.

[12]Brewed an intramural hoax: *ibid.*, pp. 263–64.

[13]"Corrupt the young": *Congressional Record*, February 24, 1969, p. 4223.

[14]Singer Pat Boone touted: *Dallas Morning News*, May 17, 1970, p. 4.

[15]At least three U.S. Representatives: See *Congressional Record*, February 24, 1969, p. 4223 (Rep. Louis C. Wyman, R-New Hampshire); October 30, 1969, pp. 32517–18 (Rep. John M. Slack Jr., D-West Virginia); January 22, 1970, p. 881 (Rep. Joe Skubitz, R.-Kansas).

[16]Columnist James J. Kilpatrick responded: *Seattle Times*, July 2, 1970.

[17]"My right-wing friends": *Portland Oregonian*, July 16, 1970.

[18]"The streets of our country": *Saturday Review*, May 17, 1969.

[19]Repeated on talk shows: Jerome Beatty Jr. tells the subsequent story of the Hitler "quote" in "Funny Stories," *Esquire*, November 1970, pp. 44–50.

[20]*The Progressive* reprinted it: *The Progressive*, July 1969, p. 9.

[21]*Newsweek* and CBS asked: Beatty, "Funny Stories," *Esquire*, November 1970, p. 44.

[22]"A professor at California State": *ibid.*

[23]Library of Congress couldn't verify: *ibid.*

[24]Beatty ran a followup: *Saturday Review*, Dec. 20, 1969.

[25]Points of Rebellion: William O. Douglas, *Points of Rebellion* (New York: Random House, 1969), 1st and 2nd printings.

[26]"When researchers try": Beatty, "Funny Stories," *Esquire*, November 1970, p. 44. In a letter to the authors, August 21, 1971, Beatty verifies that publicity about the Hitler "quote" never produced any proof of its authenticity.

[27]Protocols of the Elders: See MacDougall, *Hoaxes*, pp. 201–2.

[28]Henry Ford waged: Booton Herndon, *Ford* (New York: Weybright and Talley, 1969), pp. 348–49. For discussion of the history of the Protocols hoax, see Norman Cohn, *Warrant for Genocide* (New York: Harper & Row, 1967).

[29]Six college students blinded: UPI story in *Seattle Post-Intelligencer*, January 14, 1968, p. 12.

[30]"Distraught and sick" man: AP story in *Seattle Times*, January 18, 1968, p. 26.

[31]Swipe at the sauce: *Seattle Times*, November 9, 1959, p. 1. The subsequent story of efforts to counteract the cranberry scare is told in "PR Puts Cranberries Back in Thanksgiving," *Editor & Publisher*, November 28, 1959.

[32]Somebody is dealing with public relations: A standard textbook about public relations is by Scott M. Cutlip and Allen H. Center, *Effective Public Relations* (Englewood Cliffs, N.J.: Prentice-Hall, Inc., 1962).

[33]"There are a million definitions": Alan Harrington, "The Self-Deceivers," *Esquire*, September 1959, p. 59.

[34]Ivy Lee told: See Ray Eldon Hiebert, "Ivy Lee: Father of Modern Public Relations," Princeton University Library Chronicle, Winter 1966, pp. 113–20. Contrary to most accounts, Lee was not the first public relations practitioner. See Scott M. Cutlip, "The Nation's First Public Relations Firms," *Journalism Quarterly*, Summer 1966, pp. 269–80. For general history of public relations, see L. L. L. Golden, *Only By Public Consent* (New York: Hawthorn Books, Inc., 1968); Alan R. Raucher, *Public Relations and Business, 1900–1929*, Johns Hopkins University Studies in Historical and Political Science, Ser. 86, No. 2 (Baltimore: Johns Hopkins Press, 1968).

[35]Ludlow Massacre: See Arthur S. Link, *American Epoch* (New York: Alfred A. Knopf, Inc., 1956), p. 61.

[36]Lee urged the Rockefellers: Hiebert, "Ivy Lee," Princeton University Library Chronicle, Winter 1966, p. 113.

[37]"Fire this whole department": Robert Townsend, "Up the Organization," *Harper's*, March 1970, p. 84.

[38]The Journal customarily refuses: Carol J. Loomis, "One Story," *Fortune*, August 1971, p. 202.

[39]Herbert Denenberg was plucked: Subsequent material about Denenberg is based on Morton C. Paulson, "Dr. Denenberg: How a Brash, Breezy State Official Makes Waves and Enemies," *National Observer*, September 18, 1971, p. 1.

[40]"The first bag of loot": Diane K. Shah, "A Fashionable Bacchanal," *National Observer*, February 15, 1971, p. 1.

[41]"Sears may not have": *ibid.*

[42]"There's nothing hucksterish": *ibid.*

[43]The Associated Press: For discussion of policies, see The Unsatisfied Man, March 1971, p. 10 (AP and New York Times), and January 1971, p. 11 (*Louisville Courier-Journal*); Loomis, "One Story," *Fortune*, August 1971, p. 207 (*Wall St. Journal*); and *Philadelphia Journalism Review*, September/October 1971, p. 11–12 (*Philadelphia Inquirer*).

8. The Reporter: Advocate? Messenger?

[1]"If I'm any good": *Time*, February 25, 1957, p. 66.

[2]"A person presumably is expected": Interview on Public Broadcast Laboratory, December 22, 1968.

[3]"I don't see": *Newsweek*, March 9, 1970, p. 84.

[4]"A staff member cannot": *Editor & Publisher*, December 20, 1969, p. 52.

[5]"Being a reporter": Edmond Taylor, *Awakening from History* (Boston: Gambit Incorporated, 1969), p. 449.

[6]"(Objectivity) produces something": *Time*, October 22, 1956, p. 57.

[7]"Objectivity is the determination": A. M. Rosenthal, *If everybody screams, nobody hears*, pamphlet published by *New York Times*, 1969.

[8]Meaning listed for objective: *The American Heritage Dictionary of the American Language* (New York: Houghton Mifflin Company, 1969), p. 905.

[9]Rashomon: *Rashomon, a film by Akira Kurosawa* (New York: Grove Press, Inc., 1969).

[10]Uncertainty Principle: "Uncertainty Principle," *Encylopaedia Britannica* (1971), XXII, pp. 486–87.

[11]A thin, earnest figure: See Snyder and Morris, eds., "Jerusalem 1961: The Eichmann Trial Recalls the Faces of Six Million Dead," *Treasury of Great Reporting*, pp. 772–79.

[12]"The trouble with Eichmann": Quoted in *Newsweek*, June 17, 1963, p. 95. For more discussion of Eichmann and his trial, see Hannah Arendt, *Eichmann in Jerusalem* (New York: The Viking Press, 1963).

[13]Sen. Joseph McCarthy: For discussion of McCarthy's tactics in using the news media, see Richard H. Rovere, *Senator Joe McCarthy* (New York: Harcourt, Brace and Company, 1959).

[14]"What editors and politicians call": *Editor & Publisher*, July 4, 1970, p. 44.

[15]"I think you're mad": Kathryn Kenyon, "Advocacy Comes to the Newsroom," *Freedom of Information Center Report* #250, October 1970, p. 2.

[16]"I could not even say": *Editor & Publisher*, November 14, 1970, p. 18.

[17]"Von Hoffman has caught": *FOI Center Report*, October 1970, p. 1.

[18]"The ready capacity of reporters": *Editor & Publisher*, July 4, 1970, p. 44.

[19]"Every news story": *Editor & Publisher*, November 14, 1970, p. 18.

[20]"If ever a nation": Emery, *Press and America*, p. 152.

[21]N.Y. *Journal* headlines: *ibid.*, p. 425.

[22]New York Times had enjoyed: For an account of the *Times* when it was founded in 1851 by Henry J. Raymond, see Gay Talese, *The Kingdom and the Power* (New York: Bantam Books, 1970), pp. 180–84.

[23]ABC television tried: Robert Higgins, "It Fizzled When It Should Have Crackled," *TV Guide*, April 5, 1969, pp. 4–9.

[24]More than 130 prize contests: David Zinman, "Should newsmen accept PR prizes?" *Columbia Journalism Review*, Spring 1970, p. 37.

[25]Bribe Award: *Columbia Journalism Review*, Spring 1969, p. 2.

[26]Chicago Journalism Review caused protests: See *Chicago Journalism Review*, June 1970, pp. 7, 8, 10; October 1970, p. 15; November 1969, pp. 3–6; *Editor & Publisher*, October 10, 1970, p. 56.

[27]"Our contract with the guild": *Chicago Journalism Review*, October 1970, p. 15.

[28]"When a reporter": *ibid.*

[29]In Syracuse: *Editor & Publisher*, October 10, 1970, p. 56.

[30]Tim Reiterman: Tim Reiterman, "Two faces of Berkeley—and the news," *Chicago Journalism Review*, April 1970, pp. 7–8. Reprinted from *Chicago Journalism Review*, 11 E. Hubbard St., Chicago, Ill., 60611, subscription $5 for one year.

[31]Le Monde's operation: Leslie R. Colitt, quoted in David Deitch, "Case for Advocacy Journalism," *The Nation*, November 17, 1969, p. 531. See also Leslie R. Colitt, "The Mask of Objectivity," *The Nation*, June 17, 1968, pp. 789–91.

[32]"If you want to exert": Jean Schwoebel, "The miracle 'Le Monde' wrought," *Columbia Journalism Review*, Summer 1970, p. 9.

[33]*Kansas City Star* and *Milwaukee Journal: FOI Center Report*, October 1970, p. 2.

[34]"Should the press be": Robert J. Donovan, "The Rules Have Changed," *Neiman Reports*, March 1970, p. 9.

[35]"It is difficult to report": A. J. Liebling, *The Earl of Louisiana* (Baton Rouge: Louisiana State University Press, 1970), p. 93.

[36]"For the truth": Quoted in Herbert Brucker, "What's Wrong With Objectivity?" *Saturday Review*, October 11, 1969, p. 78.

[37]Murrow fought back at McCarthy: Two of Murrow's long-time colleagues at CBS have written accounts of the telecast. See Fred W. Friendly, *Due to Circumstances Beyond Our Control* (New York: Random House, 1967), pp. 23–67; Alexander Kendrick, *Prime Time: The Life of Edward R. Murrow* (Boston: Little, Brown & Co., 1969), pp. 35–71.

[38]Police assassinated twenty-eight Panthers: See Edward Jay Epstein, "The Panthers and the Police: A Pattern of Genocide?" *New Yorker*, February 13, 1971; Robert L. Bartley, "Those 28 Panthers—and the Press," *Wall Street Journal*, March 17, 1971, p. 16.

[39]H-bomb lost in Spain: This 1966 incident, which was kept as quiet as possible for several weeks, is worth reading about as a classic of military misinformation. See Leopoldo Azancot, "The Day H-Bombs Fell on Palomares," *Saturday Review*, January 28, 1967, pp. 21–27; Flora Lewis, *One of Our H-Bombs Is Missing* (New York: McGraw-Hill, 1967); Tad Szulc, *The Bombs of Palomares* (New York: Viking, 1967).

[40]Nat Hentoff cited: *Village Voice*, November 9, 1967, p. 7.

[41]Two weeks later Hentoff's column: *ibid.*, November 23, 1967, p. 6.

[42]"It just won't do": Carol Neiman, editor of *New Left Notes*, responded to Hentoff: ". . . You're right—it shouldn't have been buried on the third page. My lame excuses are that at the time it was printed, I could find absolutely no details on the situation, and had gotten no response at all from the article. (I suppose I had an irrational hope that it had been ignored.) As you'll notice, a larger retraction in a more prominent place appeared in the following issue." *Village Voice*, December 21, 1967, p. 6.

[43]"It seems my source": *Village Voice*, July 8, 1971.

[44]Decorative facts: For discussion of non-news facts by a former newsmagazine writer, see Otto Friedrich, "There Are 00 Trees in Russia," *Harper's*, October 1964, pp. 59–65. It should be pointed out that both *Time* and *Newsweek* are under different editorships than in their heyday of trivial facts.

[45]"When I was with": Wallace Carroll, "Ralph Waldo Emerson, Thou Shouldst Be Living At This Hour," *Nieman Reports*, June 1970, p. 22.

[46]"Is the writer": Brucker, "What's Wrong With Objectivity?", *Saturday Review*, October 11, 1969, p. 79.

9. What's Missing?

[1]"Is there any point": Arthur Conan Doyle, "Silver Blaze," *The Complete Sherlock Holmes* (Garden City, N.Y.: Doubleday & Company, 1930), p. 347.

[2]Broder said: David S. Broder, "A British Look at American Politics," *Washington Monthly*, June 1969, p. 75.

[3]McFarlane's summary: Quoted by Lewis Chester, Godfrey Hodgson, and Bruce Page, *An American Melodrama* (New York: The Viking Press, 1969), p. 211.

[4]"The serious point": *ibid.*, p. 212.

[5]Riots against the draft: See Samuel Eliot Morison, *The Oxford History of the American People* (New York: Oxford University Press, 1965), p. 666.

[6]In World War I: See H. C. Peterson and Gilbert C. Fite, *Opponents of War, 1917–1918* (Madison: University of Wisconsin Press, 1957), p. 234.

[7]At least 170 communes: Total compiled from Arthur E. Bestor Jr., *Backwoods Utopias* (Philadelphia: University of Pennsylvania Press, 1950) pp. 231–42; and Frederick A. Bushee, "Communistic Societies in the United States," *Political Science Quarterly*, December 1905, pp. 661–64.

[8]The New York hearings: For newspaper accounts of the Kefauver Committee hearings on television, see *Boston Globe*, March 21, 1951, p. 1; *Chicago Daily News*, March 13, 1951, p. 41; and March 23, 1951, p. 25; *Cleveland Plain Dealer*, March 16, 1951, p. 27; *Detroit News*, March 19, 1951, p. 12; *Indianapolis News*, March 20, 1951, p. 1; *Minneapolis Tribune*, March 19, 1951, p. 35; *Nashville Banner*, March 20, 1951, p. 11; *New York Times*, March 14–22, 1951; *Providence Journal*, March 22, 1951, p. 15; *Washington Post*, March 20, 1951, p. 10. For a general account, see "The Crime Story," *Broadcasting–Telecasting*, March 26, 1951, p. 61; *Newsweek*, March 26, 1951, p. 52.

[9]Downey Rice conceded: Letter to Ivan Doig, May 9, 1962.

[10]Rufus King recalled: Interviewed by Ivan Doig, May 3, 1962.

[11]"The Chairman": Hearings before a Special Committee to Investigate Organized Crime in Interstate Commerce, 81 Cong., 2nd Sess.-82nd Cong., 1st Sess., 1950–51, pt. 7, p. 401.

[12]Branigan was monumental: Chester, Hodgson and Page, *American Melodrama*, p. 158.

[13]Eleven have two-year terms: The 1970 World Almanac, p. 57.

[14]U.S. squeeze play: *Vancouver Sun*, May 29, 1970, p. 1.

[15]"Never negotiate": *ibid.*

[16]Column by Peter Thomson: Peter Thomson, "Too Tough Anti-American?", *Toronto Telegram* Syndicate feature in *Seattle Times*, May 31, 1970, p. 12.

[17]A few U.S. newsmen: Harry C. Ashmore, William Baggs, and Harrison Salisbury. Ashmore writes of the visit by him and Baggs in "The Public Relations of Peace," *The Center Magazine*, October/November 1967, pp. 4–11; for an account of the Salisbury visit, see Talese, *Kingdom and Power*, pp. 531–37.

[18]Typical issue of Atlas: *Atlas*, July/August 1971.

[19]Bureau of Census counted: AP story in *Seattle Post-Intelligencer*, April 22, 1971, p. 2.

[20]UPI cleared up: UPI story in *Seattle Post-Intelligencer*, August 22, 1971.

[21]Lemberg Center: See Paul G. Keough, "Probers charge press created riot 'myths',"* Editor & Publisher*, March 15, 1969, p. 18.

[22]Vigilante gave speech: Clipping in authors' possession.

[23]"I challenge Vigilante": Clipping in authors' possession.

[24]Criminals have been drawn: "Capital Punishment," *Encyclopedia Americana* (1968), V, p. 596.

[25]"Regarding deterrence": "Capital Punishment," *Encyclopaedia Britannica* (1963), IV, p. 848.

[26]UPI reporter uncovered: UPI story in *Seattle Post-Intelligencer*, August 27, 1971.

[27]Fellmeth admitted: *ibid.*

[28]Los Angeles Times uncovered: *Los Angeles Times*, August 27, 1971, p. 28. Copyright, 1971, *Los Angeles Times*. Reprinted by permission.

[29]Editing a news story: Remarkably, little has been written about the craft of news editing. Notable articles have been written by two magazine editors, however; see John Fischer, "The Editor's Trade," *Harper's*, July 1965, pp. 20–24; Norman Podhoretz, "In Defense of Editing," *Harper's*, October 1965, pp. 143–47.

[30]Do a telephone impersonation: One of the legendary editors known for finagling news on the phone was Harry Romanoff of Chicago's *American*, who retired in 1969. See *Chicago Journalism Review*, June 1969, pp. 4–5.

[31]"The body of a person": "1909 guide for reporters still fresh," *Editor & Publisher*, August 21, 1971, p. 26.

[32]"Most of the copy": Carol J. Loomis, "One Story *The Wall Street Journal* Won't Print," *Fortune*, August 1971.

[33]"Require a continuous": UPI story in *Seattle Post-Intelligencer*, March 31, 1971.

[34]The House refused: UPI story in *Seattle Post-Intelligencer*, July 14, 1971.

[35]"Every effort should be made": Fred W. Friendly, "The Unselling of The Selling of the Pentagon," *Harper's*, June 1971, p. 33. Another viewpoint on television editing may be found in "Melvin Laird and CBS," *The New Republic*, July 10, 1971, pp. 29–30.

10. Putting One Word After Another

[1]"The natural progress": Quoted by H. C. Allen, *Bush and Backwoods* (East Lansing: Michigan State University Press, 1959), p. 24.

[2]Moses On Sinai: *Newsweek*, March 13, 1961, p. 87.

[3]Melvin Maddocks concluded: *Time*, March 8, 1971, p. 36.

[4]Peace: *American Heritage Dictionary of the English Language* (New York: American Heritage Publishing Co., Inc., and Houghton Mifflin Co., 1969), p. 963.

[5]War: *ibid.*, p. 1444.

[6]Yet some forty-five wars: A succinct summary of "40 Wars Since '45" can be found in *Time*, September 24, 1965, p. 31. To that accounting can be added several conflicts since then: Nigeria v. Biafran rebels, Israel v. Egypt (1967), U.S.S.R. invasion of Czechoslovakia (1968), civil war in Northern Ireland, and India v. Pakistan.

[7]"The peace of God": Philippians, iv:7.

[8]Semantics: A clearly written textbook about semantics is S.I. Hayakawa's *Language in Thought and Action* (New York: Harcourt, Brace & World, Inc., 1964).

[9]Tasaday tribe: AP story in *Arizona Daily Star*, July 16, 1971, p. D9.

[10]Basic changes in boundary: Even the manner and policy of changing the country's political boundaries has been different at different times. See Jack E. Eblen, *The First and Second United States Empires* (Pittsburgh: University of Pittsburgh Press, 1968).

[11]Leo Rosten explained: Leo Rosten, "The Myths by Which We Live," *The Rotarian*, September 1965, p. 32.

[12]Californian Is Charged: *Newsweek*, July 8, 1963, p. 48.

[13]Critic Vincent Canby: *New York Times* story in *Seattle Post-Intelligencer's Arts and Book World*, September 19, 1971, p. 1.

[14]Rutgers Gets U.S. Grant: *Asbury Park* (N.J.) *Press*, January 24, 1962, p. 34.

[15]U.S. Grant to Study: clipping in author's possession.

[16]Bare Writer's Marriage: *Chicago Daily News*, January 12, 1962.

[17]3 Baddies: *New York Daily News*, July 20, 1965.

[18]Jehovah Resting: *Newsweek*, March 13, 1961, p. 87.

[19]French Are Urged: *ibid.*

[20]Rolling Moss: *Editor & Publisher*, September 26, 1959.

[21]"Conjures up visions": *St. Louis Journalism Review*, October/November 1970, p. 4. The trio of headlines was in the *Post-Dispatch* of July 17, 1970.

[22]Jean de Roye tells: Quoted by J. Huizinga, *The Waning of the Middle Ages* (Garden City, N.Y.: Doubleday Anchor Books), p. 234.

[23]"Such preparations shall be": Roy H. Copperud, "Gobbledygook," *Editor & Publisher*, November 28, 1959.

[24]Tell them, he said: *ibid.*

[25]Bureaucratic language called gobbledygook: *American Heritage Dictionary*, p. 564.

[26]"This change in procedure": Noted by one of the authors.

[27]Says linguist Paul Roberts: Paul Roberts, *Understanding English* (New York: Harper, 1958), p. 412.

[28]"I believe the government": Herb Caen's column in *San Francisco Chronicle*, December 7, 1960.

[29]"One of the inevitable": *NBC Nightly News*, September 24, 1971.

[30]*1984*: George Orwell, *1984* (New York: Harcourt Brace and Co., Inc., 1949).

[31]Entered Laos in an incursion: See Russell Baker's column from *New York Times* News Service in *Seattle Post-Intelligencer*, February 17, 1971.

[32]Truly euphemistic days: For discussion of military euphemisms in Southeast Asia, see Josiah Bunting, "Going Home Alone," *The Atlantic*, October 1971, pp. 125–28.

[33]General Millan Astray: Hugh Thomas, *The Spanish Civil War* (New York: Harper & Brothers, 1961), p. 272.

[34]Welfare was a euphemism: Column by Jack Smith, *Los Angeles Times/Washington Post* News Service feature in *Seattle Times*, August 9, 1970.

[35]Loss of 50,000 jobs: *Seattle Post-Intelligencer*, January 14, 1970, p. 1.

[36]George E. Allen: Beverly Smith, "When a President needs a friend," *Saturday Evening Post*, May 5, 1956, pp. 30–31.

[37]*Time* described Truman: See John C. Merrill, "How *Time* Stereotyped Three U.S. Presidents," *Journalism Quarterly*, Autumn 1965, pp. 563–70.

[38]"After God had finished": Authors' copy from a Seattle Liberation Front Pamphlet, 1969.

[39]David Brinkley has been charged: See Bruce A. Kauffman, "Fairness in TV News," *Freedom of Information Center Report* #235, January 1970, for results of a survey of viewers' responses to network newsmen.

[40]"Its virtue is": *NBC Huntley-Brinkley Report*, September 23, 1969.

[41]"From the ten candidates": *Seattle Times*, September 18, 1969.

[42]"The basic issue": *ibid.*

[43]Newswomen: See *Editor & Publisher*, July 3, 1971, p. 26.

[44]"Betty Garrett is 35": Cornelia M. Parkinson, "She aims for the gut," *Editor & Publisher*, July 17, 1971, p. 11.

[45]"Shapely Miss Witkowski": Quoted in *Chicago Journalism Review*, July 1971, p. 7.

[46]"For years," she says: Lois Wille, "Our Girl at the Daily News," *ibid.*, p. 5.

[47]"Our girl" is a put-down: For discussion of sexual tokenism and other topics related

to women's rights, see the special supplement "Woman's Place," *The Atlantic*, March 1970, pp. 81–126.

[48]"Late or early": Florence Howe, "Sexual Stereotypes Start Early," *Saturday Review*, October 16, 1971, p. 77.

[49]Just plain "Golda": *Chicago Journalism Review*, July 1971, p. 4.

[50]"Maybe when she resigns": Letter to the editor from *Chicago Daily News* reporter Jay Bushinsky, *Chicago Journalism Review*, September 1971, p. 3.

[51]Russell Baker remarked: Russell Baker column from *New York Times* News Service in *Seattle Post-Intelligencer*, September 18, 1971, p. 11.

[52]Harry Reasoner has observed: *The Strange Case of the English Language*, 1968 film produced by CBS News.

[53]"All he's doing is": James M. Perry, "Out of Yesteryear, a New Populist," *National Observer*, October 9, 1971, p. 5.

[54]Lie-discount mechanism: Russell Baker, *New York Times* feature in *Seattle Post-Intelligencer*, September 6, 1967.

11. When Rights Collide: Information versus Privacy

[1]Pulitzer arrived: Emery, *Press and America*, p. 376.

[2]William Randolph Hearst hones: *ibid.*, pp. 417–20; Tebbel, *Compact History*, pp. 166–69.

[3]Brandeis and Warren: See Gillmor and Barron, *Mass Communication Law*, pp. 482, 485.

[4]"Overstepping in every direction": Samuel D. Warren and Louis D. Brandeis, "The Right to Privacy," *Harvard Law Review*, December 15, 1890, p. 196.

[5]June, 1971, decision: Rosenbloom v. Metromedia. For the decision, see *Supreme Court Reporter*, July 1, 1971, pp. 1811–41. For discussion, see *Editor & Publisher*, June 12, 1971, p. 9; *New York Times* editorial, June 12, 1971, p. 28; Robert H. Phelps, "Now the Private Citizen Is Fair Game, Too," *New York Times*, June 13, 1971; for criticism, see interview with Louis Nizer, "They have gone too far," *Editor & Publisher*, July 31, 1971, p. 15.

[6]1964 turning point: New York Times Co. v. Sullivan. See Gillmor and Barron, *Mass Communication Law*, pp. 254–66.

[7]To include public figures: Associated Press v. Walker. See *ibid.*, pp. 272–76.

[8]Then political candidates: Ocala Star-Banner v. Damron, Monitor-Patriot v. Roy, Time v. Pape. See *Supreme Court Reporter*, March 15, 1971, pp. 621–42.

[9]"In libel cases we view": *Editor & Publisher*, June 12, 1971, p. 9.

[10]Marshall and Stewart dissenting: *ibid.*

[11]Ramsey Clark warned: Quoted by Phelps, "Now the Private Citizen," *New York Times*, June 13, 1971.

[12]"Voluntarily or not": *New York Times*, June 12, 1971, p. 28.

[13]Blind Judge Gets License: Clipping in authors' possession. As noted later in the chapter, the judge's name and minor details of the story have been changed by us so as not to compound the invasion of privacy.

[14]Sen. Edward Kennedy entitled: For details of the Chappaquiddick story, see entries listed in *Reader's Guide to Periodical Literature*, beginning in June 1969, or the *New York Times Index* for the same period. For comment, see James Reston, "The Strange Case of Senator Kennedy," *New York Times* News Service column in *Seattle Post-Intelligencer*, January 9, 1970.

[15]John Lindsay's daughter: See " 'No pix at wedding!' lensmen outwit mayor," *Editor & Publisher*, June 13, 1970, p. 13.

[16]"My camera was fastened": *ibid.*

[17]"This carefully planned setup": *ibid.*

[18]Wrote Ralph Holsinger: *Editor & Publisher*, July 4, 1970, p. 5.

[19]"This is to inform": Clipping in authors' possession. Again, names and minor details have been changed to protect privacy.

[20]Freedom of Information Act: For text of the law, see Gillmor and Barron, *Mass Communication Law*, pp. 453–55.

[21]"Pentagon Papers": See *Newsweek*, June 28, 1971; *Editor & Publisher*, June 19, 1971, p. 7.

[22]"Congress has recognized": See *I. F. Stone's Bi-Weekly*, July 12, 1971, p. 1.

[23]Five of nine justices: For text of the Supreme Court opinions, see *Editor & Publisher*, July 10, 1971, pp. 11–19.

[24]It hasn't been much used: An opposite view from the Freedom of Information Center, which helped bring the law into being, is in "Press Use of the Freedom of Information Act is Criticized Unduly," *FoI Digest*, July/August 1971, p. 4.

[25]Lyndon Johnson's archives: For the best continuing coverage of the Lyndon B. Johnson Presidential Library, see entries in *New York Times Index*, beginning in 1968.

[26]William G. Florence said: UPI story in *Seattle Post-Intelligencer*, June 25, 1971.

[27]"Related solely": Gillmor and Barron, *Mass Communication Law*, p. 455.

[28]"Personnel and medical files": *ibid.*

[29]Nader's task force charged: *Report of the 1969 Sigma Delta Chi Advancement of Freedom of Information Committee*, pp. 7–9.

[30]"Newsmen do not appear": *Report of the 1970 Sigma Delta Chi Advancement of Freedom of Information Committee*, p. 7.

[31]Robert Mardian: *Newsweek*, June 28, 1971, p. 27.

[32]Neil Sheehan: *ibid.*, p. 26.

[33]President of GM apologizing: See *New York Times*, March 23, 1968, p. 1.

[34]Elliot Horne used: Elliot Horne, *The Hiptionary: A Hipster's View of the World Scene* (New York: Simon and Schuster, 1963), p. 18. Copyright 1963 Elliot Horne and Jack Davis. Reprinted by permission.

[35]Sen. Ervin convened: *Time*, March 8, 1971.

[36]"Today," he wrote: Christopher H. Pyle, "CONUS Intelligence: The Army Watches Civilian Politics," *Washington Monthly*, January 1970, p. 5.

[37]Staffers of *Washington Star*: Nat Hentoff, "Me and My Shadow," *Civil Liberties*, March 1971, p. 2.

[38]Nat Hentoff has chastised: *ibid.*

[39]That hadn't been done: *Life*, March 26, 1971, p. 25.

[40]Ogden Reid points out: Quoted by Jeff Greenfield, "Army surveillance: euphemisms for 1984," *Village Voice*, June 3, 1971, p. 9.

41"The Army plan was sent": *ibid.*

42"What is most disturbing": *Saturday Review,* January 30, 1971, p. 21.

43"When a Senator": *New York Times,* May 2, 1971.

44*Post-Dispatch* series: See *Congressional Record,* April 30, 1971, pp. E3812–19.

45"When it becomes known": Chief counsel Lawrence Baskir, *ibid.,* p. 3816.

12. How Do You Know If It's Right?

1October evening in 1938: See Barnouw, *Golden Web,* pp. 85–89.

2Announced three more times: See Hadley Cantril, *The Invasion from Mars* (New York: Harper & Row, 1966), p. 43. Cantril points out, however, "that the most terrifying part of the broadcast came before the station break." *ibid.,* p. 44.

3*Chicago Today* and *Chicago Daily News* headlines: *Chicago Journalism Review,* May 1970, p. 15.

4*Post-Dispatch* and *Globe-Democrat* headlines: *St. Louis Journalism Review,* December 1970, p. 5.

5In 1969 a blowout: *Sierra Club Bulletin,* February 1971, p. 12; *Newsweek,* March 3, 1969, pp. 59–60.

6What happened was: *Newsweek,* March 3, 1969, pp. 59–60.

7Admitted Edward Cony: *ibid.,* p. 60.

8Otto Friedrich gives examples: Otto Friedrich, "Of Imaginary Numbers," *Time,* August 2, 1971.

9In another case, estimates: *ibid.*

10*Seattle Times* receiving: Don Duncan, "How *Times* readers have their say," *Seattle Times Sunday Magazine,* June 20, 1971, p. 4.

11*NY Times* 40,000: *Editor & Publisher,* Dec. 5, 1970, p. 45.

12Aimed at Jack Newfield: In the past year and a half, the authors have noted and filed 10 published comments about inaccuracies by Newfield, besides the *Harper's* statement below. See letters to the editor in the *Village Voice,* Dec. 25, 1969; March 12, 1970; April 30, 1970; May 28, 1970; June 4, 1970; June 25, 1970; July 2, 1970; July 23, 1970; April 9, 1971; and Victor S. Navasky, " 'Changeling Who Matured Late,' " *Life,* June 13, 1969.

13The scurrilous attack: *Village Voice,* June 4, 1970, p. 4.

14Mr. Oakes is correct: *ibid.,* p. 62.

15It is my impression: *Village Voice,* May 28, 1970.

16Newfield won special recognition: *Editor & Publisher,* May 22, 1971, p. 36.

17Article about *NY Post:* Jack Newfield, "Goodbye, Dolly!" *Harper's,* September 1969, pp. 92–98.

18*Erratum:* We are advised: *Harper's,* July 1970, p. 3.

19Forty-three reporters and cameramen: *Rights in Conflict: The Walker Report to the National Commission on the Causes and Prevention of Violence* (New York: Bantam Books, Inc., 1968), p. 330.

20Eight other cities: Atlanta, Cleveland, Holyoke (Thorn: *Connecticut Valley Media Review*), Honolulu, Long Beach (*The Review of Southern California Journalism*), Philadelphia, Providence, and New York.

[21]Author Norman Hill: Norman Hill, "The Growing Phenomenon of the *Journalism Review*," *Saturday Review*, September 11, 1971, p. 60.

[22]Squaw Valley: Roger Rapoport, "For sale: One hunk of American history," *Sports Illustrated*, May 3, 1971, pp. 72–75.

[23]There are strong indications: "The word from Olympus," *The Unsatisfied Man*, April 1971, p. 3.

[24]The review recommended: "Olympics," *The Unsatisfied Man*, May 1971, p. 6.

[25]Official sourceitis: See "The Panthers and the rest of us," *Chicago Journalism Review*, December 1969, p. 3.

[26]Grand jury indictments: *Washington Post*, August 25, 1971, p. 1; *Time*, September 6, 1971, pp. 49–50. The indictments accused the fourteen defendants, including the State's Attorney, of "unlawfully, willingly and knowingly destroying, altering, concealing and disguising physical evidence by planting false evidence and by furnishing false information."

[27]Ethic of mega-dollar: J. Anthony Lukas, "Life in These United States," (*MORE*), June 1971, pp. 3–4. Only eight advertisers finally were represented in the supplement. Charles D. Hepler, *Digest* publisher, said several advertisers stayed out because "they decided to adopt a low profile." See column by Joe Cappo, *Chicago Daily News*, August 23, 1971, for Hepler's comment; for the supplement itself, see *Reader's Digest*, September 1971, pp. 171–90.

[28]Diligence on half shell: See "The 13-minute half hour TV news," *St. Louis Journalism Review*, December 1970/January 1971, p. 9.

[29]Lineup in typical issue: *Columbia Journalism Review*, July/August 1971.

[30]FoI Center: See *Editor & Publisher*, December 20, 1958, p. 13; M. L. Stein, "Missouri's Freedom of Information Center," *Saturday Review*, March 13, 1971, pp. 93–94.

[31]In a typical span: *FoI Center Reports*, March-June 1971.

[32]"We recommend the establishment": *A Free and Responsible Press* (Chicago: University of Chicago Press, 1947), p. 100.

[33]"If the council finds": Alfred Balk, "Minnesota launches a press council," *Columbia Journalism Review*, November/December 1971, p. 26.

[34]"The chances are only one": Donald E. Brown, "Press Council rulings serve as guidelines for journalists," *Editor & Publisher*, April 24, 1971, p. 17.

[35]"To set up": Donald E. Brown, "British journalists change their attitudes toward reorganized Press Council," *Editor & Publisher*, April 17, 1971, p. 22.

[36]Will Irwin wrote: See *Collier's*, January 21-July 29, 1911; Robert V. Hudson, "Will Irwin's Pioneering Criticism of the Press," *Journalism Quarterly*, Summer 1970, pp. 263–71.

[37]Robert Benchley began: A. J. Liebling, *The Press* (New York: Ballantine Books, Inc., 1964), p. 74.

[38]Samuel Newhouse the archetype: *ibid.*, p. 7. As this is written, more than a decade after Liebling's gibe, Newhouse owns twenty-two dailies.

[39]James Aronson, author: James Aronson, *The Press and the Cold War* (New York: Bobbs-Merrill, 1970).

[40]*Louisville Courier-Journal*: Ombudsman John Herchenroeder to the authors, September 29, 1971: ". . . My duties encompass both functions—that of being an internal critic and also a reader's representative. . . . The morning paper carries the correction under a heading 'Beg your pardon' . . . The afternoon paper carries such corrections on the

jump page, the back page of the first section, under a heading 'We Were Wrong.' "
See *Time*, July 6, 1970, pp. 44–45.

[41]*St. Petersburg Times*: See "Coping with reader's gripes becomes task for specialists,"
Editor & Publisher, January 30, 1971, pp. 7–8.

[42]The problem begins with: Richard Harwood, "The News Business: Can Newsmen
Do Better on the Facts?" *Washington Post*, August 22, 1971, p. B6.

[43]A disgruntled Mexican-American: *Broadcasting*, August 9, 1971, p. 19.

[44]Accouterments of hippiedom: Ivan Doig, "Diverse Readership," *Editor & Publisher*,
May 22, 1971, p. 44.

[45]Boston melodrama: Rufus Crater, "Those high-stakes rollers in Boston," *Broadcasting*,
August 23, 1971, pp. 26–32.

[46]Richard Townley's series: Richard Townley, "Television Journalism—An Inside Story,"
TV Guide, May 15; May 22; May 29; June 5, 1971.

[47]Doing great things: Lee Kottke, "She's the woman in *Spokeswoman*," *Chicago Daily
News*, August 23, 1971, p. 23. In a letter to the authors, October 4, 1971, Editor Davis
verifies the quote, and says "about 250 of the 2600 subscribers to *Spokeswoman* are
media outlets."

[48]Oil spills: The total between the Torrey Canyon spill in March, 1967, and the San
Francisco collision of January, 1971, was twenty-seven. See "Oil Spill!" *Sierra Club
Bulletin*, February 1971, pp. 12–13.

[49]Bay Guardian: See Phil Sutin, "Newspaper preservation act challenged in court;
outcome could upset Post-Globe arrangement," *St. Louis Journalism Review*, May 1971,
p. 13.

[50]Reading of alternative sources: A guide to publications across the political spectrum
is Robert H. Muller, ed., *From Radical Left to Extreme Right: Current Periodicals of
Protest, Controversy, or Dissent* (Ann Arbor: Campus Publishers, 1967).

[51]After he gave: John McPhee, "Encounters with the Archdruid, II—An Island," *New
Yorker*, March 27, 1971, p. 44.

13. Thou Shalt Not Commit Mockery

[1]"It may be news": *Rocky Mountain News* editorial quoted in *The Unsatisfied Man*,
September 1970, p. 15.

[2]"That when people want": Garrick Utley, "Why the French are starting to believe
what they see," *TV Guide*, May 23, 1970, p. 9.

[3]Researchers for the ACE: *Time*, October 4, 1971, p. 74: ". . . The report's authors,
ACE Research Director Alexander Astin and his deputy, Alan Bayer, solicited their information from campus officials, pinning them down on specific details to guard against
exaggeration. The researchers discovered that far from being pacific, nearly half of the
campuses had experienced protests . . . Astin and Bayer are quick to point out that
the figures represent a clear 'downturn' from 1969–70, when incidents were so numerous
that no one counted them precisely. . . . Last year's turmoil became 'diffused,' moving
to the 'invisible' campuses that newsmen rarely visit and educational leaders seldom
discuss. . . ."

Index

Bundy, McGeorge, 75
Burlington (Vt.) Free Press, 82

Cable television, 27
Caen, Herb, 149
Caldwell, Earl, 63
Canby, Vincent, 146
Carroll, Wallace, 123–24
CBS, 32, 54, 63, 87, 139–40
Celebrities as sources, 83–84
Censorship, 66–68 (see *also* Government and
    media)
Chesley, Frank, 12–14
Chester, Lewis, et al., *An American Melodrama,*
    127–28, 130
Chicago Daily News, 33, 174
Chicago Journalism Review, 113, 179, 181, 194
Chicago Today, 33, 174
Chicago Tribune, 10, 63
Chronolog, 51, 194
Clark, Ramsey, 63, 161
Cohen, Jerry S., 193
Colitt, Leslie R., 118–19
Collier's, 24, 83
Columbia Journalism Review, 91, 112–13, 181,
    193
Columns, 112
Comer, Harry R.J., 64
Commission on the Freedom of the Press (Hutch-
    ins Commission), 182
Consumer:
    aware of advertiser pressure, 31
    blames messenger for message, 61
    defense against hoaxes, 96–97
    defense against messenger and advocate, 124
    and discomfiture caused by news, 189–91
    distorts message, 18–19, 173–74
    and diversity of media, 175
    evaluates attribution, 77
    evaluates political statements, 69–70
    evaluates sources of news, 78–84
    evaluates TV news, 53
    and letters to editor, 177–78
    and media critics, 179–87
    and overheated language, 156–57
    skepticism of statistics, 176–77
    stereotypes, 19
    suspects media conspiracy, 35–36, 38–39
    tension between newsmen and consumers, 20
    watches later developments in news stories,
        175–76

Crawford, Kenneth, 49
Credibility gap (see Government and media)
Cristy, Austin P., 139
Critics of media (see Media critics)
Cronkite, Walter, 3, 8, 48
Cuba, invasion of (see Bay of Pigs)
Cuban missile crisis, 72–73

Daley, Richard J., 3, 43
Daniels, Jonathan, 59
Davis, Elmer, 121
Davis, Susan, 186
Denenberg, Herbert, 101–2
Denver Post, 180
de Roye, Jean, 147–48
Dewey, Thomas E., 65
Diamond, Edwin, 184, 195
Donovan, Robert J., 119
Dorfman, Ron, 111
Douglas, William O., 94–95
Dusseldorf Rules hoax, 93–94

Editor & Publisher, 185, 194
Editorials, 112
Edwards, Douglas, 26
Eichmann, Adolf, 109–10
Eisenhower, Dwight D., 56, 65, 152
Electronic media (see Radio; Television)
Environmental Protection Agency, 41
Ervin, Sam, 168–69
Esquire, 34
Ethics, news:
    advocacy reporting, 109–24
    corporate conflicts of interest, 32
    editing, 138–40
    language problems, 144–56
    newsmen and advertising, 29–32
    newsmen and public relations, 102–5
    newsmen and sources, 42–44, 63, 76
    parochialism, 39–40
    patriotism, 40–42
    prizes for news stories, 112–13
    public service vs. profit, 46–47, 50
    simultaneous rebuttal, 134–38
    violations of privacy, 161–65
Everett (Wash.) Herald, 35

Features, 28
Federal Communications Commission, 34
    totals of licensed broadcasting stations,
        201–2